"Why Ask My Name?"

"Why Ask My Name?"

Anonymity and Identity in Biblical Narrative

ADELE REINHARTZ

New York   Oxford
Oxford University Press
1998

Oxford University Press

Oxford   New York
Athens   Auckland   Bangkok   Bogotá   Buenos Aires   Calcutta
Cape Town   Chennai   Dar es Salaam   Delhi   Florence   Hong Kong   Istanbul
Karachi   Kuala Lumpur   Madrid   Melbourne   Mexico City   Mumbai
Nairobi   Paris   São Paulo   Singapore   Taipei   Tokyo   Toronto   Warsaw

and associated companies in
Berlin   Ibadan

Copyright © 1998 by Adele Reinhartz

Published by Oxford University Press, Inc.
198 Madison Avenue, New York, New York 10016

Oxford is a registered trademark of Oxford University Press.

Library of Congress Cataloging-in-Publication Data
Reinhartz, Adele, 1953–
"Why ask my name?": anonymity and identity in biblical narrative /
Adele Reinhartz.
   p.   cm.
Includes bibliographical references and index.
ISBN 0-19-509970-2
1. Names in the Bible.   2. Bible. O.T.—Psychology.   3. Bible.
O.T.—Criticism, interpretation, etc.   I. Title.
BS1199.N2R45   1998
221.6—dc21   97-44216

9 8 7 6 5 4 3 2 1
Printed in the United States of America
on acid-free paper

For Barry

PREFACE

MY INTEREST IN ANONYMOUS CHARACTERS began in a single moment, during a conversation with a young student preparing for her bat mitzvah. The portion that Milena was preparing was Judges 13, the story of Manoah's wife, the mother of Samson. In addition to chanting this portion, Milena was also to present a short talk on the passage itself. As we studied the passage together, I felt a sense of mild discomfort. Something seemed out of kilter. It took me some time to realize that I was troubled by the absence of the woman's proper name. This gap seemed inconsistent with her starring role and obvious superiority to her doltish husband.

On the appointed day, Milena chanted beautifully, spoke insightfully about this anonymous wife and mother, and moved on to the other challenges that await the post–bat mitzvah woman. I, however, became increasingly interested in anonymity as a feature of biblical narrative. My interest lay specifically in the impact of anonymity on the ways in which readers construct their images of the characters within the narrative. Although I had largely overcome my presuppositions concerning the incompatibility of anonymity and narrative stardom, I had other assumptions to contend with. The most imposing of these was my sense that it was primarily women whose names were absent from the biblical narrative. I studied the women in the books of Samuel and Kings and, indeed, discovered a considerable number of female characters whose names are not recounted.

Initially I considered a longer and more comprehensive study of anonymous women in biblical narrative. But no sooner had I embarked on this project than I realized that alongside the many unnamed mothers, wives, daughters and wise women in biblical narrative stood an even larger number of unnamed menfolk, servants, slaves, messengers, angels and animals. Only a comprehensive study, inclusive of unnamed men, women, children and nonhuman characters, would do.

My thanks go out to the friends, colleagues and students who helped in many ways at all stages of this project. To Milena Romalis, my thanks for launching me into an area of unexpected riches. To my graduate and under-graduate students at McMaster University and to all who participated in less formal courses and workshops at the National Havurah Institute and a variety of venues in Toronto and Hamilton, my gratitude for their interest in biblical characters and the prodding questions they asked. Conversations in Jerusalem with Moshe Greenberg, Alan Rosen and Esther Chazon helped me step back from the thicket of characters and stories to contemplate the broader patterns and significance of anonymity. Ellen Frankel, Lori Lefkowitz, Amy-Jill Levine, Eileen Schuller and Barry Walfish took the time to comment with care on an earlier draft. Their comments were invaluable as I proceeded with the intensive task of revision. My appreciations go to Amy-Jill Levine and to Barry Walfish for speedy response to queries, bibliographical and otherwise, and to Cynthia Read, Will Moore, Joy Matkowski, and all others at Oxford University Press for their support and skill.

Research support provided by McMaster University and its Arts Research Board is gratefully acknowledged, as is the research assistance given by Lorenzo Ditommaso, Jennifer Nettleton, Leonard Van Dyke and Jane Webster. Thank you to Jennifer Nettleton for proofreading, reference checking and myriad other time-consuming tasks, all performed accurately and expeditiously.

My thanks to Sheffield Academic Press for permission to use "Samson's Mother: An Unnamed Protagonist," *JSOT* 55 (1992): 25–37 (reprinted in Athalya Brenner, ed., *A Feminist Companion to Judges* [Sheffield: Sheffield Academic Press, 1993], 157–70), and "Anonymous Women and the Collapse of the Mon-archy: A Study in Narrative Technique" from *A Feminist Companion to Samuel and Kings* (Sheffield: Sheffield Academic Press, 1994), 43–66, and to Scholars Press for permission to draw on "Anonymity and Character in the Books of Samuel," *Characterization in Biblical Literature, Semeia* 63 (1993): 117–41.

Family and friends provided moral support, encouragement and laughter and thoughtfully refrained from complaining about the long hours required to prepare the final manuscript. On the home front, Barry and our two teens, Mordechai and Miriam-Simma, took over more than their fair share of kitchen and childcare responsibilities to allow me uninterrupted time in front of the computer. Shoshana and Simcha kept my spirits up with hugs, jokes and antics. My thanks and love to them all.

Hamilton, Ontario   A. R.
August 1997

CONTENTS

ABBREVIATIONS

AB	Anchor Bible
ABD	D. N. Freedman, ed., *The Anchor Bible Dictionary*, 6 vols. (New York: Doubleday, 1992)
Ant.	Josephus, *Jewish Antiquities*
b.	Babylonian Talmud
BDB	F. Brown, S. R. Driver, and C. A. Briggs, eds. *A Hebrew and English Lexicon of the Old Testament* (Boston: Houghton Mifflin, 1906)
BHS	*Biblia Hebraica Stuttgartensia*
BibAnt	Pseudo-Philo, *Biblical Antiquities*
BibRev	*Bible Review*
BJS	Brown Judaic Studies
BKAT	Biblischer Kommentar. Altes Testament
BT	*The Bible Translator*
BTB	*Biblical Theology Bulletin*
CBQ	*Catholic Biblical Quarterly*
ET	*Evangelische Theologie*
Gen. Rab.	Genesis Rabbah
HAR	*Hebrew Annual Review*
HCSB	Wayne A. Meeks, ed., *HarperCollins Study Bible* (New York: HarperCollins, 1993)
HSM	Harvard Semitic Monographs
HTR	*Harvard Theological Review*
HUCA	*Hebrew Union College Annual*

       IB   George Arthur Buttrick, ed., *Interpreter's Bible,* 12 vols. (New York:
             Abingdon-Cokesbury Press, 1951–57)
      ICC   International Critical Commentary
       Int   *Interpretation*
  JANESCU   *Journal of the Ancient Near Eastern Society of Columbia University*
      JBL   *Journal of Biblical Literature*
     JETS   *Journal of the Evangelical Theological Society*
       JJS   *Journal of Jewish Studies*
       JPS   Jewish Publication Society
       JQR   *Jewish Quarterly Review*
      JSOT   *Journal for the Study of the Old Testament*
   JSOTSup   Journal for the Study of the Old Testament—Supplement Series
       JSP   *Journal for the Study of the Pseudepigrapha*
       MT   Masoretic Text
     NJPSV   New Jewish Publication Society version, *Tanakh: A New Translation
             of the Holy Scriptures according to the Traditional Hebrew Text* (Phil-
             adelphia: Jewish Publication Society, 1988)
      NLH   *New Literary History*
      NRSV   New Revised Standard Version
      OTL   Old Testament Library
       RB   *Revue Biblique*
      RSV   Revised Standard Version
     SBLDS   Society of Biblical Literature Dissertation Series
      TDNT   Gerhard Kittel and G. Friedrich, eds., *The Theological Dictionary of
             the New Testament,* trans. Geoffrey W. Bromiley, 10 vols. (Grand
             Rapids, Mich.: Eerdmans, 1964–76)
      USQR   *Union Seminary Quarterly Review*
       VT   *Vetus Testamentum*
     VTSup   *Vetus Testamentum Supplements*
      ZAW   *Zeitschrift für die alttestamentliche Wissenschaft*

"Why Ask My Name?"

Introduction

R EADING THE BIBLE for its unnamed participants is akin to examining the negatives of beloved family photographs. Initially I could make out only a few familiar figures: a sacrificial daughter, a seasoned family servant, a hero's mother. But as my eyes grew accustomed to this new perspective on a familiar text, I found unnamed characters wherever I looked, in virtually every corner of biblical narrative and in every social circle: among the ostracized lepers at the city gates, among the widowed and poor, in the households of Israel's founding families, in the courts and armies of the monarchs, and in the heavens themselves. As their numbers grew and their features became clearer to me, I began to view the anonymous as a society unto themselves—fully integrated into the human landscape of the biblical narrative, to be sure, but nevertheless set apart by the absence of their names.

The demography and the demeanor of this population was surprising. Where I had expected only a small number of unnamed characters, I discovered more than a hundred individual actors and countless others who appear in groups or whose existence is mentioned or presumed by biblical narrative. Where I had anticipated a preponderance of women, I found abundant men, children and angels, as well as a talking animal or two. Whereas I had associated anonymity with indistinctness, impersonality, and distance, I was soon absorbed with these characters, whose personalities and stories became vital, vibrant, and vivid to me.

The community of the unnamed not only challenged my prior views about anonymity but also revised my understanding of personal identity. The assumption that the absence of a proper name denotes the absence of individuality was simply not borne out by my reading. Nor was I unique in my ability to imagine the appearance and the behavior of these characters, to analyze their motivations and their relationships. Despite the dearth of direct attention to the phenomenon of anonymity in biblical narrative, many unnamed characters themselves—the queen of Sheba, Lot's wife, the primordial couple, for example—have captured the imagination of scholars, artists, poets, and all manner of other readers. Maurice Samuel's paean to the "supporting cast" of biblical narrative articulates the perspective that emerges from the written and artistic record of these readings:

> I see them with my own eyes, and nothing that I see is of my own invention or by anyone else's suggestion. Many of them are given only a few lines, and yet their presence can be as solid as that of the principals. They are like great actors with short roles; they are there for a few moments, but they are mightily there.[1]

The view that personal identity somehow belongs to, or is inherent in, the individual himself or herself is implied by Samuel's insistence that he sees nothing of his or anyone else's invention. Nevertheless, the variety of readings proposed for biblical characters, both named and unnamed, suggests that identity hovers in the encounter between character and reader and is demanding of both.

Though difficult to define with precision, personal identity connotes individuality, uniqueness, and personality. The presence of personal identity may be taken for granted in the case of characters named Moses, Samuel, and David. What of those known only as Abraham's servant, Pharaoh's daughter, Jeroboam's wife? Their distinctiveness emerges from their particular circumstances and the ways in which they respond to them. At the same time, their identities blend with the others of their ilk, the other servants, daughters, and wives to whom they are bound by these labels. Even as I reveled in their company, the anonymous danced just outside my grasp.

This book serves two purposes. One is to introduce these many figures to other readers of biblical narrative. The relative paucity of written material on anonymous characters suggests that many readers are as oblivious to their presence and role as I was before undertaking this study. The second is to explore the interplay of anonymity, understood in the narrow sense denoting the lack of a proper name, and identity, denoting the palpability of individuality or personality. Three aspects of this interplay are considered: the ways in which

---

[1]Maurice Samuel, *Certain People of the Book* (New York: Union of American Hebrew Congregations, 1955), 94.

anonymity effaces or veils the personal identity of the character; the ways in which the personal identities of unnamed characters nevertheless emerge from the narrative; the impact of anonymity on the clarity of character.

ANONYMITY AND THE EFFACEMENT OF PERSONAL IDENTITY

Historical and tradition critics frequently omit consideration of anonymity. One exception is Martin Noth, whose main interest is in tracing the tradition history of biblical texts. Commenting on the anonymity of the infant Moses' parents and sister (Exod 2:1–10), Noth notes that their names are provided at other points in the Pentateuch (Exod 6:20; Num 26:59). On this basis, Noth argues that the early tradition represented in the infancy story was not acquainted with the names of Moses' family members. Furthermore, the details of Moses' birth story are paralleled in other ancient Near Eastern birth stories. At the birth of King Sargon of Akkad, for example, his anonymous mother put him into a little box made of reeds, sealed it with pitch and set it afloat on the Euphrates. For Noth, the absence of names in Exod 2:1–10 is due to the narrator's ignorance and to the genre of literature to which the story belongs.[2]

Literary critics, both outside and within the biblical guild, also largely ignore anonymity as an aspect of characterization.[3] But implicit in studies of or remarks about specific anonymous characters is the assumption that the absence of their proper names veils or effaces personal identity. Literary critic W. J. Harvey notes that anonymity creates narrative texture and "the perspective of depth—in which certain characters become important because they stand out from, or are immersed in, a world of other human beings seen briefly, shallowly or in fragments."[4] E. J. Revell comments that "an individual who was not named was not sufficiently prominent in the [biblical] narrative, or in the history of the community to warrant specific identification."[5] The general tendency of literary studies of biblical texts to ignore or downplay anonymous characters suggests that Revell is here expressing a widely held assumption.

Some feminist readings take this principle one step further by arguing that anonymity not only bespeaks unimportance but also actively suppresses the

---

[2]*Exodus: A Commentary* (OTL; Philadelphia: Westminster, 1962), 25. For the story of Sargon, see James A. Pritchard, *Ancient Near Eastern Texts*, 2d ed. (Princeton, N.J.: Princeton University Press, 1955), 119.

[3]The only full-length work on anonymity that I have come across is the excellent study of postmodern characterization by Thomas Docherty, *Reading (Absent) Character: Towards a Theory of Characterization in Fiction* (Oxford: Clarendon Press, 1983).

[4]*Character and the Novel* (London: Chatto and Windus, 1965), 55.

[5]*The Designation of the Individual: Expressive Usage in Biblical Narrative* (Kampen, The Netherlands: Kok Pharos, 1996), 51.

identity of the unnamed woman and symbolizes her lack of power and person-hood within her narrative context. About the Levite's concubine, gang-raped and then left for dead while a guest in Gibeah (Judg 19), Phyllis Trible writes:

> Of all the characters in scripture, she is the least. Appearing at the beginning and close of a story that rapes her, she is alone in a world of men. Neither the other characters nor the narrator recognizes her humanity. She is property, object, tool, and literary device. Without *name*, speech, or power, she has no friends to aid her in life or mourn her in death (emphasis added).[6]

This unnamed woman's identity is both veiled and violated. Her effacement from the story through death is foreshadowed narratively by the absence of her proper name. Guilty are not only the men in the story but also the teller of the tale.

The assumption that anonymity veils or effaces personal identity is a natural corollary of the central role played by the proper name in the construction of character. The proper name fulfills four related functions with respect to literary characterization. First, the proper name in itself may carry meaning. This meaning may be derived from its etymology or from its associations with or similarities to other names in various literary contexts.[7] Second, as a peg on which the other traits and features of the character may be hung, the proper name unifies disparate bits of information under one rubric.[8] Third, insofar as it unifies the character and labels the set of traits from which that character may be constructed, the proper name is a convenient way of referring to the character. Fourth, the proper name distinguishes one character from another. This function is particularly useful for characters with overlapping or similar traits.[9]

These four functions are as detectable in biblical narrative as in other forms of narrative literature. First, the meanings of biblical names are frequently given in the form of an etymology or conveyed through the narrative content and the context. The name Moses, bestowed by the Pharaoh's daughter upon the infant whom she "drew ... out of the water (כי מן־המים משיתהו"; Exod 2:10), embodies, and reminds the reader of, the means of this child's survival.[10] Benjamin is

---

[6]*Texts of Terror: Literary-Feminist Readings of Biblical Narratives* (Philadelphia: Fortress, 1984), 80–81.

[7]As, for example, in Herman Melville's *Moby Dick*, in which some of the characters carry biblical names such as Ahab and Ishmael. For discussion of the relationship between name and identity in this novel, see Peter J. Bellis, *No Mysteries out of Ourselves: Identity and Textual Formation in the Novels of Herman Melville* (Philadelphia: University of Pennsylvania Press, 1990), 61 and passim.

[8]Shlomit Rimmon-Kenan, *Narrative Fiction: Contemporary Poetics* (London: Methuen, 1983), 39.

[9]See Joel Weinsheimer, "Theory of Character: Emma," *Poetics Today* 1 (1979): 195.

[10]The name Moses (משה pronounced "Mosheh") literally means "drawing out." In sound, it resembles the verb משיתהו (pronounced "meshitihu"), meaning "I drew him

named Ben-Oni ("son of my sorrow") by his dying mother, Rachel, but then he is renamed Benjamin ("son of the right hand") by his father, Jacob (Gen 35:18), perhaps to avoid the tragic meaning of Ben-Oni.[11] For named characters who appear only fleetingly in the text, this symbolic meaning may be the main feature of their characterization. For example, the infant born to the priest Eli's daughter-in-law after the Philistines capture the ark of God is named Ichabod, "the Glory has departed from Israel" (1 Sam 4:21). His name, which ties him to the historical moment of his birth, is all that we know of him.

Second, biblical names impute unity to character. Few readers doubt that the child drawn out of the water in Exod 2:5 became the man who killed the Egyptian (Exod 2:12), fled to Midian (2:15), spoke to God at the burning bush (3:1–4:17) and led the Israelites out of Egypt (12:37–42). This impression is re-inforced by the continuity of the name Moses. Unity of character is called into question when figures are accorded several proper names. Moses' father-in-law Reuel (Exod 2:18; Num 10:29) is called Jethro in Exod 18:5–12 and perhaps also Hobab in Judg 4:11.[12] The unity of his character is established not by the proper name, which varies, but by the consistent relational designation of the charac-ter as the father-in-law of Moses.[13] The proper name is often supplemented by other identifiers, which appear alone or in combination with the proper name. For example, Hamor, the father of Shechem, who had defiled Dinah, refers to her as Jacob's daughter (Gen 34:8), whereas the brothers call her "our sister" (Gen 34:31). In this example, the identifiers express the perspective of the speaker with respect to Dinah; they help to explain why Hamor initially ap-proaches Jacob (34:6) and why the brothers avenge her rape (34:31). The proper name Dinah unifies these other identifiers and ascribes them to a single char-acter.

---

out," though these two words are not related etymologically. As Noth explains, the Egyptian princess provides a Hebrew etymology, which does not quite fit with the story. The name is, in fact, Egyptian, a shortened form of Egyptian names like Ahmosis and Thutmosis. S. R. Driver, *The Book of Exodus*, rev. ed. (Cambridge: Cambridge University Press, 1953), 11. Noth, *Exodus*, 26. English scriptural citations are from the New Revised Standard Version (1989) unless otherwise stated; all Hebrew citations are from the *BHS*.

[11]So Claus Westermann, *Genesis 12–36: A Commentary*, trans. John J. Scullion, S.J. (Minneapolis: Augsburg, 1985), 555.

[12]According to Num 10:29, however, Hobab is the name of Jethro's son. A similar profusion of names occurs in Judg 7:1, in which the name Jerubbaal is used as an alter-native to Gideon.

[13]The father-in-law of Moses is present in each of these contexts except Exod 2:18, where he is not yet the father-in-law but rather the father of Moses' future wife. Noth (*Exodus*, 146–47) suggests that the father-in-law of Moses was unnamed in the basic material of the Elohist, to whom Exod 18:5–12 is attributed, contributing to a fluidity in the traditions concerning his proper name.

Third, in biblical narrative as in everyday parlance, the proper name is the clearest and most convenient way of referring to a character. The name by which the child is called at birth, though it may have a symbolic dimension, functions first and foremost as the "label" by which the child is known to others. The standard naming formula, "he/she called his/her name..." in itself embodies this notion (cf. Gen 29:32–30:24; 35:18). The narrator, in turn, uses the proper name to introduce new characters to the reader. In Judg 13:2, we meet the future father of Samson as "a certain man of Zorah, of the tribe of the Danites, whose name was Manoah."[14] Although the provenance and tribal affiliation of Manoah are important for situating him socially, it is by his proper name that he is identified throughout the pericope. Often the proper name does not accompany the first introduction of the character but is provided at a later point. The infant of Exod 2:1–10, saved by his mother from the Pharaoh's evil decree, is named Moses only at the end of this initial episode in his biography (Exod 2:10). Nevertheless, after the name has been introduced, it becomes the primary referent for this figure.

Fourth, the proper name distinguishes one biblical character from another. This function is implicit in every act of naming and is particularly clear in the case of twins, such as Jacob and Esau (Gen 25:25–26) and Perez and Zerah (Gen 38:29–30). A rabbinic comment illustrates the use of this function in the midrashic interpretation of scripture. In Gen 22:2 God tells Abraham : קח נא את בנך את יחידך אשר אהבת את יצחק: "Take your son, your only one, the one whom you love, Isaac..."(my translation). To the question of why God refers to Isaac by three additional descriptors ("your son," "your only one, "the one whom you love"), the rabbis respond that of these designations only the final one, the proper name, distinguishes one of Abraham's sons from the other.[15]

The proper name therefore defines biblical character. In doing so, it ascribes unity and a full identity to the character and gives the reader a convenient way of referring to the figure and distinguishing it from others. The name may also carry symbolic meaning, which provides insight into the nature, appearance, or significance of the character in the larger story of the Israelite people.

The integral relationship between name and identity is apparently self-evident to biblical characters themselves. For example, when David inquires about the bathing woman whom he had spied from his rooftop, he is supplied with a series of identifiers, most prominent of which is her name: "Bathsheba daughter of Eliam, the wife of Uriah the Hittite" (2 Sam 11:3). Similarly, he requests the identity of a man summoned to his presence by asking, "Are you

---

[14]On this introduction, see Yairah Amit, " 'There was a man whose name was...' Redactional Variation and Its Tendencies," *Beth Mikra* 30/3 (1985): 388–99 (in Hebrew).

[15]Gen. Rab. In M. A. Mirkin, ed., *Midrash Rabbah*, vol. 2 (Tel Aviv: Yavneh, 1957), 262 (Hebrew).

Ziba?" (2 Sam 9:2) and identifies the son of Saul with the single word "Mephibosheth!" (2 Sam 9:6). In each case, the name conveys the other's identity to David.

The centrality of the proper name to the perception and construction of identity implies the converse: that the absence of the proper name contributes to the effacement, absence, veiling, or suppression of identity. Having waxed eloquent on the vividness of unnamed biblical characters, I must now admit that a good many of them, perhaps even the majority, make scarcely a ripple on the surface of the narrative. Not only are they unnamed but also they are described only minimally, and they speak and act briefly if at all. These bit players, like the mother of Rebecca (Gen 24:53, 55) and the consort of Gilead (Judg 11:2), are whisked off the stage before their measure may be taken.

ANONYMITY AND THE EXPRESSION OF PERSONAL IDENTITY

If the bit players are here and gone, other anonymous characters surprise exegetes with the amount and detail of their portrayal. The wife of Manoah, to whom an angel appears to announce the impending conception and birth of her son Samson (Judg 13), is a case in point. Her anonymity is "most striking," says Ed Greenstein.[16] J. Cheryl Exum comments, "It is surprising that neither the introduction nor the remainder of chapter 13 gives the name of this woman. . . . The absence of the woman's name . . . is all the more striking when we consider the fact that she has a central role here and is more favorably pictured than her husband."[17] For Greenstein and Exum, the wife of Manoah unexpectedly takes on personal identity.

Manoah's wife is not exceptional in this regard. Indeed, the most striking feature of the corpus of unnamed characters is the variety in amount, type, and depth of characterization and the degree to which they live on in the imagination of their readers. Some are shadows, their existence unmentioned in but assumed by genealogical lists, such as the mothers and wives of the many male descendants of Adam (Gen 5:3–32)[18]; others act briefly but are speechless, such as the man who built the city Luz (Judg 1:26) or the man who dreams of Gideon and his army (Judg 7:13–14). Some, such as the wise woman of Tekoa and the medium of Endor, are secondary to named characters but indispensable to the plots of their respective narrative segments; others, like Abraham's servant (Gen 24) and Manoah's wife (Judg 13), are themselves richly drawn protagonists of

[16]"The Riddle of Samson," *Prooftexts* 1 (1981): 240.
[17]"Promise and Fulfillment: Narrative Art in Judges 13," *JBL* 99 (1980): 45.
[18]See Phyllis A. Bird, "Images of Women in the Old Testament," in *Religion and Sexism: Images of Woman in the Jewish and Christian Traditions*, ed. Rosemary Radford Ruether (New York: Simon and Schuster, 1974), 41.

particular pericopes. Still others, such as the queen of Sheba (1 Kgs 10:1–10) and the squabbling harlots of Solomon's reign (1 Kgs 3:16–28), have enjoyed successful postbiblical careers in literature, art and drama.[19]

Anonymity renders the reader unable to distinguish the character from others by name. But even the brief comments here on the range and variety of unnamed characters demonstrates our ability to speak of them and, indeed, to refer to them. Identity creeps in as soon as characters are described, referred to, act, or speak.

Perhaps we readers simply cannot keep ourselves from ascribing identity to the characters we meet in print. As Thomas Docherty points out, character identity cannot be suppressed even in postmodern texts that deliberately set out to do so.[20] In a number of their *nouveaux romans*, Nathalie Sarraute and Alain Robbe-Grillet studiously avoid proper names.[21] Their hope is to destabilize character and hence subvert the conventional modes of characterization.[22] In marking the presence of character, the personal pronouns or initials these authors use also impute unity and character to the figures so marked.[23]

The postmodern use of anonymity is intended to subvert mimesis—that is, the view that a narrative imitates life and hence can and should be read as a reflection of reality. Biblical narrative, by contrast, manifests no such intention. The variety of literary forms within the Bible suggests that it belongs to that category of "idiosyncratic texts whose extreme singularity keeps them from belonging to any genre at all."[24] Nevertheless, some critics insist that the Bible itself *is* mimetic. Jacob Licht states that biblical authors "reproduce reality, . . . create an image of it; in most cases it is ordinary human reality, and therefore eternally interesting. Many other works of literature do this; it is a basic aesthetic phenomenon technically called mimesis."[25] Shimon Bar-Efrat comments that "few of the characters in biblical narrative are depicted extensively and in detail, most being sketched in with only a few lines. Nevertheless, they are convincingly *real* and *human*, and have unique features" (emphasis added).[26]

The Bible is therefore open to a mimetic reading in which characters are endowed with life in a world analogous to our own. Readers adopting a mimetic stance draw heavily on their experience in the real world to construct a narrative

[19]See James Pritchard, ed., *Solomon and Sheba* (London: Phaidon, 1974).

[20]*Reading (Absent) Character*, 72.

[21]E.g., Sarraute's novel *Portrait d'un inconnu* (Paris: Gallimard, 1956) and Robbe-Grillet's *La Jalousie* (Paris: Les Éditions de Minuit, 1959).

[22]Docherty, *Reading (Absent) Character*, 42.

[23]Docherty, *Reading (Absent) Character*, 70–72.

[24]Gérard Genette, *Fiction and Diction*, trans. Catherine Porter (Ithaca, N.Y.: Cornell University Press, 1993), 16.

[25]*Storytelling in the Bible* (Jerusalem: Magnes Press, 1978), 10.

[26]*Narrative Art in the Bible* (JSOTSup 70; Sheffield: Almond Press, 1989), 92.

world from the various features of the text being read. In doing so, they often consider the narrative world of the Bible to mirror, if only obliquely, the real world in which it originated. To Athalya Brenner, for example, the book of Judges reflects the social reality of Israelite women. Brenner observes that whereas only four of the nineteen female characters or character groups in Judges are named, virtually all male characters are given proper names, with the notable exclusion of those in Judges 19. She concludes:

> The reverse ratio of nameless versus named female/male figures must be a reflection of un/conscious social norms. Female figures, even when indispensable for a narrative framework or even when active within it, do not cease to be configurations of a certain extratextual "reality"; and that reality, given away by the namelessness of most of these female figurations, is plainly androcentric.[27]

For Brenner, the absence of the proper name not only effaces narrative identity but also symbolizes the suppression of women in Israelite society.

A mimetic reading of character assumes a certain commonality not only between the narrative world and the real world but also between individual characters and real people. If this assumption is at all valid, perhaps mimetic readers construct the identity of unnamed characters in the same way as we do the identities of the real individuals whose names are not known to us—store clerks, bus drivers, fellow pedestrians.[28] If so, then it will be useful to consider how, or perhaps whether, we construct the identities of the anonymous people in our own environment.

Phenomenologist Maurice Natanson defines anonymity as "the state of being unknown . . . a kind of hiddenness."[29] In everyday life, Natanson observes, we do not know anonymous individuals in the fullness of their individuality. Nevertheless, we know them partially, as "agents, that is, in the typified roles they play or the functions they perform."[30] The typified roles by which anonymous others are known to us are not necessarily stable aspects of their identities. A bus driver may also be a mother, daughter, and, at times, a pedestrian. Nor is anonymity itself a fixed state; indeed, all individuals are anonymous to us until we discover their names and learn more about them.

If biblical literature is read mimetically—that is, evokes a response based on our experience of the real world—then is it also the case that its anonymous characters will be perceived in their typified roles? The answer to this question

[27]"Introduction," *A Feminist Companion to Judges* (Sheffield: Sheffield Academic Press, 1993), 13.
[28]Maurice Natanson, *Anonymity: A Study in the Philosophy of Alfred Schutz* (Bloomington: Indiana University Press, 1986), 24.
[29]*Anonymity*, 23.
[30]Natanson, *Anonymity*, 25.

has been present, if not obvious, throughout this discussion. What are "the wise woman of Tekoa," "the servant of Abraham," "the queen of Sheba," and "the wife of Manoah" if not role designations? Even "Mr. So and So"(פלני אלמני), the John Doe of Ruth 4:1, is identified by his social role, a potential redeemer of Elimelech's land and posterity.[31]

Role identity in and of itself does not constitute personal identity. Natanson argues that although it is only persons who take on typified roles, the affirmation of a role means relinquishing personhood for the time being, resulting in a bracketing of the person himself or herself.[32] To the extent that the agent achieves dominance in the role taking, the person is set aside or obscured. The opposite of anonymity or pure agency is recognition, in which "the person is recovered in his full integrity."[33] If there is indeed a dichotomy between social role and personal identity, as Natanson suggests, then the role designations that label anonymous characters should further obscure their individuality.

But personhood emerges despite the best efforts of the narrative to keep it under wraps. Similarly, biblical narrative contains a variety of unnamed characters whose individuality, far from being veiled or eclipsed by the social roles by which they are designated, is expressed in and through those very roles. In Natanson's terms, they are persons at the same time as they are agents. For illustration, we return to the anonymous protagonist of Judges 13. Though defined throughout the passage as Manoah's wife, her words, actions, and interactions both amplify and challenge this mode of identification, just as her centrality to the passage belies the insignificance implied by her anonymity. In forcing the reader to use "the wife of Manoah" rather than, say, Eluma (as she is called in *BibAnt*, 42), anonymity draws attention to the interplay between the wifely role and her narrative portrayal and thereby to the uniqueness and individuality which personal identity expresses.

ANONYMITY AND THE BOUNDARIES OF PERSONAL IDENTITY

Even the most vivid of our anonymous company are nonetheless blurred around the edges, as if the outlines of their identities were traced by dotted lines rather than encased in a solid frame. Individuality is compromised by the generic nature of the role designations themselves. Anonymity allows us to see Manoah's

---

[31]The designation "Mr. So and So" is obscured in the NRSV, which translates פלני אלמני as "friend."

[32]Maurice Natanson, *Phenomenology, Role, and Reason: Essays on the Coherence and Deformation of Social Reality* (Springfield, Ill.: Charles C. Thomas, 1974), 163, 164, 170.

[33]Natanson, *Phenomenology*, 164, 168.

wife as a representative of the general category *wife*, despite the uniqueness of her experience. Furthermore, our ability to distinguish among unnamed characters may be hampered by the use of personal pronouns. The phrase "he said to him" (1 Kgs 13:18) makes it difficult to sort out the dialogue between the Judahite man of God and the old prophet of Bethel. Passages such as Judges 19–21, in which some or even all the characters are anonymous, call to mind the cliché that you can't tell the players without a program.

Anonymity in postmodern literature not only challenges conventional assumptions concerning anonymity and identity but also obscures the distinctions between the reader outside the text and the voices within it. This effect, too, is an element of postmodern characterization in the *nouveau roman*. Through the anonymity of his characters, Robbe-Grillet manages the point of view in his fiction in such a way as to make the reader the central character. In doing so, he places the reader in the locus from which the world of the novel is seen.[34] Robbe-Grillet's endeavor is "tantamount to having the reader inscribe his or her own name in the empty *locus* in this text, to ascribe a position to the self of the reader."[35] The reader therefore "becomes" the character and is invited by the anonymity of the character to adopt his or her position or point of view in the text.

Then again, argues William Flesch, perhaps the lesson to be learned from the anonymous mode of characterization concerns not the commonality of human life but its fictionality: "There is something fictional about all people, something susceptible to anonymity, in the vanishing space beyond generality where pure interiority ... and pure exteriority ... coincide; and that this fictionality requires our deepest attentiveness, even if it perpetually defeats our acknowledgement."[36]

This study is comprised of three parts, each corresponding to one of the aspects just outlined. Part I focuses on the role of anonymity in the effacement of personal identity. The first chapter looks at the bit players as a general category and the factors that combine to hide their individuality. The following two chapters examine two subsets of the bit players. Personal attendants, such as servants and armor-bearers, are the subject of chapter 2; purveyors of information, such as messengers and informers, are discussed in chapter 3. Many of these figures are eminently forgettable. A number of them, however, unveil themselves through the amount and nature of their narrative portrayal.

[34]Natanson, *Phenomenology*, 164, 168.
[35]Natanson, *Phenomenology*, 164, 168.
[36]"Anonymity and Unhappiness in Proust and Wittgenstein," *Criticism* 29 (1987): 475.

Part II, on the emergence of personal identity, considers two groups of characters. Chapter 4 focuses on anonymous characters who are defined in terms of their professional roles. The depiction of these figures focuses on their success or lack of success in fulfilling the terms and requirements of their professional roles. Chapter 5 presents a range of female characters whose narrative portrayal stretches or calls into question the stereotypical attitudes and behaviors associated with the familial roles of wife, mother, and daughter. These female characters are frequently trapped between the competing demands of their gendered roles. Diverse as their stories are, the figures considered in these chapters share two features. Unlike most of the bit players discussed in part I, these figures are in the narrative spotlight within their respective pericopes. Moreover, their personal identities, including character traits, self-interest and worldview, emerge precisely in the ways in which they act out their social roles.

Part III, on the blurring of boundaries, begins by looking at the ways in which anonymity destabilizes character. Chapter 6 looks at the permeability of personal identity that exists among unnamed characters and between the categories of the named and unnamed themselves. Chapter 7 explores the impact of anonymity on our reading of the divine-human relationship on the basis of blurred boundaries among humans, angels and the divine. Finally, postmodern literature and theory suggest that anonymity can transcend the borders between the readers and the text. The question of whether and to what degree this occurs in the reading of biblical literature is addressed in chapter 8.

In considering the complex relationship between anonymity and identity, we make the acquaintance of most of the individual unnamed characters in biblical narrative. Doing so will allow us to fill out our demographic survey by addressing issues of gender and social realities that are raised by Trible and Brenner.

My sojourn with the unnamed has challenged many of the expectations with which I entered their world. Nevertheless, some basic assumptions remain. First, the details of and gaps within the text, such as role designations and the absence of the name, are meaningful. I do not mean that these features necessarily encode the intentions of the historical author(s) but rather that they are available for the reader's use in constructing character and making meaning. Second, the ambiguities and indeterminacies of the text will be resolved by different readers in different ways. My own view is that it is often preferable, or at least more interesting, to allow narrative tensions to inform one's interpretations without necessarily aiming for resolution. Finally, as elements of narrative, I consider both God and the narrator to be singular and masculine. The use of "he" for God does not reflect my views on the nature of the deity as such, but it is consistent with the usage of masculine pronouns for God within biblical narrative itself. Similarly, the use of "he" for the narrator is not a statement regarding biblical authorship but simply a way of signaling the generally androcentric worldview of the text.

The analysis I present here is fundamentally a description of my own encounters with the anonymous characters of biblical narrative. I have no doubt that other readers respond in different ways to these figures and configure the relationship between anonymity and identity in their own terms. I hope that my explorations will open a door through which others will enter the intriguing domain of the unnamed.

PART I

ANONYMITY AND
THE EFFACEMENT OF
PERSONAL IDENTITY

1

⊞   ⊞   ⊞

The Bit Players

THE MAJORITY OF UNNAMED BIBLICAL CHARACTERS are obscure, incidental figures, who make only fleeting appearances in the narrative. Some are defined by the most general of terms: *man* (איש) and *woman* (אשה), *boy* (נער) and *girl* (נערה),[1] amplified, if at all, by place name or tribal affiliation only. Many of them carry out a single act and then disappear. These bit players, minor as they are, have major literary functions in the narrative as a whole. In this chapter, I examine their contribution to the plot and characterization as well as their role in conveying the narrator's ideology to the reader.

PLOT

Unnamed incidental characters often provide crucial links in the plot and contribute to its impact upon the reader.[2] Had not a man told Joseph where to find his brothers (Gen 37:15, 17), Joseph might be wandering in the fields still, and the Israelites might never have emigrated to Egypt. Had not "a man from the house of Levi" (איש מבית לוי) married a "Levite woman" (בת-לוי), Moses would

---

[1]The latter terms frequently denote servants or messengers. See chapters 3 and 5 in this book. The designations *son* (בן) and *daughter* (בת) appear infrequently as sole designations.

[2]This is true of named minor characters as well. See Uriel Simon, "Minor Characters in Biblical Narrative," *JSOT* 46 (1990):11–19.

not have been born.[3] Similarly active are the captive boy (נער) who draws up a list of officials and elders of Sukkoth for Gideon (Judg 8:14), the boy (נער) who leads the blind Samson by the hand to his final exploit (Judg 16:26) and the man (איש) who draws his bow at random and hits the king of Israel (1 Kgs 22: 34). Though most of these characters remain obscure, their momentary presence moves the narrative line along from one point to the next.

In some cases, the specific role designation is a central aspect of the character's portrayal and accounts for the figure's role in plot development. For example, Mr. So and So (Ruth 4:1) is the next-of-kin (literally, "redeemer"; גואל), who, according to the laws of levirate marriage, technically was required to marry Ruth and to father a son and heir for her late husband.[4] This "redeemer" was apparently unknown either to Ruth or Naomi; he is first mentioned as a potential obstacle to the marriage of Ruth and Boaz during their night together at the barley harvest (Ruth 3:12–13). On the morrow, Boaz craftily confronts the man and offers, "If you will redeem it [Naomi's property], redeem it; but if you will not, tell me . . . for . . . I come after you" (4:4). The man immediately agrees to redeem it (4:4) but changes his mind as soon as Boaz tells him that along with the land comes Naomi's daughter-in-law Ruth. He then relinquishes his right of redemption to Boaz. "I cannot redeem it for myself without damaging my own inheritance" (4:6), he explains, thereby redeeming the romantic situation for Boaz and Ruth. His anonymity corresponds to his disappearance from the lives of Ruth and Boaz and from the narrative itself.

This figure draws the reader through a range of emotions. Boaz's mention of him as a potential impediment to his marriage with Ruth and the redeemer's initial eagerness create tension and suspense. The redeemer's rapid retreat releases the tension. It paves the way for a satisfying ending to the pastoral romance and for the birth of their child, who is the ancestor of King David (Ruth 4:18–22). The brief glimpse of the story that might have been—Ruth's marriage to Mr. So and So—adds depth without detracting from the book's idyllic quality.

Other examples focus not on the activity of the unnamed actors but on their passivity. Chilling is the reference to the firstborn son (בנו הבכור) offered up on the wall as a burnt offering by his father, the Moabite king, in an attempt to gain military victory over Edom. In the wake of this act, "great wrath came

---

[3]These two figures are anonymous in Exodus 2, though their names are given as Amram and Jochebed in Exod 6:20.

[4]The introduction to the book of Ruth does not specify whether Ruth was married to Mahlon or Chilion; Ruth 1:1–5 thus provides a rare example of an unclear distinction between two named characters.

upon Israel" forcing them to withdraw from battle and return to their own land (2 Kgs 3:27). The implied causal connection between the human offering and the Israelite retreat shocks, for it suggests that human sacrifice, proscribed elsewhere in the biblical corpus,[5] has effected Israel's defeat.

Unnamed figures contribute to biblical plot not only causally but also materially and symbolically. Job's seven sons and three daughters head the enumerated list of his considerable worldly possessions (Job 1:2–3), the loss of which constitutes Job's trial and provides the occasion for the theological discourses at the core of this work. Along with the restoration of Job's wealth at the conclusion of the book, Job receives a new set of children (42:13). At this point, the names of Job's daughters—but not his sons—are given. Jemimah, Keziah, and Keren-Happuch, all named for perfumes and cosmetics,[6] are beautiful and rich, for they inherit Job's estate together with their brothers (42:14–15). This conclusion surprises both by its greater emphasis on the daughters than on the sons and by its apparent reversal of inheritance practices.

The unnamed children in the frame narrative of the book of Job contribute materially to the rise and fall in their father's fortunes. Their death constitutes a large part of his tragedy; new offspring crown the restoration of his wealth. Along with their material contribution, the children also symbolize the pattern of reversal around which the frame narrative is built. It is not the anonymity of the second set of sons that stands out so much as the contrast between the seven unnamed sons and the three lavishly detailed daughters. Why describe the daughters and not the sons? Perhaps it is simply too cumbersome to name ten children, though biblical narrators have been known to do so,[7] or perhaps, as Marvin Pope suggests, the naming of the daughters and the omission of the sons' names is an ancient Near Eastern literary motif, parallel to the Ugaritic myths in which the three daughters of Baal are named but seven or eight boys remain nameless.[8] Pardes attributes these names and Job's delight in his daughters to the new world Job has discovered after the restoration of his fortunes, "a world of beauty, of fragrance, of cosmetics—of feminine grace."[9]

But the most salient point is the reversal of social norms implied by the narrative. The anonymity and minimal characterization of Job's sons contrast

---

[5]See 2 Kgs 16:3; 21:6.

[6]Marvin Pope, *Job* (AB 15; Garden City, N.Y.: Doubleday, 1964), 293. The presence of the naming formula implies that these are newborn children. See *IB*, 1196. Ilana Pardes (*Countertraditions in the Bible: A Feminist Approach* [Cambridge: Harvard University Press, 1992], 153) comments that this is the only place in the Bible in which a father names his daughters.

[7]For example, Esth 9:7–9 names the ten sons of Haman.

[8]*Job*, 292.

[9]*Countertraditions*, 153.

with the detailed and individual identities bestowed upon his daughters. Whereas the biblical convention is to name and describe sons, the conclusion of Job focuses on daughters.[10] Although biblical law specifies that sons alone inherit, Job's daughters, too, are his heirs.[11] This reversal of norms parallels the reversal in Job's fortunes, which surprises in its extravagance. It must be noted, however, that if the narrator and Job contravene convention by providing the daughters with names and estates, respectively, they immediately retreat from this radical position to emphasize the numbers of Job's male descendants, many of whom no doubt were provided by these same daughters (42:16).

CHARACTERIZATION

At the same time as they contribute to narrative plot, incidental characters also flesh out the portrayal of major named figures. Rebecca's mother (Gen 24:55), Ishmael's wife (Gen 21:21), and the consort of Gilead (Judg 11:1) amplify the portrayals of Rebecca, Ishmael and Jephthah and imply their place within a family constellation, although these unnamed relatives do not themselves act in the narrative.

Many figures, however, contribute more substantially to the characterization of others. The life-giving powers of the prophet Elijah are manifest in his revival or resurrection of the unnamed son of the (also unnamed) widow of Zarephath (1 Kgs 17:17–23).[12] This story is repeated with some variations with respect to the son of the Shunammite woman and Elijah's successor, Elisha (2 Kgs 4:35). Similarly, Elisha provides a miracle for the wife of one of the disciples of the prophets so that she will not be forced to sell her children as slaves (2 Kgs 4:1–7). A man from Baal-Shalishah brings Elijah some grain, which the prophet miraculously multiplies (2 Kgs 4:42). A dead man illustrates the power resident in Elisha's very body: At death, the man is buried in Elisha's grave and

---

[10]This convention is attested by biblical genealogies, virtually all of which include only male characters. In addition, biblical parents (or perhaps the narrator) pay significantly greater attention to sons. See, for example, the accounts of the births of Jacob's children in Gen 29:31–30:24. These verses recount the births of twelve children; the names of the eleven sons are explained, but that of the daughter, Dinah, is simply noted (30:21).

[11]According to biblical law, daughters do not inherit, but the story of the daughters of Zelophehad in Numbers 22 and 27 suggests that at least in the story world implied by biblical narrative, and perhaps in biblical society itself, there were exceptions.

[12]John Gray (*I and II Kings: A Commentary*, 2d ed. [OTL, London: SCM Press, 1970], 383) argues that the child had not died; in his view, the verb ויחי ("and he brought back to life") signifies the revival, not the resurrection, of the child. Jerome Walsh (*1 Kings* [Berit Olam: Studies in Hebrew Narrative and Poetry; Collegeville, Minn.: Liturgical Press, 1996], 232) argues the opposite: that the child had indeed died and been resurrected by Elijah. No doubt a reader's belief in the possibility of resurrection, or the lack of such belief, may influence the reading of this verse.

returns to life upon coming into contact with Elisha's bones (2 Kgs 13:21). The predicaments of these players allow Elijah and Elisha to demonstrate their prophetic prowess.

THE NARRATOR'S POINT OF VIEW

Morality (2 Sam 12:15–24)

Unnamed incidental characters also convey the narrator's moral evaluation of a particular character's behavior. The unnamed first child of David and Bathsheba, born of their adulterous union (2 Sam 12:15–24), bears the unhappy distinction of being one of the very few anonymous characters not to have a name even within the story world.[13] Not only is his name not conveyed to us but also the brevity of his life suggests that he may not have been named at all. As a newborn, he has no speaking role; all that matters are the facts of his illegitimate conception, his illness, and his death. His conception led to the death of Uriah and the marriage between David and Uriah's widow. His birth and his illness provide the narrator with occasion to describe David's grief and the servants' puzzlement at its mode of expression (2 Sam 12:21).[14] Finally, the child's death atones for David's sin, legitimizes morally the marriage of David and Bathsheba, and clears the narrative path for the next son, Solomon, to the throne as David's successor. The anonymity of this child is consonant with his tragic role, the main feature of which is his death and effacement from the story and the Davidic line. Unnamed and only barely present in the story, the infant contributes to the main plot line of the books of Samuel and Kings and to the characterization of his father, whose torment, guilt, and grief add depth to his character. Finally, the child illustrates the narrator's judgment that "the thing that David had done displeased the LORD" (2 Sam 11:27b).

Political Ideology (1 Sam 4:19–22)

The political stance of the narrator is conveyed in the brief account of the unnamed daughter-in-law of the priest Eli, the wife of Eli's evil son, Phinehas (1 Sam 4:19–22). The early chapters of 1 Samuel establish Eli as a priest of Shiloh (1:9), along with his two sons Hophni and Phinehas (1:3). Unlike their father, these two sons are "scoundrels; they had no regard for the LORD or for the duties of the priests to the people" (2:12–13), "treated the offerings of the LORD

---

[13]The son of one of the prostitutes in 1 Kings 3 may also have died before being named.

[14]David reverses the norm by engaging in mourning behavior throughout the week before the death of his son and arising from mourning immediately after the child's death. See P. Kyle McCarter, *II Samuel* (AB 9; Garden City, N.Y.: Doubleday, 1984), 300.

with contempt" (2:17), and "lay with the women who served at the entrance to the tent of meeting" (2:22). A man of God came to Eli and prophesied that his sons would both die by the sword on the same day as a sign to Eli that the Lord has cut off the strength of his priestly family (2:27–36). The prophecy comes to pass in the Philistine victory over Israel. In an attempt to call the Lord into battle on Israel's behalf, the elders decide to bring the ark of the covenant, the symbol of God's presence, from Shiloh to the battlefield. The Philistines capture the ark, and many Israelites, including the two sons of Eli, perish (4: 11). Upon hearing the news, Eli, too, dies (4:18).

When his pregnant daughter-in-law, the wife of Phinehas, hears the news of the capture and the death of Eli and her husband, she immediately gives birth. Silent and unresponsive to the women attending her, she names her baby Ichabod (אי־כבוד; literally, "without glory"), meaning "the glory has departed from Israel" (4:21). According to the narrator, this name refers to the ark of the covenant as well as to her dead father-in-law and husband (4:22).

The duality of her identity is emphasized by the order and proximity of her twofold designations in her initial introduction: "Now his daughter-in-law, the wife of Phinehas (כלתו אשת־פינחס), was pregnant" (4:19). She is identified first in relationship to Eli, whom the narrative portrays as good, and second in relationship to Phinehas, who is evil. This dual identification circumscribes her fate and implies an ultimately untenable conflict in her identity. Although she is defined solely in terms of her familial relationships, the woman's words are prophetic. They focus not on her personal loss but on the divine judgment of the people of Israel. The prophecy and her death mark this moment as a turning point in the narrative and highlight the symmetry between the fortunes of Israel and the fortunes of the priestly family of Eli. The child to whom she gives birth will not be the bearer of an illustrious line but, in the name she has given him, a symbol of national misfortune and the moral barrenness of his house—all, of course, from the point of view of the narrator.

Social Values (Judg 9:53–54 and 1 Kings 3–11)

Unnamed characters are vehicles not only for the moral evaluation of major characters but also for many other aspects of the narrator's point of view and value system. The woman of Thebez (Judg 9:53–54) is remembered for the fact that she dropped a millstone on the wicked Abimelech and cracked his skull. Abimelech immediately orders his armor-bearer to kill him, "so people will not say about me, 'A woman killed him' " (Judg 9:54). The shameful death of Abimelech at the hands of a woman apparently went down in the annals of Israelite military history. Joab later fears that David will be angry at the Israelites for their proximity to the walls of Rabbah during their siege of the Ammonite capital and that the king will rail: "Who killed Abimelech son of Jerubbaal? Did not a woman throw an upper millstone on him from the wall, so that he died at Thebez?" (2 Sam 11:21). Abimelech's distaste at being killed by a woman reflects the view that war is men's business.[15]

An extended example of the ways in which incidental figures convey the narrator's system of values is found in 1 Kings 3–11. The beginning of this section mentions a daughter of Pharaoh who becomes Solomon's wife (1 Kgs 3:1; cf. 9:16, 24; 11:1).[16] The gift of the Pharaoh to Solomon, this woman is the token by which the bond between these two kings, and their nations, is forged. She neither speaks nor acts directly in the narrative. We learn little of her beyond the following details: She is taken to live in the city of David until David has finished building his house, the temple, and the wall around Jerusalem (3:1; 9:24); she is given Gezer as dowry, after her father captures and razes the city and kills its Canaanite inhabitants (9:16). Finally, to her falls the dubious distinction of being the first of Solomon's numerous wives to be taken from the nations that the Lord had forbidden to the Israelites for marriage purposes. As such, Pharaoh's daughter bears some responsibility for Solomon's downfall, which the narrator attributes to the idolatrous worship to which his foreign wives enticed him.

Because neither her words nor her actions are conveyed, the reader has no basis on which to evaluate her culpability. To a sympathetic reader, the woman appears caught between two sets of norms that entail different assessments of the alliance that her dual role as Pharaoh's daughter and Solomon's wife symbolizes. According to the norms of statesmanship, which Solomon followed in marrying her (3:1), the woman binds the states of Egypt and Israel as allies. According to the covenantal norms God has set out for Israel, such a conjugal bond is forbidden because of its perceived consequences—namely, the worship of other gods.[17] Her anonymity focuses attention on this critical undercurrent to her minimal narrative portrayal.

This woman's presence at the beginning of the list of Solomon's wives in 1 Kgs 11:1 accords her a role as the exemplar of Solomon's harem as a whole. According to 11:3, Solomon had seven hundred royal wives and three hundred concubines. Of these, only one is named, and then only in passing. As the mother of Rehoboam, the Solomonic scion who rules Judah after the division

---

[15]Exceptions are the wise woman of Abel (2 Kings 20); Deborah and Jael (Judges 4–5). The latter story focuses attention on the fact that Sisera was killed by a woman (4:9); this may have been a source of pride for Jael (4:22), who shows off the corpse to Barak, and for Deborah, who exults over Jael's act in her song of triumph (5:14–21).

[16]For a detailed study of this figure, see Shaye J. D. Cohen, "Solomon and the Daughter of Pharaoh: Intermarriage, Conversion, and the Impurity of Women," *JANESCU* 16–17 (1984–5): 823–37.

[17]Cf. Ezra 10:2–5.

of the monarchy, Naamah the Ammonite is named in the formula with which the narrative normally introduces the kings of Judah (1 Kgs 14:21).[18] She receives no further characterization in the narrative. The king's other consorts are designated as "Moabite, Ammonite, Edomite, Sidonian, and Hittite women, from the nations concerning which the LORD had said to the Israelites, 'You shall not enter into marriage with them, neither shall they with you; for they will surely incline your heart to follow their gods' " (11:1–2; cf. Deut 7:3–4; 23:3). Solomon's motivations in acquiring these women as wives and concubines were likely both diplomatic and political. Once acquired, however, he "clung to these in love" (1 Kgs 11:2), and they turned his heart away from the Lord and toward other gods, such as "Astarte the goddess of the Sidonians, and Milcom the abomination of the Ammonites" (11:5)—proof, suggests the narrator, that "his heart was not true to the LORD his God, as was the heart of his father David" (11:4).

The negative judgment of the narrator upon Solomon for loving foreign women, expressed explicitly in 1 Kgs 11:1–3, is also conveyed by silence regarding the offspring of these unions. That there *were* offspring is indicated in the formulaic reference to Naamah the mother of Rehoboam (15:21) and the naming of several daughters of Solomon who married his prefects (4:11–15). This silence regarding Solomon's offspring is emphasized by the reference to the son of his archenemy, King Hadad the Edomite (11:14). In some respects, Hadad is the mirror image of Solomon. Like Solomon, he married a close relative of the Pharaoh, and an anonymous one at that (11:19). But unlike Solomon, Hadad is portrayed as the father of a son, Genubath, borne of the Pharaoh's sister-in-law and raised in the Pharaoh's palace (11:20). It is a mark of Solomon's disgrace that his adversary is accorded the kind of conventional treatment by the narrator that Solomon himself is denied.

The principal comparison in 1 Kings 1–11 is not between Solomon and Hadad, however, but between Solomon and his father, David. Solomon's spiritual inferiority to David is stated explicitly by God, who informs Solomon that his punishment—the loss of his kingdom—is deferred to the era of Solomon's son, "for the sake of your father David" (11:12). The superiority of David is also implied by a comparison of the narrative treatment of their wives and children. In contrast to Solomon's many marriages, David's complex relationships with Michal, Bathsheba, and Abigail are recounted in detail.[19] Similar attention is

---

[18]For other examples, see 1 Kgs 15:2; 22:42 and 2 Kgs 8:26; 14:2; 15:2; 18:2; 22:1; 23:31, 36; 24:8, 18; not all mothers of Judahite kings are mentioned in the text, however. Cf. 2 Kgs 16:2.

[19]See the portrayal of Michal in 1 Samuel 18–19, Abigail in 1 Samuel 25 and Bathsheba in 2 Samuel 11 and 1 Kings 1–2. For studies of these royal women, see David J. A. Clines and Tamara C. Eskenazi, eds., *Telling Queen Michal's Story: An Experiment in Comparative Interpretation* (JSOTSup 119; Sheffield: JSOT Press, 1991).

given to David's royal issue. The narrative explains why Michal did not produce any offspring (2 Sam 6:23)—her lack of children is attributed to the fact that she despised and mocked David for leaping, dancing, and uncovering himself publicly after bringing the ark of God to Jerusalem (2 Sam 6:12–23)—and describes how Solomon was born and destined for kingship (2 Sam 12:24).

The anonymous royal consorts are therefore made to bear a heavy load as the rationale for the downhill process that results in division of the kingdom and the eventual destruction of both Israel and Judah. They also create a picture of the foreign consort as a type: married off by their fathers to a king in order to create political alliances, responsible for dragging an Israelite spouse into the mire of idolatry, passive and silent. The narrative absence of their names and offspring—prime markers of identity—not only expresses the narrator's disapproval of exogamy but also suggests a wish that these women themselves had been absent from Solomon's life. The narrator's disapproval of exogamy is not specific to Solomon alone but rather is conveyed numerous times throughout the biblical corpus, most vigorously in Ezra 9–10, which tells how the men returning to Jerusalem from Babylonian exile are forced to send away their foreign wives. The unnamed foreign women and their alliance to Solomon indirectly constitute a negative paradigm of behavior.

Other unnamed figures appear explicitly as negative role models. A man in Num 15:32 is found gathering wood on the Sabbath, a violation for which he is executed at God's command (15:35–36). The "man whose mother was an Israelite and whose father was an Egyptian" suffers the consequences of blasphemy and perhaps the idolatrous influence of his father's foreign origins when he is put to death for cursing the (divine) Name (Lev 24:10–23). Of course, many named characters also serve as role models and convey the value system of the narrator.[20] The bit players deliver the message directly and unencumbered by the distractions of plot, full characterization and lengthy dialogue.

The use of paradigmatic stories to affect the audience's perceptions and behavior is illustrated explicitly with respect to David. The prophet Nathan forces David to face the enormity of his adultery with Bathsheba and his role in the death of her husband, Uriah, by telling him a parable featuring two anonymous men (שְׁנֵי אֲנָשִׁים). The rich man of the parable takes the lamb of the poor man to feed his own guest (2 Sam 12:1–4). The story provokes David's anger: The rich man deserves to die. Nathan proclaims to David, "You are the man!" (12:7) and conveys God's judgment against him. David acknowledges, "I have sinned against the LORD" (12:13).

In a similar fashion, the wise woman of Tekoa convinces David to bring his banished son, Absalom, back to Jerusalem (2 Sam 14:1–24). The woman

[20]For example, Abraham is the model of hospitality, Moses of prophecy, Solomon of wisdom.

delivers a dramatic monologue in which she plays a distressed widow asking for the king's intervention in a family feud. During a fight, one of her sons killed the other; now her family demands the life of the killer. The woman begs for the life of her son, her "one remaining ember" and sole heir of her husband's name and posterity (14:7). After David promises to intercede, the wise woman draws the analogy to David's own actions with respect to his son. David allows Absalom to return to his house as long as he stays away from David (2 Sam 14:24). Just as these parables force David to recognize the effects of his behavior, so, too, do the vignettes featuring unnamed characters stress the consequences of actions that are unacceptable within the worldview conveyed by the biblical text.

In performing their literary roles, anonymous incidental characters further deflect attention from themselves. Within the social world created by the text, these bit players have full identities, unique personalities and joys and sorrows of their own. Their anonymity and their minimal characterization veil their individuality from the reader and provide meager opportunity or encouragement for a reader to bring them to life.

But occasionally, such bit players do engage the attention of the reader, if only momentarily. The series of unnamed individuals involved in Absalom's search for Ahimaaz and Jonathan, David's allies (2 Sam 17:17–20) is a case in point:

> Jonathan and Ahimaaz were waiting at En-rogel; the female servant (השפחה) used to go and tell them, and they would go and tell King David; for they could not risk being seen entering the city. But a *boy* (נער) saw them and told Absalom; so both of them went away quickly, and came to the house of a *man* (איש) at Bahurim who had a well in his courtyard; and they went down into it. The *woman* (האישה) took a cloth, stretched it over the well's mouth, and spread out grain on it; and nothing was known of it. When Absalom's servants came to the *woman* at the house, they said, "Where are Ahimaaz and Jonathan?" The *woman* said to them, "They have crossed over the brook of water." And when they had searched and could not find them, they returned to Jerusalem. (translation mine; emphasis added)

Through their bit parts in the tragic conflict between David and his son Absalom, these figures not only expose the pro-Davidic perspective of the narrator but also reveal themselves to be resourceful and creative in their support of the king against his enemies.

Some incidental figures are remembered for an unusual act or word. Lot's wife is famous, or perhaps notorious, for her backward glance at Sodom and Gomorrah. As punishment for violating the rescuing angels' explicit command not to look back at the burning cities, she is transformed into a pillar of salt

(Gen 19:26).[21] No reason for this transgression is given, but various motives are imputed to her by later readers. According to von Rad, she could not resist a fascinated glimpse at the terrible fate of her town.[22] In the *Interpreter's Bible*, her act of looking back is thought to illustrate her reluctance to leave (e.g., Gen 19:16).[23] Pirke de Rabbi Eliezer attributes to her a rather more maternal motivation: "The pity of Edith the wife of Lot was stirred for her daughters . . . and she looked behind her to see if they were coming after her or not. And she saw behind [her] the Shekhinah [the presence of God], and she became a pillar of salt."[24] Yet this concern is nowhere evident in the biblical account itself. Indeed, we wonder at her absence from or silence during the scene of her husband's offer of their virgin daughters to the mob outside their Sodom home.[25] Whether this silence implies her feelings toward the children or simply the narrator's lack of interest in her response, it underscores the power of Lot as the father over his as yet unmarried daughters, against which the mother's voice may not have been heard in any case.

Her unusual fate and the absence of explanation still move contemporary writers. In "Looking Back at Lot's Wife,"[26] novelist Rebecca Goldstein, too, looks back. Recalling the fear that the story aroused in her as a child, Goldstein describes the answers her teachers and father had attempted to give to her persistent question of why the woman had looked when ordered not to. None of these answers satisfied a child who herself was aware of the many ways in which school, family, and society forbid her from looking.

More voluble than Lot's spouse is Job's wife, who, at the time of his calamities, urges him to "Curse God, and die" (Job 2:9). In its consistent focus

[21]For a structuralist interpretation of this verse, see D. Alan Aycock, "The Fate of Lot's Wife: Structural Mediation in Biblical Mythology," in *Structuralist Interpretations of Biblical Myth*, ed. Edmund Leach and D. Alan Aycock (Cambridge: Cambridge University Press, 1983), 113–19.

[22]Gerhard von Rad, *Genesis: A Commentary*, rev. ed. (OTL; Philadelphia: Westminster Press, 1972), 121.

[23]*IB*, 630.

[24]Pirke de Rabbi Eliezer chap. 25; *Pirke de Rabbi Eliezer*, trans. Gerald Friedlander, 2d ed. (New York: Hermon Press, 1965), 186. Despite the fact that she is an actor only in this one verse, Lot's wife stirred the imagination of many, no doubt because of her bizarre fate. The pillar of salt is mentioned in many postbiblical sources, including Josephus, *Ant.* 1.203); Philo, *De Abrahamo* 27, *De Vita Mosis* 2.10; Wisdom of Solomon 10:6, 7; Tosefta Berakhot 54a and 54b. Von Rad (*Genesis*, 221) suggests that the biblical story may present the etiology of an unusual rock formation.

[25]That his wife is present in the house is indicated in Gen 19:15, when she, along with Lot and their daughters, is brought out of the house by the angels and taken out of the city.

[26]*Out of the Garden: Women Writers on the Bible*, ed. Christina Büchman and Celina Spiegel (New York: Ballantine, 1993), 3–12.

on Job and his responses to tragedy, the Hebrew text ignores the fact that his losses are hers as well. This point, however, is made explicit in the Septuagint, which gives Job's wife a much longer speech, thereby allowing the reader to glimpse her own pain:

> How long will you hold out, saying, Look, I wait yet a little while, expecting the hope of my deliverance? For, look, your memorial is abolished from the earth, that is, your sons and daughters, the pangs and pains of my womb which I bore in vain with sorrows; and you yourself sit down to spend the nights in the open air among the corruption of worms, and I am a wanderer and a servant from place to place and house to house, waiting for the setting of the sun, that I may rest from my labours and my pangs which now beset me: but say some word against the Lord, and die.[27]

Chrysostom declared that "when indeed the wife of Job speaks, a Devil is at work."[28] But Job's subsequent speeches indicate that he, too, sees his experience as unjust in light of his faith and piety.[29] As Pardes notes "Job's wife spurs her husband to doubt God's use of His powers, but in doing so she does him much good, for this turns out to be the royal road to deepen one's knowledge, to open one's eyes."[30]

Despite their minimal characterization, the wives of Lot and Job have long invited speculation as to their motives, personalities, and their relationships with family members. Although briefly portrayed and then removed from the narrative by death, the women emerge as individuals because of their contrary behavior and unusual fates. The very brevity of their depictions entice interpreters, ancient and modern alike, to fill the gaps in their own way.

The incidental, unnamed characters whom we have dubbed the bit players are, on the whole, eminently forgettable. The effacement of their personal identities is achieved through narrative neglect. This neglect, manifested in the absence of proper names, actions, and other details, creates distance between these characters and the reader; the reader is thereby discouraged from dwelling on them as individuals. This effect is enhanced by their specific role designations. Unnamed "men," "women," and "youths" are not designated by a role that situates them more specifically within the social landscape of the narrative. The personal identities of figures defined through kinship are eclipsed by their fa-

---

[27]Translation based on *The Septuagint in English*, vol. 2, trans. L. C. L. Brenton (London: Samuel Bagster and Sons, 1844), 547.

[28]*Homilies on Second Corinthians*, III, 8. *Works of St. Chrysostom*, trans. Talbot W. Chambers, in *Nicene and Post-Nicene Fathers of the Christian Church*, vol. 12 (1889; reprint, Grand Rapids: Eerdmans, 1983), 292.

[29]*Countertraditions*, 150–51.

[30]Pardes, *Countertraditions*, 151.

milial roles. As wives, daughters, husbands, and children, they are not important for who they are as individuals but for the mere fact of their relationship to named and more developed characters. In all cases, the incidental figures advance the plot, contribute to the characterization of other figures, and express the moral judgments and values of the narrator. These narrative functions themselves deflect attention from the unnamed characters toward the major figures to whose stories they contribute or toward the behaviors and values they illustrate.

Personal identity creeps in even under these circumstances, particularly with respect to characters who behave in unexpected or unusual ways. The merest morsel of information endows the most shadowy of characters with a name and personal history, even if they are absent from the text. Personal identity itself is not absent but simply hidden from the reader, suppressed by a narrator whose interests lie elsewhere.

2

◈   ◈   ◈

Servants, Stewards and Armor-Bearers

A LARGE GROUP WITHIN the category I have called the bit players is comprised of personal attendants: the servants, stewards, armor-bearers or "lads" of kings, prophets and other dignitaries. Like the briefly mentioned and unnamed mothers, husbands, and children, they are given scant narrative attention. What distinguishes personal attendants from unnamed family members, though, is the nature of the designated role itself. The servant participates in a hierarchical relationship in which he or she is the subordinate party. Because the task of the servant is to serve, the servant's activity draws attention to the needs and desires of the one being served. In this way, servants identify the one they serve as a person of wealth and power. The nature of the servant role itself therefore adds another layer to the veil over the personal identity of these sketchy characters.

Personal attendants are formally identified in a variety of ways. A youth (נער, נערה) is not necessarily a personal attendant except when defined as such by the possessive form, such as "his young man" (נערו; 1 Sam 9:5, "the boy who was with him"), or the narrative context, as in 1 Sam 20:21, in which Jonathan tells David that he will send "the boy" (הנער) to tell him whether he should flee from Saul. The designations *servant* (עבד) and *youth* (נער) can denote either a slave or servant.[1] Most narratives featuring slaves/servants do not address their legal status. One exception is 2 Kgs 5:1–5, in which the maidservant (נערה קטנה)

---

[1]*ABD* 6:62.

of the Syrian Naaman's wife is explicitly described as an Israelite captured in battle by Syria (2 Kgs 5:2). The most specific term in this category is *armor-bearer* (נשא כלים), which defines the formal function that the attendant performs for his master. Finally, almost all unnamed personal attendants are male. Exceptions are the aforementioned servant to Naaman's wife (2 Kgs 5:1–5) and the female attendants of Rebecca, including her nurse (מנקתה, Gen 24:59; the nurse is later referred to as Deborah, 35:8), and her other "girls" (נערתיה, 24:61). None acts in the narrative except to accompany Rebecca.

Servants are found primarily, though not exclusively, in the books of Samuel and Kings. This distribution no doubt reflects the preoccupation of those books with the monarchy, in which servants had an important function. Servants are frequently portrayed as group characters, such as the obedient entourage of kings and would-be kings. The servants of Saul (עבדי־שאול; 1 Sam 16:15–16), David (עבדי המלך; 2 Sam 15:15) and David's son and rival Absalom (נערי אבשלום; 2 Sam 13:29) act in concert on behalf of their masters. No differentiation is made between the personal identities of one servant and another[2] or, indeed, between one group of servants and another, except in their allegiances.

Inherent in the role of servant is obedience to one's master. Most often this obedience is rendered without consideration of the morality or legality of the acts themselves, as illustrated by Absalom's servants (נערי אבשלום), who obey his command to murder Amnon for the rape of his sister Tamar (2 Sam 13:29). Obedience is emphasized explicitly in 2 Sam 15:15, in which the king's servants express their readiness to obey David's order to flee Jerusalem in order to escape from Absalom: "Your servants are ready to do whatever our lord the king decides." One wonders, however, exactly what behavior was expected of—or fate anticipated for—the ten anonymous concubines left behind to "look after the house" (2 Sam 15:16).

The role of the king's entourage is not limited to unquestioning obedience but includes giving counsel. Even a young maidservant can provide advice that proves advantageous to her masters. Second Kings 5:1 describes the situation of Naaman, commander of the Syrian army, who was in high favor with the king of Syria—and leprous. The Israelite girl in service to Naaman's wife sparks a lengthy chain of events by suggesting in the most deferential terms that Naaman's leprosy could be cured by Elisha, the "prophet who is in Samaria" (5:3). The subsequent story proves her right.

Both obedience and counsel ideally express the personal devotion of a servant to his master. Jonathan's armor-bearer, who accompanies Jonathan to the Philistine garrison (1 Sam 14:1, 6), declares his willingness to participate in a very dangerous mission by telling Jonathan: "Do all that your mind inclines to.

[2]An exception is Esth 1:14, which names Ahasuerus's seven eunuchs.

I am with you; as your mind is, so is mine" (14:7). This verse is translated more literally—and evocatively—in the *Revised Standard Version*: "Do all that your mind inclines to; behold, I am with you, as is your mind so is mine." The devotion implied here is further underscored by descriptions in 14:11–14 of the brave acts of Jonathan and his armor-bearer, who scramble up a rocky crag and kill twenty of the enemy Philistines.

PLOT AND CHARACTERIZATION

Servants provide obedience, devotion and allegiance. These qualities deflect attention away from the servants as autonomous individuals with will, desires, and opinions and toward those who benefit from their fidelity and service. In doing so, they contribute to the narrative portrayal of their superiors and to the plot in which they act. By their very presence, and by their designations as servants to the mighty, they ascribe wealth, power, and status to their superiors. They also provide a background against which their masters' personality traits are etched clearly. To illustrate these points, we turn to two extended sagas in which servants are the linchpins in both plot and characterization.

Servants in the Joseph Saga (Genesis 37–50)

The early chapters of the Joseph saga feature three unnamed servants of Pharaoh, the butler, the baker, and the captain of the guard. When Pharaoh becomes angry with the butler and the baker, he throws them into the prison where Joseph is also being detained (Gen 40:1–3). In jail, the two anonymous servants and Joseph are in the custody of, and subject to, the captain of the guard. The remainder of the chapter describes the dreams of the butler and baker, Joseph's interpretations of the dreams as prophecies of death for the baker and of restoration for the butler (40:5–19), and their subsequent fulfillment (40:20–23). The chief butler reappears briefly in 41:9 in order to recommend Joseph, albeit belatedly, to Pharaoh as an accurate interpreter of dreams. This recommendation marks the beginning of Joseph's meteoric rise to power in Egypt.

Although the butler, baker, and captain are formally defined as Pharaoh's attendants, their narrative portrayal focuses on their relationship to Joseph. The captain puts Joseph in charge of the baker and the butler, effectively giving over to Joseph some of the power that Pharaoh had vested in him. This act foreshadows the powerful role that Joseph will soon play in Pharaoh's court, and the authority that he, as an agent of Pharaoh, will have over Pharaoh's subjects and over visitors such as his brothers. The action of the captain contributes to the narrative structure of the Joseph saga, which depicts Joseph's cyclical fortunes in his repeated rise to ever-greater power within the family constellation, Potiphar's household, prison and the pinnacle, Pharaoh's kingdom.[3]

Minimally characterized servants fill out the saga. Before hiring Joseph as the overseer, Pharaoh consults with his servants (41:37). Servants are implied though not explicitly mentioned in Joseph's orders to return the brothers' money to them, an act that makes the brothers fear his reprisal (42:25–28). Joseph's steward is ordered to invite the brothers into his home for the dinner at which he sees Benjamin (43:16) and to fill the men's sacks again with food, return their money and place Joseph's silver cup in Benjamin's sack (44:1–2). These servants both emphasize and mediate the gap between Joseph and his brothers. This gap pertains to the brothers' ignorance of the Egyptian governor's true identity and to the emotional distance between them. Most of all, the servants highlight the differences between them with respect to status. Whereas Joseph was their victim as a boastful adolescent, they are now his humble servants dependent upon his beneficence (42:10), just as his adolescent dreams had foretold (37:5–10). After the reconciliation between Joseph and his brothers, servants are no longer mentioned. Instead, Joseph interacts directly with his father and brothers, indicating that the relationships have been restored.

Servants in Saul's Story (1 Samuel 9–30)

Servants play crucial roles throughout the long narrative sequence devoted to Saul, the first king of Israel. Saul's saga begins when the young Saul and his "boy" (נערו; 1 Sam 9:5) search at length for Saul's father's lost donkeys. When Saul is ready to turn back, for fear that his father, Kish, will be worried about them (9:5), the young servant brushes aside Saul's suggestion and presses him to consult the local man of God in a last attempt to find the donkeys. Although the man of God is anonymous in this pericope, his identity is already known to the reader, who has encountered Samuel in the previous chapters of this work. His name will shortly be made known to Saul as well (10:14).

After some discussion, the boy's plan prevails. Saul meets the prophet Samuel, who not only assures Saul of the donkeys' whereabouts but also anoints him king (9:15–10:8). The resourceful and patient advice of Saul's "boy" provides a sharp contrast with his more immature, impatient and worried master. The servant's actions contribute directly to plot development by creating the opportunity for the encounter between Saul and Samuel, who will anoint Saul king. Having facilitated this encounter, the boy is dismissed by Saul (9:27). Samuel's message about Saul's future kingship is for Saul's ears alone.

---

[3]See Donald A. Seybold, "Paradox and Symmetry in the Joseph Narrative," in *Literary Interpretations of Biblical Narratives*, ed. Kenneth R. R. Gros Louis, et al. (Nashville: Abingdon, 1974), 59–73.

Early in his monarchy, Saul's servants introduce him to David, a lyre player whom they hire to soothe Saul's evil spirit (16:14). David begins as Saul's favorite and ends as his rival and nemesis. Servants are drawn into both sides of the conflict between them. Saul's servants must participate in the traps that Saul has devised so that David might meet an "accidental" death. When Saul sends David out to kill one hundred Philistines—a mission from which Saul hopes that he will not return alive—it is the servants who convey the inducement, marriage to Saul's daughter Michal (18:25–26). On the other side, the "little boy" (נער קטן) of Saul's son Jonathan is the means by which Jonathan confirms that Saul is, indeed, seeking his life (20:35–42). The servants of King Achish of Gath, to whom David has run for protection, identify him to their master and tell him of the rivalry between David and Saul. Fearing that they will harm him, David feigns madness in order to avoid entering the king's house (21:10–15). Finally, Saul's fear and jealousy cause him to suspect his servants of conspiring against him. He accuses them of withholding information concerning David's alliance with Jonathan and the help that the priest Ahimelech is providing David (22:6–10). Saul orders the servants to kill Ahimelech and the other treasonous priests, but his servants refuse (22:17).

Finally, Saul attempts to involve his unnamed armor-bearer in his own death (1 Sam 31:4–6). After the Philistines have vanquished Israel and killed Saul's three sons, Saul orders his armor-bearer to draw his sword and kill him "so that these uncircumcised may not come and thrust me through, and make sport of me" (31:4). Caught between the principles of personal devotion and obedience, the armor-bearer is unwilling to comply[4]; Saul then takes his sword and falls upon it. Upon Saul's death, the armor-bearer imitates his master and dies alongside him.

The Saul saga, opened by an episode that features an anonymous servant, is closed out symmetrically in the same way. Saul's final armor-bearer contributes strongly to the reader's assessment of Saul. By the end of the Saul saga, the reader has been fully impressed with the depth of Saul's hatred of David and his relentless efforts to kill him. This devoted and conflicted servant is the narrative counterpart to—and forms an *inclusio* with—the "boy" of the young Saul, whose guidance led to the encounter with the prophet Samuel that brought Saul to power in the first place. Both servants demonstrate their complete loyalty to their master, whether by refusing to acquiesce to his suggestion (1 Samuel 9) or to obey his express command (1 Samuel 31). These two relationships subtly mitigate or qualify the negative impression of Saul created by the plot of the Saul story.

---

[4]David M. Gunn, *The Fate of King Saul: An Interpretation of a Biblical Story* (JSOTSup 14; Sheffield: JSOT, 1980).

In the Joseph and Saul stories, servants propel the plot line by placing Joseph in the Pharaoh's government, by introducing David to Saul, stalking David, and aiding in the latter's flight. They also help to illuminate these and other characters by exposing the complexity and intensity of their relationships with other characters. In these ways they perform the same sorts of narrative functions as the other incidental characters that we have looked at.

NARRATIVE IDEOLOGY

The nature of their role rarely permits servants to expose narrative ideology. Because servants must obey and demonstrate their allegiance to their superiors, their actions and deeds reflect the point of view and carry out the agendas of the major named characters they serve. Exceptions to the pattern occur in those few stories in which servants disobey their masters. The possibility of disobedience exists, of course, in any servile relationship, as Saul recognized with respect to the servants whom he suspects of treason (1 Sam 22:6–23). Two stories in 2 Kings and their parallels in 2 Chronicles provide explicit examples.

The Rebellious Servants of King Joash
(2 Kgs 12:19–21 // 2 Chr 24:23–27)

In 2 Kgs 12:19–21, Joash, the king of Judah, is killed by his servants, who "arose, devised a conspiracy, and killed Joash in the house of Millo, on the way that goes down to Silla" (12:20). The narrator provides no reason for this event but simply identifies the servants as Jozacar son of Shimeath and Jehozabad son of Shomer. The more detailed version in 2 Chr 24:23–27 provides greater narrative detail. It sets the assassination in the context of the Aramean conquest of Judah and Jerusalem. The narrator explains Aram's victory as the Lord's judgment on Joash and Judah "because they had abandoned the LORD, the God of their ancestors" (24:24). The servants' conspiracy is attributed to "the blood of the son of the priest Jehoiada" (24:25), whom "they" (other royal minions) had stoned to death in the court of the temple at Joash's behest (24:21). After Joash was severely wounded in the battle, his servants killed him on his bed and buried him in the city of David, though not in the royal tombs (24:25). According to both versions, these servants, in turn, were killed by Joash's son and successor, Amaziah. The servants' children were not killed, however, "according to what is written in the book of the law of Moses . . . [that] 'The parents shall not be put to death for the children, or the children be put to death for the parents.' " (2 Kgs 14:6 // 2 Chr 25:1–4).

In 2 Kings 12, the servants' rebellion and murder appear to be random violence. In 2 Chronicles 24, however, the servants' acts are tied into the narrative and reflect a clear political perspective. The latter version suggests that

Joash deserved death; the man he killed was possessed by the spirit of God and prophesied against the king for transgressing the commandments of the Lord (24:20). The servants carry out God's vengeance as the dying man had implored (24:21); they thereby express the negative judgment of the narrator upon the idolatrous king.

The Treasonous Servants of Amon
(2 Kgs 21:19–26 // 2 Chr 33:21–25)

This episode, too, involves a king of Judah, Amon, who "did what was evil in the sight of the LORD" (2 Kgs 21:20); he worshiped idols and abandoned the Lord (21:21–22). His servants conspired against him and killed him in his house (21:23). Like the rebellious servants of Joash, these men were killed in turn. Their killer was not Amon's successor, as were the assassins of Joash, but "the people of the land," who installed Amon's son Josiah in his place (21:24). The rebellion of the servants initially plays out the narrative point of view concerning the evil King Amon. But the servants' own deaths at the hands of the people imply that a contrary ethic is at stake: rebellion, even against an evil king, is not to be condoned and must be punished by death.

Aside from those who conspire against their kings, unnamed biblical servants are faithful to their superiors and commit acts both honorable and odious at their command. Although they are not vehicles for the political or social convictions of the narrator, they illustrate the values of loyalty, devotion, obedience and allegiance and imply their centrality to the narrator's worldview.

PERSONAL IDENTITY DESPITE ANONYMITY

The Israelite Servant Girl (2 Kgs 5:1–5)

The emphasis on service and obedience leaves little room for the expression of a servant's individuality, beyond the degree to which he or she is capable of carrying out the required duties. However impressed we may be by the unflagging devotion their armor-bearers show to Saul and Jonathan and the willingness of Absalom's servants to kill Amnon, these aspects tell us little about these servants as individuals. Slightly more vivid is the servant girl who refers the leprous Naaman to the Israelite prophet who can cure him. Her knowledge is attributable to the fact that she herself is an Israelite captive. Her youth is emphasized by her designation as a young girl (נערה) and her forthrightness allows us to imagine her as spirited and bold (5:2–3). Maurice Samuel refers to her as the "indispensable instrument" of a famous affair; he senses "a quiet assurance . . . from her brief presence, adding a permanent note of goodness to the world's consciousness."[5] For these reasons, he holds her in special affection and singles her out that she "not be lost in the tumult of the events she set in motion."[6] Little narrative encouragement, indeed, is required in order for Samuel to breathe life into this anonymous figure.

Abraham's Servant (Gen 24:1–67)

More fodder for the reader's imagination is provided by the venerable servant of Abraham (Genesis 24), whom the elderly Abraham delegates to secure a wife for Isaac. After he is given his commission by Abraham (24:1–9), the servant meets Rebecca by the well and bestows gifts upon her (24:10–27). He is then welcomed at her family's home (24:28–33). The servant launches into a lengthy monologue, describing the financial resources of his master and recapitulating the first two scenes of the pericope (24:34–49). By the conclusion, he has succeeded in persuading Rebecca's parents to allow the match. Negotiations ensue over the timing of Rebecca's departure. The next morning, Rebecca herself makes the final decision to accompany the servant back to his home that very day (24:50–61). The final section describes the meeting of Isaac and Rebecca and the consummation of their marriage (24:62–67).

This brief summary points to the servant's major role in the pericope. Of the sixty-seven verses of this chapter, forty of them are occupied with the narration of this servant's words and deeds. He is the major actor in each of the narrative segments and interacts significantly with each of its other actors—Abraham, Rebecca, and her family—except Isaac. The anonymity of this figure was an irritant to ancient commentators, perhaps because it was assumed to be inconsistent with his central role. Rabbinic midrash identifies him with the Damascan steward Eliezer, whom Abraham regretfully considered to be his heir before his own natural sons were born (Gen 15:2–3). This identification is also made by von Rad, on the grounds that his role as supervisor of all that is Abraham's (24:2) would befit the heir-designate of Gen 15:2.[7] Nevertheless, many contemporary scholars honor his anonymity and adopt the designation of the biblical text by referring to him as Abraham's servant.[8]

Anonymity also affects scholars' evaluation of his centrality to the story. John Van Seters insists that there is no consistent focal point in the story, though the behavior of the servant is striking. Abraham's wish propels the story, but

---

[5]Samuel, *Certain People of the Book*, 77.
[6]Samuel, *Certain People of the Book*, 77.
[7]Von Rad, *Genesis*, 254.
[8]John Van Seters (*Abraham in History and Tradition* [New Haven: Yale University Press, 1975], 247 note 45) believes that there is no justification for identifying the servant with "Eliezer" of 15:2. Cf. E. A. Speiser (*Genesis* [AB 1; New York: Doubleday, 1964], 183), who notes that 15:2 appears to refer to the same servant as Genesis 24.

the patriarch himself quickly fades from view. Van Seters recognizes the prominence of the servant but comments that "he remains nameless and easily becomes a secondary figure in the final scene."[9] Wolfgang Roth, by contrast, does not assume that his anonymity necessarily relegates the servant to a lesser narrative role. Roth argues that the servant "fulfills his mission selflessly, patiently and prudently; he is, though unnamed, the central figure of the . . . story."[10] For Van Seters, the servant's anonymity outweighs his narrative prominence. Roth is convinced of the servant's centrality despite his anonymity. Although these judgments differ in substance, both subscribe to the view that anonymity is inconsistent with narrative significance.

Rather than privilege one view over the other, however, we can fruitfully look at the interplay between the servant's role designations and his behavior. Like other servants, this one is defined solely with respect to his master. The consistent use of "servant" or "servant of Abraham" to designate the man and of אדון (lord, master) to identify Abraham stresses this point. The terms appear not only in the words of the narrator, as in 24:10, "the servant took ten of his master's camels (מגמלי אדוניו) and . . . all kinds of choice gifts from his master (וכל טוב אדוניו בידו)," but also, repeatedly, in the servant's long monologue (five times in 24:35–39 alone).

The relentless emphasis on this hierarchical relationship, however, carries the seeds of its own undoing. Though subordinate, the servant is hardly effaced by the narrator. No lowly household employee, he is "the oldest of his house" and "had charge of all that [Abraham] had" (24:2). The term זקן (elder) denotes not only age but also, or preeminently, a role of respect and authority. He, like most other servants, serves his master without fail. But he does not enter his oath with Abraham unquestioningly. Rather, he seeks to establish the degree of personal risk, should his mission fail. The servant embarks only after Abraham promises to release him from his oath if the woman is unwilling to return with him (24:8). Abraham's assurances ease the servant's mind enough for him to accept the mission (24:9). They also emphasize the serious nature of the undertaking. Should the servant fail, Isaac will remain unmarried, for his father will not allow him to travel (24:8) or consent to have Isaac find a local bride (24:3).

As befits his role, the servant acts on his master's behalf and not on his own. But the nature of the mission requires that he exercise considerable judgment and initiative. In the absence of clear guidelines from Abraham, the servant prays: "O LORD, God of my master Abraham, please grant me success today and show steadfast love to my master Abraham" (24:12). He then proposes the following test for identifying the woman suitable as a bride for Isaac (24:

---

[9]*Abraham*, 244, 247.
[10]"The Wooing of Rebekah: A Tradition-Critical Study of Genesis 24," *CBQ* 34 (1972): 181.

14): "Let the girl to whom I shall say, 'Please offer your jar that I may drink,' and who shall say, 'Drink, and I will water your camels'—let her be the one whom you have appointed for your servant Isaac. By this I shall know that you have shown steadfast love to my master."

This prayer adds further substance to the servant's character by depicting his piety. As Nahum Sarna notes, "Be it coincidental or otherwise, one cannot fail to be impressed by the fact that it is this man who is the first person of whom it is expressly recorded in the Bible that he prayed for personal divine guidance at a critical moment of his life."[11] The prayer also situates the events within the context of God's covenantal relationship with Abraham. Although the servant is under Abraham's authority, both of them are ultimately governed by God.

Most indicative of his personal identity, however, is the servant's loquaciousness or, to be precise, the length at which his words are reported by the narrator. The centerpiece of the chapter is the servant's extended presentation of Abraham's case to Rebecca's family in 24:34–39. Its length and content magnify the importance of the servant in the whole affair. As a reporter, he accentuates his own role in the events he narrates and refers to himself in virtually every verse. The overall presentation is hardly self-effacing. Rather, it emphasizes his piety, his importance in serving so great a master, and his resourcefulness in achieving his goal. Of course, one might say that even this grand picture is in the service of his task; after all, he is the only representative of Abraham's household to have direct contact with the family of Isaac's prospective bride. Yet the servant controls the story.[12]

In this way the story sets up a tension between the servant's narrative authority and the centrality of divine providential authority.[13] Of course, the servant has much at stake. His monologue must serve a twofold purpose. The first is to obtain the family's agreement to the match in principle; the second is to persuade them to allow Rebecca to depart with him immediately. Failure at the first stage would have meant failure of the entire project because Abraham was not willing to have his son travel to her home (24:8). Such failure would have meant loss of face and status on the part of the servant, as the one who had failed despite his best efforts to remedy Isaac's unmarried state.

The servant's persuasive abilities benefit from his astute measure of his audience. The fate of his mission rests formally with the father, Bethuel, and the brother Laban, who are defined in 24:28 as "her mother's household."[14]

[11]*JPS Torah Commentary: Genesis* (Philadelphia: JPS, 1989), 173.

[12]Sarna, *JPS Genesis*, 173.

[13]George W. Savran, *Telling and Retelling: Quotation in Biblical Narrative* (Bloomington: Indiana University Press, 1988), 46.

[14]Sarna (*JPS Genesis*, 166) suggests that it is usual for a girl to refer to her home as her mother's house. Cf. Song 3:4; 8:2.

These men greet the servant, invite him in, and make the final decision regarding his proposition. But the servant recognizes that it is also important to persuade the girl. To this end, he rehearses the events at the well at length, mentioning her frequently (24:45–49). He speaks passionately of his encounter with her and his well-founded conviction that she is the divinely intended bride of Isaac. That he has convinced the family is indicated in their assertion, "The thing comes from the LORD; we cannot speak to you anything bad or good" (Gen 24:50). But the decision to depart immediately comes from Rebecca (24:58), further testimony to his persuasive powers and to the family dynamics in which her decision carries weight.

The story conveys a delightful dissonance between the anonymity of the servant and his narrative centrality. His anonymity might signify self-effacement and eclipsing of personal identity, particularly when this pericope is read against the background of the other stories in which unnamed servants are actors. But the high degree of his participation, the initiative and prayer attributed to him, and the demonstration of his persuasive powers all belie his anonymity and allow us to construct a more complex and detailed picture of him.

Anonymity serves an additional purpose here. The gap created by the absence of the proper name provides the servant with just enough narrative flexibility to serve as a proxy for named characters. It is clear from the outset that the servant substitutes for Abraham, who saw it as his role to search out a wife for his son. As Lise Teugels notes, the servant is a full representative of Abraham, to an extent that at some points verges on complete identification.[15] But the literary structure of the passage suggests that the servant may also be a stand-in for Isaac.[16] In the other biblical examples of the betrothal-type scene—namely, the meeting of Jacob and Rachel (Gen 29:1–14) the meeting of and Moses and Zipporah (Exod 2:16–21)[17]—the prospective groom himself meets the woman at the well, becomes enamored of her, goes home to meet her family and eventually weds her. In Genesis 24, the servant functions as the groom's proxy: He meets the girl and her family, showers them all with gifts and then brings Rebecca back, relinquishing her to Isaac just prior to the consummation of the marriage.[18]

---

[15]"The Anonymous Matchmaker: An Enquiry into the Characterization of the Servant of Abraham in Genesis 24," *JSOT* 65 (1995): 17.

[16]Sharon Pace Jeansonne (*The Women of Genesis: From Sarah to Potiphar's Wife* [Minneapolis: Fortress, 1990], 56) considers it striking that Isaac was not sent; Robert Alter (*The Art of Biblical Narrative* [New York: Basic, 1981], 52) refers to the servant as Isaac's surrogate.

[17]Alter, *Art*, 52; Jeansonne, *Women*, 57.

[18]Meir Sternberg (*The Poetics of Biblical Narrative: Ideological Literature and the Drama of Reading* [Bloomington: Indiana University Press, 1985], 512) refers to the servant as the Wooer.

This point leads us back—playfully or perhaps ironically—to Gen 15:2 and Abram's plaintive plea: "O Lord GOD, what will you give me, for I continue childless, and the heir of my house is Eliezer of Damascus?" Had not God (with the help of Sarah and Hagar) provided sons for Abraham, it would, indeed, have been the Damascan Eliezer who would have carried on the covenantal community through the appropriate marriage and offspring. On an earthier note, the servant's role as Isaac's substitute may lie behind the ribald rabbinic tradition, which speculates on whether the servant and Rebecca, who spent so much time together on the journey back to Canaan, had sexual relations. Some midrashic treatments assume that Rebecca was no longer a virgin by the time she reached Isaac's tent.[19] Perhaps, they suggest, Rebecca lost her virginity when she fell off her camel (24:64), a fact that needed to be proven to Isaac, who otherwise suspected adultery between her and "Eliezer." Whether or not the aggadic tale reflects a prebiblical version of the biblical story, as Yair Zakovitch and Avigdor Shinan tentatively suggest, it makes entertaining use of certain details of the biblical story, including an emphasis on her virginity, the servant's gift of the nose-ring and two bracelets frequently used in the Torah in an erotic sense, and the field, associated with sexual misdemeanors, as the place where Isaac and Rebecca meet.[20]

Abraham's steward focuses relentlessly on the interests of his master. In this sense, his personal identity, like his name, is veiled by his social role, to which he himself repeatedly draws our attention. But the sheer quantity of narrative detail, the creativity with which he approaches his task and the almost exaggerated emphasis on his servile role single him out from among his fellow anonymous servants as a vivid personality in his own right.[21]

The individual identities of servants, armor-bearers and other personal attendants most often remain hidden beneath the veils of their social roles and the prominence of their masters. The distance that their largely impersonal portrayal creates between themselves and the reader contributes to their effectiveness in unobtrusively moving the plot along and accentuates the personalities, status, agendas, and aspirations of the major characters. The preponderance of servants in the books of Samuel and Kings relegates them primarily to the royal court and to the complex events and relationships that those books relate. The Israelite servant girl and, even more, Abraham's servant are exceptional in this regard. They reveal two points that continue to be important as we proceed through

---

[19]E.g., Pirke de Rabbi Eliezer 16:38.

[20]Yair Zakovitch and Avigdor Shinan, "Rebecca's Fall from the Camel: On the Metamorphosis of a Strange Traditional Tale," *Hasifrut* 29 (1979): 104–9 (in Hebrew).

[21]In this respect, the servant is similar to Gehazi, the amusing and crafty servant of the prophet Elisha. See 2 Kgs 5:19–25 for illustration.

this study. First, they indicate that anonymity and low social status do not necessarily suppress personal identity. Second, they show that personal identity often emerges in the contrast between the role designations by which the anonymous character is identified and his or her behavior as recounted in the narrative.

3

❖   ❖   ❖

Transmitters of Information

IN THE ABSENCE OF fax machines, telephones, and computers, biblical kings, prophets, and other dignitaries required the services of individuals to carry information, convey intentions, and act as their agents. It is not surprising, therefore, to find an abundance of characters whose main role is to transmit information. Some messengers are named, such as Bathsheba's husband, Uriah the Hittite, who carries a letter from David to Joab that details the instructions for his own murder (2 Sam 11:14), and Elisha's servant Gehazi, through whom the prophet speaks to the Shunammite woman (2 Kgs 4:12–13).[1] The majority, however, are as anonymous and lacking in personal identity as the technology we now use to accomplish the messenger's task.

Some messengers are implied rather than directly portrayed in the narrative. The plot of Genesis 38 is propelled by specific pieces of information that Judah and his daughter-in-law Tamar acquire about one another. The knowledge that Judah is going up to Timnah for the sheep shearing (38:13) prompts Tamar to meet him at Enaim in the guise of a prostitute. The message that Tamar is pregnant (38:24) provokes Judah to condemn her to death. Similarly, David

---

[1]With respect to named professional messengers in the ancient Near East, Samuel A. Meier (*The Messenger in the Ancient Semitic World* [HSM 45; Atlanta: Scholars Press, 1988], 15, 116) notes that "the evidence clearly points to many individuals who appear specifically as envoys over periods of up to several years." Occasional messengers in the ancient Near East, as in the Hebrew Bible, are not named.

sends for information about Bathsheba (2 Sam 11:3). The NRSV translation specifies an agent for this request: "David sent someone to inquire about the woman." But in the *BHS*, the agent is implicit rather than explicit: "And David sent and asked after the woman" (וישלח דוד וידרש לאשה). Such examples take the effacement of personal identity to its extreme by omitting any but the most ephemeral narrative traces of the messenger.

In many other passages, however, the messenger is more visible than in these two examples. A number of the terms attached to those who carry information, such as "man" (איש),[2] "young man" (נער),[3] or "servant" (עבד),[4] do not in themselves designate the person as a messenger.[5] Others are more specific. The person who informs David of the po$pular following gained by his son and rival Absalom is designated as "one who tells" (מגיד)[6]; the ones who scout out the land on Joshua's behalf are called "spies" (מרגלים).[7] The most prevalent designation, however, is messenger (מלאך). In most cases the context ensures that the human מלאך is not mistaken for his divinely sent counterpart, for whom the same Hebrew designation is used.[8]

Human messengers appear either as individuals or in groups of two or more. A specific number may be given. For example, the narrator specifies that David sends ten young men (נערים) to Nabal to ask for support (1 Sam 25:5). Most often, the number of messengers remains vague, as in Josh 7:2, in which Joshua sends men (אנשים) to spy out the land. No explicit rationale is given for sending an individual or a group of messengers, though scholars have attempted to create a meaningful distinction between the role of the one and the role of the many. Samuel Meier offers a set of suggestions based on the geographical and social realia of the ancient Near East. In his view, the plurality of messengers reflects the dangers and adverse conditions faced by long-distance messengers, which necessitated traveling in numbers.[9] The status of the sender and the importance of the mission may also have affected the number of emissaries and their identities. Balak sends numerous and distinguished messengers to Balaam, rather than lowly servants, suggesting to Meier that "the greater the size of the delegation the more honor applies or pressure is applied to the recipient."[10]

[2]E.g., Josh 7:2.

[3]E.g., Gen 22:3, 5, 19; 1 Kgs 18:43.

[4]For example, 1 Sam 25:39d–42; 2 Sam 10:1–5. Cf. 1 Kgs 20:2–12, in which the terms *messengers* and *servants* are used interchangeably in the NRSV.

[5]For detailed analysis of roles of messengers, the different terms used, and parallels in ancient Near Eastern texts, see John T. Greene, *The Role of the Messenger and Message in the Ancient Near East* (BJS 169; Atlanta: Scholars Press, 1989); and Meier, *Messenger*.

[6]2 Sam 15:13.

[7]Josh 6:22–23.

[8]For discussion of angels, see chapter 7.

[9]*Messenger*, 96.

[10]*Messenger*, 117.

Literary considerations may also be relevant. Meier comments that "biblical literature, when uninterested in messenger activity per se, employs a limpid cliche assuming more than one messenger. However, when biblical literature treats specific messengers, they tend to function alone."[11] While these suggestions are plausible, there is, in fact, very little narrative distinction between a single emissary or a group. The members of messenger groups are rarely individuated; they speak and act as one, as the examples in this chapter show. This lack of differentiation between individual members of the messenger group is only reinforced by their pervasive anonymity.

THE MESSENGERS' JS DESCRIPTION

The biblical messengers can be examined from two perspectives: their role or function within the society implied by biblical narrative and their literary function within the biblical stories as such.

Transmitting Messages

The variety and generality of the terms used to identify messengers requires readers to look beyond role designations to the specific tasks associated with biblical messengers. John Greene argues for five major types of messengers: the ambassador, a high-ranking diplomatic agent sent by one sovereign or state to another (2 Kgs 18:17); an emissary-courier, an agent sent on a specific errand or mission (2 Sam 10:1–5); an envoy, a representative sent by a ruler or state to transact diplomatic business with another (2 Kgs 20:12–19); a harbinger, who goes before the people or their leaders to make known their approach (Josh 2:1–7); and a herald, who either carries state messages from one capital or headquarters to another or proclaims and announces significant news or tidings (2 Sam 18:19–19:1).[12]

These differentiations draw fine lines within the generally coherent portrayal of the messenger in biblical narrative. The principal Hebrew designation for all such characters is the same—that is, מלאך—as is their main function: to transmit a message, whether written or oral, from a sender to a recipient.[13] When transmitting the message, the messenger frequently speaks in the name of the one who sent him or her. Through this device, we are meant to understand that the content of the message is uttered by the messenger but originates with and expresses the will of the sender. In Num 21:21, the Israelite messengers sent to King Sihon of the Amorites speak in Israel's name. They convey Israel's request in the first person singular (collective), saying, "Let me pass through

[11]Meier, *Messenger*, 119.

[12]*Messenger and Message*, xvi–xvii.

[13]In a slight variation, 1 Sam 11:9 depicts the commissioning of a group of messengers by a large group of people, the 73,000 who had been mustered by Saul.

your land" and utter their promises in the first person plural: "we will not turn aside into field or vineyard; we will not drink the water of any well; we will go by the King's Highway until we have passed through your territory . . ."

Pick-up and Delivery

Messengers may be commissioned for tasks other than the delivery of communiqués. Some are asked specifically to fetch particular people or items. Joshua sends the two men who had spied out the land to retrieve Rahab; they do so, but the words they surely would have spoken on this occasion are not conveyed (Josh 6:22–23). Later, Joshua sends messengers to the tent of Achan the Judahite to recover stolen goods (7:22); they bring the goods to Joshua and the Israelites and spread them out before the Lord (7:23) as a prelude to the judging, sentencing, and execution of Achan.

Messengers may be employed for sinister purposes. In 1 Sam 18:22–26, for example, servants of Saul are commissioned as messengers to express privately Saul's delight with David and, a second time, to order David to bring back one hundred Philistine foreskins. This plan, as the reader is informed (18:25), is intended to provide occasion for David's death. The failure of this mission forces Saul to continue his attempts, in the service of which Saul sends messengers to kill David at the home he shared with his wife, Saul's daughter Michal (1 Sam 19:11).

Occasionally, messengers expedite marriage or romantic liaison. Like Abraham, who successfully utilized his servant's services to find a wife for Isaac, David uses messengers to procure a lover or spouse. After the death of her husband, Nabal, David summons Abigail through his servants (עבדי דוד; called "the messengers of David" (מלאכי דוד) in 25:42), who tell her that "David has sent us to you to take you to him as his wife" (1 Sam 25:40). In 2 Sam 11:4, David sends messengers to bring Bathsheba to him.

Spying and Informing

Messengers are central to tales of political intrigue. Joshua sends two men as spies (מרגלים; cf. Josh 6:17, 25, where they are called messengers, מלאכים) to Jericho, charging them to view the land. They report that "Truly the Lord has given all the land into our hands; moreover all the inhabitants of the land melt in fear before us" (2:24). The nature of the messenger's role downplays his personal identity and characteristics and focuses exclusively on the message, its sender and recipient. The name, will and personality of the messenger are not described, presumably because they have no bearing on the message itself. Other "spies" are informers, who, in contrast to messengers, are not sent by one party to another but rather take it upon themselves to impart information to select individuals or groups.

LITERARY FUNCTIONS

Like other minimally characterized figures, unnamed messengers or, more precisely, the messages they carry, contribute to plot development, enrich the narrative portrayal of major figures such as Saul and David, and provide a vehicle for the narrator's ideology and viewpoints.

Characterization and Plot Development

Many messengers both move the plot along and add depth to the personality of the sender, recipient, or both. They do so by providing opportunity for other characters to reveal their personality traits. The story of David's interest in Abigail begins when he sends ten young men as envoys to Nabal to acquire provender and other aid (1 Sam 25:2–42). Nabal rebuffs the request, thereby enraging David. David's desire for vengeance is averted by Abigail, who intercedes with a long, obsequious, but politic speech. David is immediately taken with her, and he showers blessings upon God, her good sense, and her person (25:18–31). The failure of the envoys, while discomfitting to David initially, is ultimately to his benefit (2 Sam 32:42).

Another side of David's character emerges in 2 Sam 10:2–5. David sends envoys (עבדיו) to Hanun son of Nahash, king of the Ammonites. Their mission is to express David's condolences on the death of Hanun's father. These messengers are assaulted, humiliated, and dismissed by Hanun, who has been convinced by his own servants that the messengers are spies (10:3–4). Hanun's rejection of David's sympathy sparks a war between the Ammonites and the Israelites (10:6); it also adds to our perceptions of David as a man who deals faithfully with his colleagues but does not hesitate to react when humiliated.

Passages involving the transmission of messages often convey notions regarding the relative status of the sender and the recipient. Sometimes there is parity between them, as when kings send messengers to each other; frequently, these messages pertain to battles or other situations of rivalry or competition. Judges 11:12–17 describes an exchange between Jephthah and the king of the Ammonites regarding their mutual claims to land now in Israelite possession. The exchange is facilitated by the sending of messengers (11:12, 13, 14), and it demonstrates Jephthah's attempts at peaceful negotiation with the Ammonites as a prelude to his successful conquest of their land (11:21–22). The hostile negotiations between King Ben-hadad of Aram and King Ahab of Israel take place by means of messengers who travel back and forth between them (1 Kgs 20:1–12).

In many other passages, the messengers transfer information between two parties of unequal status. Messengers play a role in the struggle for power between Queen Jezebel and the prophet Elijah. By means of a messenger, Jezebel conveys to Elijah her vow to avenge the deaths of the prophets of Baal: "So may the gods do to me, and more also, if I do not make your life like the life of one of them [i.e., dead] by this time tomorrow" (1 Kgs 19:2). In 2 Samuel, David and his general Joab frequently communicate by means of messengers, as in 2 Sam 11:19–21, which describes the success of David's plot to engineer the death of Uriah in battle. The messengers are the medium through which these power politics are played out. This narrative role, essential to both plot and characterization, draws attention away from the messengers as individuals to the content of the message and the identities of and relationship between the sender and recipient of the message.

Narrative Point of View

The point of view of the narrator or specific characters within the narrative comes to the fore in those stories in which messengers fail to complete their assigned tasks.[14] Such stories frequently exhibit a threefold structure. Two examples occur in the context of Saul's prolonged but ultimately unsuccessful attempts to kill his rival David. In 1 Sam 19:11–17, Saul's messengers are sent to watch out for David at the residence he shares with his wife, Michal, who is Saul's daughter, and to kill him in the morning. The first time they come, Michal warns David, who escapes through the window (19:12). The second time, she constructs a dummy, which she places in David's bed, and she tells the messengers that David is ill (19:14). The third time the messengers see the dummy for themselves. When Saul confronts Michal with her deception, she implies that David had threatened her: "He said to me, 'Let me go; why should I kill you?' " (19:17).

This episode is followed immediately by another in which the same three-fold structure is evident.[15] First Samuel 19:20–24 depicts the repeated attempts of Saul's messengers to capture David at Naioth in Ramah. The first set of messengers succumbs to a prophetic frenzy; the second and third follow suit. Finally Saul comes to Ramah himself, "and the spirit of God came upon him. As he was going, he fell into a prophetic frenzy, until he came to Naioth in Ramah" (1 Sam 19:23). Saul strips off his clothes, falls into a frenzy before Samuel, and lies naked all that day and night. From this event, remarks the narrator, comes the saying, "Is Saul also among the prophets?" (19:24). In implying a connection between Saul's prophetic frenzy and the spirit of God, the

---

[14]Robert Polzin, *Samuel and the Deuteronomist: A Literary Study of the Deuteronomic History* (1989; reprint, Bloomington: Indiana University Press, 1993), 217. On the motif of the deceptive or lying messenger, see Meier, *Messenger*, 168–71. Meier suggests that the unreliability of the messenger may have been one motivation for the use of letters (171–72).

[15]On threefold patterns and their variations, see Yair Zakovitch, *About Three . . . and about Four* (Jerusalem: Makor, 1979; in Hebrew).

passage places the responsibility for the messengers' repeated failures upon God, who evidently preferred that Saul not capture David.[16]

The role of messengers in expressing the narrator's political perspective is also evident in a complex tale in 2 Kgs 9:17–26. King Joram of Israel, recovering from war wounds in Jezreel, is host to King Ahaziah of Judah. Upon being told by the sentinel that a company is coming, Joram sends a horseman as messenger to ask, "Is it peace?" (9:17). The messenger transmits the message, to which Jehu retorts: "What have you to do with peace?" Jehu commands the messenger to fall in behind him—that is, to desert Joram and join his men (9:18). The sentinel, watching from above, reports to Joram that the messenger reached the company but did not return. Joram sends a second horseman. He is subjected to the same treatment (9:19–20). The sentinel then identifies Jehu, son of Nimshi, as the leader of the company, "for he drives like a maniac" (9:20); Joram and Ahaziah go out to meet Jehu's company themselves. Joram accuses Jehu of treason; Jehu kills Joram and has him thrown on the ground belonging to Naboth the Jezreelite, which Joram's parents, Ahab and Jezebel, had stolen (1 Kgs 21:1–17).

In and of themselves, these events might be read as evidence of the treasonous and evil behavior of Jehu in usurping Joram's throne. But the larger narrative context shows that the narrator's sympathies lie with Jehu. In the pericope preceding this episode, Elisha commissions a member of the company of prophets to anoint Jehu king of Israel (2 Kgs 9:1–13). Elisha tells the man to anoint Jehu and to proclaim, "Thus says the LORD: I anoint you king over Israel," after which the messenger is to flee immediately (9:3). In carrying out this mission, the man adds: "You shall strike down the house of your master Ahab, so that I may avenge on Jezebel the blood of my servants the prophets, and the blood of all the servants of the LORD" and a series of details concerning the denigration of the house of Ahab (9:6–10). Jehu's officers blow the trumpet and proclaim him king (9:13). The narrator thus provides the perspective through which Jehu's murder of Joram is to be viewed: as a welcome act confirming Jehu's role as God's anointed. The chosen King Jehu is the instrument through which the hated house of Ahab is brought low. Convoluted as this sequence of events is, it illustrates the importance of messengers not only in the transmission of messages between heads of state but also in the communication of the narrator's point of view to the reader.

MESSENGERS AND PERSONAL IDENTITY

Despite the inconspicuousness that the messenger role requires, small hints that messengers applied a personal touch to their formal duties do emerge. The

---

[16]For a detailed study of Saul, see Gunn, *Fate of King Saul*.

sentinels and spies mentioned previously exercise some discretion in the content and timing of their communication, which, in turn, opens a way for readers to impute personality and individuality to them. Possibilities for verbal improvisation in the delivery of messages may also have existed.

Greene argues that the messenger delivered the message verbatim, orally, in writing or both, though this did not preclude additional elaboration or gestures by the messengers through their own commentary or deeds.[17] Meier, by contrast, believes that the messenger's task was not the verbatim delivery of a message. Rather, he was commissioned as a defender of the sender, empowered to argue, reason, and answer questions on the sender's behalf. The messenger was thus required to be a diplomat in often tense and unanticipated circumstances and to represent the sender's interests with "tact, truth and firmness."[18]

Both Greene's and Meier's positions have biblical support. In Gen 32:4–5, "Jacob sent messengers before him to his brother Esau in the land of Seir, the country of Edom, instructing them as follows, "Thus shall you say to my lord Esau, 'Thus says your servant Jacob. . . .' " The form of Jacob's instructions implies that Jacob gave them the text of his message, which was to be delivered verbatim. In other passages, the words "Thus says," or "Thus shall you say" are absent, yet the message is presented as the words of the sender. In 2 Kgs 5: 10, Elisha sends a messenger to Naaman with Elisha's prescription for Naaman's leprosy, "Go, wash in the Jordan seven times, and your flesh shall be restored and you shall be clean." These words as spoken by the messenger are clearly attributed to Elisha.

In other passages, however, the messenger's mandate goes beyond the transmission of a verbal message and entails exhorting or encouraging the ones to whom they are sent. In these cases, the messenger has some scope with respect to the actual text of his words. In 2 Sam 11:25, David gives specific words to the messenger who had told him of Uriah's death in battle and also suggests that the man encourage Joab. In 2 Kgs 18:17, the king of Assyria sends three messengers, entitled the Tartan (viceroy), the Rabsaris (chief eunuch), and the Rabshakeh (chief butler), along with a great army, to King Hezekiah at Jerusalem. Their message for the king is transmitted by the Rabshakeh through three Israelite functionaries: Eliakim son of Hilkiah, who was in charge of the palace; Shebna the secretary; and Joah the recorder (18:18). When the latter three complain about the Rabshakeh's use of Aramaic (18:26), he retorts that his message is really for the "people sitting on the wall, who are doomed with you to eat their own dung and to drink their own urine" (18:27). The Rabshakeh then proceeds to address the people directly "in the Aramaic language" (18:26) concerning their impending conquest by Assyria. As an emissary of the

---

[17]*Messenger and Message*, xvi.
[18]*Messenger*, 250.

Assyrian king, the Rabshakeh exercised his own judgment in handling this situation.

With respect to the personal identity of the messenger, however, it matters little whether the message is transmitted verbatim. These examples illustrate that the messenger's activity is entirely in service of the sender; any improvisations do not impute to him a personal agenda or identity beyond that necessary to fulfill his task.

Almost all messengers remain indistinct and circumscribed by the social and literary roles previously described. For this reason, it is virtually impossible to construct their identities beyond the role designations by which they are named or which they enact within their narrative confines. Their anonymity goes beyond the mere absence of the proper name to include the eclipse of personal identity. Exceptions to this general pattern are a number of messengers or informers who are identified by ethnicity, such as Cushite, Benjaminite, Egyptian and Amalekite, or by other personal details, such as leprosy.

The Cushite (2 Sam 18:19–19:1)

This passage is situated in the context of civil war between David and his son Absalom. The war ends with the victory of David's forces and the death of Absalom (2 Sam 18:1–18). Ahimaaz son of Zadok asks Joab for permission to run and report the tidings to the king, though it is unclear from his request exactly what he wishes to report and how. The request of Ahimaaz may be reasonable, given his strong support of David and David's use of him as a messenger on other occasions (cf. 2 Sam 15:27). But Joab refuses, for Absalom has also died (18:21), and sends a Cushite messenger instead. Ahimaaz begs to be allowed to run also, and, reluctantly, Joab relents (18:22–23). The reasons for Joab's initial refusal are not given; the context implies Joab's concern for David's reaction upon hearing of his son's death.

The scene now switches to the city gates. David's sentinel, watching for runners, sees Ahimaaz; David interprets Ahimaaz's arrival as good news, though it is not clear what constitutes good news in this situation. Ahimaaz reports on the victory in battle but, when asked about the fate of Absalom, avers ignorance (18:28–30): "When Joab sent your servant, I saw a great tumult, but I do not know what it was" (18:29). The Cushite then arrives with the news of both David's victory and Absalom's death: "May the enemies of my lord the king, and all who rise up to do you harm, be like that young man" (18:32). David's response relates only to the news of his son's death: "O my son Absalom, my son, my son Absalom! Would I had died instead of you, O Absalom, my son, my son!" (18:33; 19:1 in *BHS*/MT).

The Cushite and Ahimaaz present contrasting models of the messenger role. The properly named Ahimaaz is an engaged messenger, deeply concerned about the outcome. The unnamed Cushite, however, is an outsider, as his tribal designation indicates, and presumably less involved emotionally with the personal and strategic outcomes of the battle. Ahimaaz's inadequacy resides in his failure to focus on the issue of most concern to David. In contrast, the Cushite is the effective messenger, who provides an excellent answer to David's question.[19] Ahimaaz is insensitive; the Cushite formulates his message so as to soften the harsh news. According to Robert Polzin, "the Cushite tells the truth but deflects his answer away from Absalom by making the young man represent all David's enemies."[20] In a similar vein, Meier comments: "One runner shows his allegiance to David by desiring to run and cushion David against the bad news; the other runner in contrast shows his insensitivity toward David in cheerfully informing the bereaved father that his son is now dead."[21] Their formal behavior also contrasts: The Cushite bows when he leaves Joab but not when he greets David; Ahimaaz does not bow to Joab, who sent him, but only to David.[22] The messenger who is behind in 18:22 crosses over in 18:23 to become the one in front, mirroring the two emotional poles of the news that David is anticipating with both hope and dread.[23]

Anonymity therefore contributes to the contrast between the appointed messenger and the self-appointed one. There appears to be no particular significance to the man's specific identification as a Cushite.[24] The term *Cushite* generally denotes a person of Ethiopian origin. Although there have been some attempts to identify this Cushite with the man named Cushi referred to as a Benjaminite in the superscription to Psalm 7, the passage does not use the term as a proper name but as an ethnic designation.

The Four Lepers (2 Kgs 7:3–10)

This passage describes the activities of four leprous men outside the gate of Samaria as it was besieged by the Aramaeans. Rather than await death outside the gate or within the famished city, they defect to the Aramean camp. To their surprise, the camp is deserted, "For the Lord had caused the Aramean army to hear the sound of chariots, and of horses, the sound of a great army" (7:6) and hence frightened them away. The lepers feast and loot, until plagued by their consciences and by fear of discovery (7:9). Having been saved from desertion by circumstance, they bring the good news of the enemy's flight back to the gatekeepers of Samaria (7:10), who relay the message to the king (7:11). In response, the king sends messengers to verify the report of the leprous men

[19]J. P. Fokkelman, *Narrative Art and Poetry in the Books of Samuel.* Vol. 1, *King David* (Assen, The Netherlands: Van Gorcum, 1981), 261.

[20]Robert Polzin, *David and the Deuteronomist: A Literary Study of the Deuteronomic History,* Part III (Bloomington: Indiana University Press, 1993), 189–90.

[21]Meier, *Messenger,* 152–53.

[22]Meier, *Messenger,* 153.

[23]Polzin, *David,* 189.

[24]McCarter, *II Samuel,* 408.

(7:12–15); the people then plunder the Aramean camp (7:16). In the course of events, the captain chosen by the king to guard the gate is trampled by the mob. The narrator interprets this act as the fulfillment of God's prophecy that the captain, who had doubted the man's earlier prediction of these momentous events, will not eat of the plunder himself (7:19).

In this story, in which all the characters remain unnamed, the informers set into motion a chain of events that result in the fulfillment of a prophecy. Although the four leprous informers are not individuated, as a group they take the narrative foreground. Their leprous condition accounts for their marginal location at the gate of the city and the despair that fuels their decision to defect. Their motivations and the decision-making processes upon which their behavior is based are presented in detail within the narrative. Hence the description and the degree of narrative attention lift them out of obscurity. In withholding their personal identities, their anonymity draws attention to their leprous condition as the primary focal point of their characterization; their behavior and motivations are seen in light of this aspect of their identities.

The Benjaminite Informer (1 Sam 4:12–18)

In 1 Sam 4:12–18, a self-appointed Benjaminite informer runs from battle to tell the priest Eli in Shiloh that Israel has fled before the Philistines, that Eli's two sons, Hophni and Phinehas are dead, and that the ark of God has been captured (4:17). The information leads to Eli's own death: He falls over backward from his seat upon hearing about the ark of God and breaks his neck, "for he was an old man, and heavy" (1 Sam 4:18). For the reader, and Eli, the Benjaminite's information confirms the fulfillment of God's earlier word to the young Samuel, that "the iniquity of Eli's house shall not be expiated by sacrifice or offering forever" (1 Sam 3:14).

Is there narrative significance to the man's tribal designation? P. Kyle McCarter confesses, "It is uncharacteristic of biblical narrative to provide such details gratuitously . . . but in this case the point escapes us."[25] It is indeed difficult to suggest a thematic or literary function for the designation of the man as a Benjaminite. In this case, the designation imputes a degree of individuality to the anonymous man, but the paucity of narrative portrayal does not allow a more specific construction of his identity. Although the combination of anonymity and tribal designation creates the expectation that the man's identity is germane to the story, the continuation of the episode focuses attention primarily on Eli's extreme response to the message borne by the Benjaminite.[26]

[25]P. Kyle McCarter, Jr., *I Samuel* (AB 8; Garden City, N.Y.: Doubleday, 1980), 113– 14.
[26]In later biblical history, the Benjaminites acknowledged Ishbaal as Saul's successor (2 Sam 2:9). Some Benjaminites later transferred to David, but most did not (2:19). It is possible that this background had some bearing on the narrator's characterization of the Benjaminite, but no indication is given in the text.

The Egyptian Informer (1 Sam 30:11–16)

The Amalekite attack on Ziklag is the subject of 1 Sam 30:1–10. Many Israelites were captured, including David's two wives, Ahinoam and Abigail (30:5). David and four hundred men take up pursuit, buoyed by a divine promise of success (30:8). In the course of this quest, David's men come upon a starving Egyptian, bring him to David and provide him with food and drink. David queries the man's identity on two points: "To whom do you belong? Where are you from?" (30:13). The man responds that he is an Egyptian, servant to an Amalekite who had abandoned him three days earlier when the Egyptian fell ill (30:13). He then describes the Amalekite raid on Ziklag, thereby confirming his involvement both to David and to the reader.

Whether the Egyptian understood that he had been rescued by Israelites and was now being questioned by their head is uncertain. What is clear to both the reader and the Egyptian himself is the power that David has over the ill man. The exchange between them indicates that the important aspect of the man's identity for David is not his name or personal history but his allegiances and origins. Most valuable to David is the man's knowledge of the whereabouts of the Amalekite raiding party, the very group David is pursuing.

Having been abandoned by his Amalekite master, the Egyptian is prepared to betray the ones for whom he had formerly fought. Indeed, the Egyptian willingly assents to David's direct request, "Will you take me down to this raiding party?" (30:15) on the condition that David neither kill him nor return him to his master (30:15). Thanks to the Egyptian, David's party raids and despoils the Amalekite band and effects the release of the captives and bounty that the Amalekites had taken from Ziklag (30:18–20). This sequence of events fulfills the divine prophecy of David's success (cf. 30:8).

In this story, the anonymity of the informer draws attention to both his ethnic origins and his self-imposed role of informer. Although his actions propel the plot and result in the fulfillment of prophecy, his individuality emerges in his concern for his own safety and freedom. As future king, David has power over the man who is dependent on his goodwill. The man himself has leverage because he possesses information David desires. He may decide to convey or to withhold this information, depending on whether his conditions are met. Although his name is not divulged, central aspects of his personal identity—ethnicity, past employment, current concerns, and motivations—may be constructed from the story itself.

The Amalekite Informer (2 Sam 1:1–27)

The most dramatic of the biblical informer stories is the account of Saul's death, which begins the second book of Samuel and ushers in David's reign. The reader of 1 Samuel 31 has already read of the death of Saul and Jonathan in battle against the Philistines and is reminded of this event in 2 Sam 1:1. David, newly victorious in battle against the Amalekites (1 Samuel 27:8; 1 Sam 30), is as yet ignorant of these events.

A man in mourning garb arrives at David's camp and does obeisance. David does not initially inquire about his identity but demands information about the battle between the Israelite and Philistine armies. The man reports on the retreat of the Israelite army and the death of many Israelites, including Saul and Jonathan (2 Sam 1:4). Pressed for more details, he describes his own role in Saul's death. Mortally wounded, Saul had asked the young man to kill him, and he had obliged, knowing that Saul had not long to live. The man has brought to David the royal crown and armlet worn by Saul in battle. They are testimony to the truth of the man's story and tokens of the monarchy, which is now David's (1:6–10).

As part of this report, the man recounts Saul's inquiry concerning his identity. In response to Saul's question, "Who are you?" reports the man, he identified himself as an Amalekite. (1:8) This declaration had apparently satisfied Saul that the man was a suitable executioner (1:9). But if the man was expecting David's thanks for dispatching his enemy and bringing the royal tokens, he was soon disappointed. David and his men tear their clothing, mourn, weep, and fast until evening for Saul, Jonathan, and all Israel (1:11–12). David then asks the man, "Where do you come from?" The Amalekite expands slightly on the answer he had reportedly given to Saul: that he is the son of an Amalekite sojourner (בן־אישׁ גר עמלקי; 1:13), a long-time foreign resident in Israel. David chastises him, "Were you not afraid to lift your hand to destroy the LORD's anointed?" (1:14). He orders one of his young men to kill him and declares that the Amalekite is responsible for his own death, for he has testified against himself.

David's question concerning the provenance of the Amalekite is puzzling, for the man has already identified himself in his account of Saul's interrogation. Coming after David's formal acts of mourning, the question and its aftermath constitute David's first utterances as the undisputed king of Israel. Just as much as his possession of the crown and armlet, his near repetition of Saul's query draws attention to his assumption of this new role, as do his formal mourning of Saul and the judgment he enacts so swiftly in vengeance of his predecessor's death.

In killing the Amalekite, David has shown that he has believed the Amalekite's story. The reader might be less inclined than David to take the Amalekite's word, for his story contradicts in important ways the story told by the narrator in 1 Samuel 31.[27] In the narrator's version, it is the armor-bearer to

---

[27]On the issue of the veracity of the Amalekite's story, see Hans Wilhelm Hertzberg, *I & II Samuel: A Commentary* (Philadelphia: Westminster, 1964), 236; Polzin, *David*, 2–4; Yairah Amit, "Three Variations of the Death of Saul," *Beth Mikra* 30 (1984–85): 96–97 (in Hebrew). On source-critical solutions to the contradictions between these stories,

whom Saul makes his last request; upon the man's refusal, the king then takes his own life (1 Sam 31:4). The Philistines behead Saul, strip his armor, and place it in the temple of Astarte (31:8, 10). The reader is placed in the position of choosing between these two versions. On the one hand, the tone and content of the narrative impute reliability and authority to the narrator, who speaks confidently of the words, deeds, and thoughts of the characters, human, and divine. Unlike the narrator, the Amalekite belongs to an enemy nation and has been engaged in some questionable activities. On the other hand, the Amalekite's version is supported by his possession of Saul's crown and armlet and by his self-confessed role in Saul's death.

As the teller of the Amalekite's tale, the narrator himself is responsible for the reader's dilemma and provides no basis for a solution.[28] What may be more fruitful than deciding between the two versions of Saul's death is a consideration of the interplay between them. The question that remains at the end of the first story concerns the response of David. How will he learn of Saul's death and what will his reaction be? The second story answers these questions. As Yairah Amit points out, the second story allows David to show spontaneous grief but also permits the narrator to consolidate David's position vis-à-vis the reader by demonstrating his innocence of Saul's death.[29] The story also demonstrates David's moral superiority to the king who had plotted his death. Saul's repeated efforts to kill David might, indeed, have turned David against him and caused him to rejoice at Saul's death and reward his killer. Instead, the news of Saul's death is met with mourning, and the Amalekite is punished for his reported role therein.

The anonymity of the informer draws attention both to his identity as an Amalekite and to his behavior and fate as described in the story. As an Amalekite, he evokes the historical enmity between the Israelites and Amalekites, which may be traced from the period of the wilderness through the early monarchy (Exod 17:8–16; Judg 3:13; 6:3, 10:12; 1 Samuel 15; 1 Samuel 30).[30] Yet he is represented not simply as an Amalekite enemy but as the specific individual through whom Saul met his death. In this role, suggests Robert Polzin, the Amalekite doubles for David:

---

see Bill T. Arnold, "The Amalekite's Report of Saul's Death: Political Intrigue or Incompatible Sources?" *JETS* 32 (1989): 290–94; McCarter, *II Samuel*, 62–63.

[28]This does not prevent scholars from worrying about historicity. For a survey of interpretations, see Amit, "Three Variations," 92–102; and Arnold, "The Amalekite's Report," 289–98.

[29]"Three Variations," 101.

[30]Amalek continues in postbiblical Jewish literature to symbolize Israel's enemies. Cf. Josephus, *Ant.* 11.209.

In the narrator's refusal, so far, to give the reader more than a few glimpses into the inner life of David, the Amalekite youth comes to us as he came to David, as a personification of David's own motivations and perhaps even as an anticipatory suggestion of David's hidden role in the fall of the house of Saul. The narrator confronts David with his alter ego, and the reader with David's double.[31]

The Amalekite physically completes the process of destroying Saul and his monarchy that had been initiated by David's own successes. In killing the Amalekite, David erases this story. He refashions his relationship with Saul by means of the words with which he eulogizes him:

> Saul and Jonathan, beloved and lovely!
>   In life and in death they were not divided;
> they were swifter than eagles,
>   they were stronger than lions.
> O daughters of Israel, weep over Saul,
>   who clothed you with crimson, in luxury,
>   who put ornaments of gold on your apparel.
> How the mighty have fallen
>   in the midst of the battle! (2 Sam 1:23–25)

The anonymity of the Amalekite not only links him to an enemy people and focuses attention on his individual behavior and responsibility but also symbolizes the erasure of his presence, his story and the emotional road that David has rejected as his response to Saul's death. Yet in his continued presence in the text, the anonymous Amalekite holds open these possibilities for the reader's consideration.

The anonymity of messengers directs the readers' attention to their role qua messengers, to the content of their messages, and to the identities of and power struggles between the sender and recipient. Messengers are rarely described in terms of their personal attributes, and the narratives give no consideration to their personal will or intentionality. But the effacement of narrative identity, to which anonymity is a major though not the only contributor, is not a signal of narrative unimportance. Indeed, the activity of messengers is absolutely essential to plot and character development. These aspects depend on the transfer of information, particularly in books in which geographical distance and military activity are prominent.

Military settings also provide the context for characters we have termed *informers*, who convey intelligence but do not mediate a relationship between sender and recipient. Informers are not designated by nouns describing their

---

[31]Polzin, *David*, 4–5.

activity (such as *informer* or *spy*). This omission may be in keeping with the secretive nature of their role. Rather, they are described in terms of features that are incidental to the function associated with them in the story. These identifiers, such as *lepers*, or a tribal or ethnic designation—Benjaminite, Egyptian, Amalekite—beg to be used in the construction of character. In each case, some measure of significance may be ascribed to them. Leprosy accounts for the marginal position and the fluid loyalties of the four men who intend to defect from the Israelite to the Aramaean camp but, instead, find themselves as informers to the Israelite cause. The responses of other characters to the Egyptian and the Amalekite are affected by these informers' association with two peoples with whom Israel has had hostile relations. The Benjaminite, while within Israel, belongs to a tribe associated with tensions and conflicts at the conclusion of the book of Judges. Their formal designations with respect to medical conditions or ethnic identities remain secondary to their actions; their self-interested behavior constitutes the primary basis for constructing their identities. Hence in these cases anonymity does not obscure identity but allows identity to emerge through the unnamed characters' actions. Anonymity may also reflect the narrator's distaste for the informers' activity. None is rewarded for his actions; each disappears from the narrative soon after providing his information.

Finally, anonymous messengers and informers allow for reflection on gender roles and social context. All anonymous members of these categories are male, although the presence of female messengers and informers within the biblical story world cannot be ruled out.[32] The absence of females from these literary roles draws attention to the military context of most of these stories, in which the active participants are men.

---

[32]It is possible, for example, to imagine that it was their female attendants who reported the pregnancies of Tamar and Bathsheba to Judah and David, respectively.

PART II

ANONYMITY AND
THE EXPRESSION OF
PERSONAL IDENTITY

4

⊞   ⊞   ⊞

Wise Women and Unworthy Levites

A MONG THE CAST OF UNNAMED BIBLICAL CHARACTERS are those designated by autonomous social roles. These designations do not define them in terms of other characters, whether by means of household relationship or by means of their function. This chapter deals with two groups of autonomous characters. The first consists of four women described positively in terms of their wisdom and skill. The second consists of two Levites toward whom the narrator is very critical. Unlike servants and family members, these characters are not defined by their relationships with others or eclipsed by the content of their communications, as are messengers. Rather, they are contracted for their professional expertise or act autonomously. The main feature that differentiates them from the majority of bit players, servants, and messengers is their narrative importance. From the time they appear, they take center stage, though they may share the spotlight with one or another named character.

WOMEN OF WISDOM AND SKILL

These characters present a less tidy and self-evident set than the messengers and servants that we have already considered. Though all are women, they play very different roles within their respective pericopes. The narrator designates them in three different ways; the two to whom the same designation is applied are otherwise dissimilar in their narrative presentation. Nevertheless, the four characters share two points that make a comparison fruitful. First, their social roles—medium, wise woman, queen—entail knowledge or wisdom of one sort or another. Second, their narratives allow us to consider the interplay between social role and gender. Their anonymity draws attention not only to their professional tasks but also to the harmony or perhaps disharmony between the behaviors related to social role and those associated with gender role.

The Wise Woman of Tekoa (2 Sam 14:1–24)

This story is set at the time of the initial rift between David and his son Absalom. David banishes his son Absalom from the kingdom after the latter has murdered his brother Amnon in revenge for Amnon's rape of their sister Tamar (2 Samuel 13). A wise woman (אשה חכמה) of Tekoa is hired by Joab to persuade David to admit Absalom back to the kingdom. Joab instructs the woman to disguise herself as a mourner and to convey his message to David (2 Sam 14: 3).

The wise woman fulfills her task with skill and talent. Acting out the part given to her by Joab, she lays out a case before the king. One of her sons has killed the other, and her family is urging her to give up the murdering son so that they can kill him. She asks the king to intercede with the family on her behalf (14:7). The king promises to do so and pledges that "not one hair of your son shall fall to the ground" (14:11). The woman then abruptly shifts from the role of supplicant to that of accuser. She declares that in rendering this decision David convicts himself, inasmuch as the king does not allow Absalom to return (14:13). The woman's mission succeeds; David orders Joab to bring Absalom back into his own house (14:21), though not into the king's presence (14:24).

This wise woman is a messenger of sorts. Her task is to overcome distance—not the physical distance between a dispatcher in the field and a recipient in the city, but the emotional distance between David and Absalom on the one hand and between David and Joab on the other. As she herself admits to David, "it was your servant Joab who commanded me; it was he who put all these words into the mouth of your servant" (14:19). Unlike the typical messenger, the Tekoite wise woman is required not to convey information but to persuade David of Joab's conviction regarding the return of Absalom. In presenting David with a persuasive analogy, the wise woman resembles Nathan, David's prophet, who, a scant two chapters earlier, had told David a story that similarly allowed the king to view his own behavior—in seducing Bathsheba and arranging her husband Uriah's death—in a different light (2 Sam 12:1–14).

Yet the Tekoite woman is designated neither as messenger nor as prophet but as wise woman. This designation is ambiguous. The concept of wisdom is well developed in the biblical wisdom literature, in which divine wisdom is personified in female form.[1] In narrative literature, however, the term has a

---

[1] E.g. Proverbs 8. See Claudia V. Camp, *Wisdom and the Feminine in the Book of Proverbs* (Decatur, Ga.: Almond Press, 1985).

variable meaning. The adjective is used of craftspeople who contribute their skills to the beautification of the tabernacle (Exod 25:25–31); wisdom is associated with the discernment and good reputation needed for effective governance (Deut 1:13), as well as with Joshua, Moses' successor as the Israelite leader (34: 9). The skill of the wise woman of Tekoa, however, lies not in handicrafts but in her words; though she does not exercise formal leadership, her discernment induces David to change his mind.

It is possible, therefore, that the identification of the Tekoite as a wise woman is simply the narrator's assessment of her personal traits. This perspective is taken, for example, by J. Hoftijzer, who perceives the wise woman as one "who knows how to present her case and how to act in a given situation."[2] According to Fokkelman, her wisdom consists in the fact that she is "in complete control of the situation," demonstrating through her speeches "depth, great eloquence, and a wealth of facts, persons, colour, expression, and emotion."[3]

The fact that Joab seeks out this particular woman from Tekoa implies that she had experience and a professional reputation. On this basis, S. D. Goitein suggests that "the wisdom of the wise woman is more than a natural talent. It is the complete ensemble of traits and training by means of which a woman acquires leadership among women, and sometimes among the public in general."[4] Similarly, Claudia Camp argues that the wise woman represented one significant political role available to women in the period of the monarchy.[5]

The woman's professional skill momentarily inverts the power relationship between her and David. She comes initially in the role of supplicant, desirous of and also subject to the judgment of her king. Her supplication and its aftermath testify to her skills of suasion. Like other messengers, however, she expresses the will and intention of the one who sends her. In acceding to her point of view, David is, in fact, bowing to Joab's will in this matter.

The anonymity of the wise woman therefore draws our attention to her professional designation and her success in fulfilling it. Readers are reminded of her identification as a wise woman by her own use of the language of wisdom in reference to David. In the course of her efforts, she flatters David by declaring "my lord has wisdom like the wisdom of the angel of God to know all things that are on the earth" (14:20). Her gender is also a significant aspect of her success; the fiction she acts out places her in the role of female supplicant. This role is reflected in the obsequiousness of her language, in which she refers

[2]"David and the Tekoite Woman," *VT* 20 (1970): 429.
[3]*Narrative Art and Poetry in the Books of Samuel.* Vol. II, *The Crossing Fates* (Assen, The Netherlands: Van Gorcum, 1986), 141.
[4]"Women as Creators of Biblical Genres," *Prooftexts* 8 (1988): 10.
[5]"The Wise Women of 2 Samuel: A Role Model for Women in Early Israel?" *CBQ* 43 (1981): 14.

to herself consistently as "your servant" (שִׁפְחָתֶךָ; e.g., 14:15). Nevertheless, through this language she successfully exerts her persuasive power.

The absence of her name also has narrative significance. Her name and other personal details may have been known to Joab, but the success of her ruse depends on David's ignorance of her identity. The story explicitly reveals little of her personal life aside from her place of residence, profession and reputation. But the drama of her presentation, the boldness of her address to David and her success suggest not only technical skill but also imagination, creativity, dramatic flair and self-confidence.

The Wise Woman of Abel (2 Sam 20:14–22)

A second wise woman appears in the story of the Benjaminite Sheba son of Bichri, who headed a rebellion against David (20:2). When Sheba and his followers enter the town of Abel of Beth-maacah, Joab's forces prepare to besiege the city and batter down the walls (20:15). At that moment a "wise woman" (אשה חכמה) calls down to him, requests him to approach, and verifies his identity: "Are you Joab?" (20:17). She then initiates negotiations with Joab, through which she hopes to avert the siege of her city. In her opening gambit, she draws upon the long-standing reputation of Abel as a place where people come to settle disputes and where the Lord is present (20:18). She also identifies herself as one who is peaceable and faithful in Israel (20:19). This declaration signals that she is not a follower of Sheba but of David. Her only wish is for the restoration of peace. To this speech, Joab responds that his primary goal is not to destroy the city but to capture Sheba (20:20). On her own authority and apparently without consulting her fellow city dwellers, the wise woman promises to throw Sheba's head over the wall (20:21). In pledging not only to deliver Sheba but also to kill him, she goes one step further than Joab has asked and saves Joab the trouble of killing Sheba himself. After the execution of her plan, Joab withdraws and returns to King David in Jerusalem (20:22).

The wise woman of Abel acts as the spokesperson for her city in order to avert an attack by Joab and his troops. She clearly has political power, as well as detailed knowledge of the political players; after all, her question regarding Joab's identity is not an open-ended "Who are you?" The question and her anonymity direct our attention not only to her designation as a wise woman and her powerful role in the narrative but also to the imbalance in her relationship with Joab. Although he has the military power to besiege the city, she has power over him in knowing his name. Because she holds Sheba hostage, she also has the leverage with which to influence Joab's behavior. As in the Tekoite's story, the theme of wisdom is evoked not only in the woman's designation but also in other references to wisdom, as when the narrator recounts that "the woman went to all the people with her wise plan" (20:22). That she is atypical in her involvement with military matters is evident by comparison to the all-male cast of participants in the battles recounted in 2 Samuel 8–10. Although the story does not provide personal details, the wise woman's individuality may be detected in the way that she performs her role. In negotiating with Joab and offering him Sheba's head, she emerges as wise, politically astute, coolheaded and powerful.

A comparison between the wise women of Tekoa and Abel reveals both similarities and differences. Both women exert power and influence over the behavior of the men of high standing with whom they interact. Both are able to identify these men while remaining essentially unknown to them apart from their formal roles. Gender is invoked by both in their speeches: The Tekoite acts out the role of mother, the Abelite refers to her city as a mother in Israel. In both cases, anonymity draws attention to their autonomous functions. Neither woman exceeds her role; her identity within the narrative is circumscribed by the behavior required in the specific situation. Despite the absence of personal details, however, each is the focus of narrative attention and, through the hints of personality inherent in her behavior, invites the reader's speculation as to her character and identity.

The Medium of Endor (1 Sam 28:3–25)

Another unnamed professional woman is the medium of Endor. Her story is told against the background of three essential facts: the death of the great prophet Samuel (28:3a), King Saul's banishment of the mediums and wizards from the land (28:3b), and the standoff between the Philistines, encamped at Shunem, and the Israelites, stationed at Gilboa (28:4). His fear of the Philistines drives Saul to inquire of the Lord by dreams, Urim, and prophets; he receives no response (28:5–6). Finally, he instructs his servants to find him "a woman who is a medium" (אשת בעלת-אוב); they inform him of a medium at Endor (28:7).

In darkness and disguise, he comes to the woman and asks her, "Consult a spirit for me, and bring up for me the one whom I name to you" (28:8). She, too, has reason to fear: His demand will cause her trouble under Saul's regime. Upon receiving assurances, she calls up Samuel as he had requested. Seeing Samuel, the medium exclaims, "Why have you deceived me? You are Saul!" (28:12). Again Saul reassures her, and she continues her work. Samuel confirms what God's apparent deafness to Saul's earlier divining efforts has implied: "the LORD has turned away from you and become your enemy" (28:16). Samuel describes Israel's impending defeat at the hands of the Philistines and the imminent death of Saul and his sons (28:19). Saul then collapses from fear and hunger (28:20). The woman and his servants cajole him into eating the fatted calf and unleavened bread the woman had prepared, and Saul departs. At the conclusion of 1 Samuel, the dead prophet's words are fulfilled.

The professional role of the medium as depicted in this story is to act as the mediator, or messenger, between the living and the dead. Like the wise woman of Tekoa, the medium of Endor is hired by a man for her professional skill. The prefatory information given by the narrator—that Saul has banished the practitioners of this profession from the land—labels the woman's role as illicit.

The medium is guilty of contravening the king's orders by remaining in the land and, even more, by agreeing to call Samuel's spirit up from the dead. The king's culpability is even more acute. In seeking out the very services that he himself has outlawed, he shows himself lacking in personal integrity. The fact that the honorable and legitimate modes of divination are closed to him is eloquent expression of the divine disfavor into which he has fallen. The deep cracks in his regime are symbolized by the servants who facilitate Saul's encounter with the medium. Not only are the banished practitioners still working but also the servants of the king himself can find them without difficulty.

The parity of the medium and Saul in this unlawful situation is signified within the narrative by their anonymity. Although the readers know the petitioner's identity, the medium and the king are anonymous to each other. Her name and other identifying information are not divulged to the reader or, it would seem, to the king. This secrecy is in keeping with the medium's illegal activity and fear of discovery. On the surface, the king is simply a man who hires her to perform a professional service. But in the context of Saul's earlier decree, this commission requires her to break the law. The narrative creates tension for the reader who knows the man's identity and is privy to the fear for which the man is directly responsible as the author of the decree and the petitioner for her services. In these ways, anonymity contributes to the theme of stealth and deception.

The arrival of Samuel's ghost disrupts this uneasy equilibrium, for in some unspecified manner the event uncloaks Saul as her client. The revelation of the petitioner's identity redraws the power dynamic between them. On the one hand, the woman is now aware that she depends on Saul's good graces not to reveal that she has defied his law. On the other hand, she has power over him, perhaps even more than he has over her. First, he is desperate. God's silence has forced him to seek her expertise to accomplish his goal of discerning his future. Second, the encounter implicates Saul more than it does the medium. The fact that she knows his name while he remains ignorant of hers symbolizes this imbalance, just as in the relationship between the Abelite wise woman and Joab. Once the medium recognizes Saul and fully comprehends the pathos of his situation, she loses her fear, takes charge, and looks after both his spiritual and physical needs.

In the absence of her proper name, the construction of the woman's identity is guided by her designation as a medium. The performance of this role requires her to call up the spirit of the dead for interrogation of the living. Though fearful and cautious, she nevertheless violates the king's decree. In context, her continued performance of her service in the wake of Saul's decree reveals something of her that goes beyond the typified role itself.

In some ways, the medium's service to Saul conforms to biblical stereotypes of female behavior. Hence Uriel Simon comments that, in urging Saul to eat, she is no longer speaking as a witch but as an ordinary woman.[6] In providing him with hospitality—the fatted calf and unleavened bread—she acts as his host, just as Abraham and Lot did with respect to their visitors. Nevertheless, it is a question as to whether this behavior must necessarily be described as typically female. In the biblical context, hospitality is associated more frequently with male hosts (such as Abraham) than with women.[7] She evinces concern for his physical well-being and in her discourse demands parity with him. Like the Tekoite, she uses obsequious language, but this subordinate role is belied by the content of her speech: "Your servant has listened to you; I have taken my life in my hand, and have listened to what you have said to me. Now therefore, you also listen to your servant; let me set a morsel of bread before you. Eat, that you may have strength when you go on your way" (28:21b–22).

The medium's concern for Saul is equivocal. It can be read as a genuine expression of human compassion. If so, she emerges as a woman who rises above professional delegitimization at Saul's hands to demonstrate hospitality and concern for a human being. On the other hand, her concern may reflect self-interest. She may be worried that Saul will collapse or even die in her presence.[8] The imminent death of both Saul and his son Jonathan has been prophesied by Samuel. Although his prediction was made in the same context as the prophecy concerning Israel's defeat, there is no direct statement that his death will be in battle rather than in the home of the medium herself. Finally, her motivation may be self-preservation. Pamela Reis argues that the food the medium offers Saul is a covenantal meal comprised of a cultic offering of raw meat with blood and sacred bread. The fact that he partakes in the meal signifies Saul's commitment to safeguard her life.[9]

These readings are not mutually exclusive. In leaving open the possibility of both altruism and self-interest, the narrative strengthens the depiction of the medium as a complex character. Her anonymity coheres well with the secrecy motif in this passage and draws attention to her typified role. But she emerges from anonymity because of the extraordinary circumstances under which she

---

[6]"A Balanced Story: The Stern Prophet and the Kind Witch." *Prooftexts* 8 (1988): 164–65.

[7]The hospitality of the medium contrasts with the hospitality of another woman, namely, Jael (Judges 4–5), whose offers of shelter and nourishment to Sisera lure him to his death.

[8]Adele Berlin, "Literary Criticism and Biblical Interpretation." Unpublished lecture delivered at Wayne State University, Detroit, 1988.

[9]"Eating the Blood: Saul and the Witch of Endor," *JSOT* 73 (1997): 3–23.

performs this role, its implications in the narrative context and other acts that go beyond her function as a medium.

The Queen of Sheba (1 Kgs 10:1–13 // 2 Chron 9:1–12)

This anonymous woman, too, is portrayed in a formal role, that of foreign monarch. The reader's construction of her role depends not only on her designation and behavior in 1 Kings 10 but also on the narrative context in which this passage appears. The first nine chapters of 1 Kings develop a dual and contradictory representation of King Solomon. On the one hand, he is favored by God with great wisdom. On the other hand, he is given to marrying foreign women, who turn him aside to their gods and hence away from the God of Israel. "Solomon loved the LORD," we are told, and walked "in the statutes of his father David; only, he sacrificed and offered incense at the high places" (3: 3). When asked by God what God should give him, Solomon asks only for wisdom: "an understanding mind to govern your people, able to discern between good and evil" (3:9). This request pleases God so much that he also grants Solomon the riches and honor for which he had not asked and promises him long life conditional on his continued observance of God's statutes and commandments (3:13–14). Solomon's wisdom is illustrated by his famous decision in the case of the two prostitutes, each of whom claimed to be the rightful mother of the same young child (3:16–28), and he developed a worldwide reputation for his wisdom (4:29–34).

Solomon undermines both his wisdom and his favored position with God by his alliances with foreign women, almost all of whom are anonymous. The queen of Sheba stands in contrast to these anonymous consorts.[10] She, too, is unnamed, and her offspring, if any, are absent from her narrative. Yet in other elements of her characterization, the queen of Sheba has little in common with the other foreign queens in Kings 3–11. Whereas they are minimally portrayed, she is the star of her own narrative segment, in which she claims narrative equality with Solomon along with symmetry in status, wealth, and wisdom.[11] Whereas they are characterized as a group of a thousand, she is unique. Whereas they are silent, she is loquacious; whereas they are passive, she actively initiates a state visit of great pomp and ceremony. Whereas they are linked to Solomon by marriage or concubinage, she is autonomous; she arrives with her entourage

---

[10]In this book, most kings and queens of foreign nations are given proper names in addition to their titles, such as Hiram, king of Tyre (1 Kgs 5:1; 5:15 in *BHS*/MT), and Queen Tahpanes (1 Kgs 11:19) or have titles that function as names, such as Pharaoh, king of Egypt (1 Kgs 11:18).

[11]Solomon is wealthier, however. According to 10:23, he "excelled all the kings on earth in wealth and in wisdom."

as a visiting foreign dignitary and departs, with her attendants, as the same. Finally, whereas they are associated with Solomon's folly and downfall, she comes to demonstrate and celebrate her wisdom.

The queen of Sheba therefore stands out boldly from the group of anonymous royals in 1 Kings 3–11. In fact, the character she most resembles is another foreign monarch, King Hiram of Tyre. Such comparison is invited by the direct reference to Hiram in the midst of the Sheba narrative (10:11). There are differences, to be sure. Hiram is a named male character, in contrast to the queen, an anonymous woman. Hiram does not initially visit Solomon himself, as she does, but communicates with him by means of envoys or messengers (5:1, 8; 5:16, 22 in *BHS*/MT). The relationship between Hiram and Solomon is ongoing, with Hiram providing materials and labor for the construction of Solomon's temple (5:8–10; 5:22–25 in *BHS*/MT), whereas our narrator presents only a one-time encounter between Solomon and the queen of Sheba.

Beyond these differences, however, these two figures have much in common. Each is impressed with Solomon's wisdom and his wealth (5:7; 5:21 in Hebrew; 10:7). Second, each is in a formal relationship of equality with Solomon, despite the fact that Solomon—according to the narrator—surpassed them both, and indeed, all kings, in wealth and wisdom (10:23). This equity is important for the narrative; only a king who was rich and wise himself could recognize Solomon's wisdom and give him the help he needed for building the temple; only a wise and rich queen could ask riddles that test Solomon's wisdom and bring gifts that he would appreciate and value.

Both Hiram and the queen of Sheba function narratively as witnesses to Solomon's divinely given wisdom. Hiram's judgment of Solomon's wisdom is apparently based on the latter's decisions to build the temple and to use Sidonian labor and wood (5:2–6; 5:16–24 in *BHS*/MT). Not explicitly called wise, the queen of Sheba is the arbiter of Solomon's wisdom. The queen's judgment is based on Solomon's ability to answer her riddles in a way that apparently exceeded her expectations and that, along with his wealth, literally left her breathless (10:5).

Yet in contrast to 1 Kgs 3:16–28, in which the readers are privy to the process by which Solomon wisely decides in whose custody to place a young child, 10:1–3 provides us with no opportunity to judge Solomon's wisdom for ourselves. The riddles are not recounted; the reader is told only that "Solomon answered all her questions; there was nothing hidden from the king that he could not explain to her" (10:3). This omission is all the more glaring in light of the length at which her speech in praise of his wealth and wisdom is reported (10:6–9).

This pattern of omission and provision attests to the strong hand of the narrator: he withholds information but asks that we trust and accept his judgment regarding Solomon's wisdom. Similarly, we are not told how and why

Solomon came to worship the idols of his foreign wives, yet we are asked to believe the narrator's negative judgment that Solomon was idolatrous and hence deserving of the punishment set out by the Lord in 9:6–9.

The queen of Sheba draws together the twin themes of Solomon's characterization in 1 Kings 3–11. Although she is not explicitly defined as wise, the very fact that she tests and judges Solomon's wisdom implies her own. That he passes muster is testimony to Solomon's surpassing wisdom and furthers the narrator's argument concerning his superiority over all his reigning peers. Her anonymity draws attention to her wisdom and royal attributes in a way that magnifies Solomon's own. Anonymity also suggests a comparison with the other foreign royal women in Solomon's life, his thousand consorts, who likewise remain unnamed. The comparison is further implied by the queen herself, who, in her paean to Solomon's wisdom, exclaims, "Happy are your wives!" (10:8). The similarity implied by their shared anonymity is negated by her narrative portrayal, however. Unlike these women, she is not a threat to his faith; rather, she functions as the mouthpiece for the narrator's perspective on Solomon's early relationship with God. Her wordy declaration—"Blessed be the LORD your God who has delighted in you and set you on the throne of Israel! Because the LORD loved Israel forever, he has made you king to execute justice and righteousness" (10:9)—echoes the description of Solomon in Kings 3–5. It also recalls the words of King Hiram of Tyre, who blesses the Lord "who has given to David a wise son to be over this great people" (5:7; 5:21 in *BHS*/MT).

As a royal woman, however, her portrayal is significant not so much for what is included but for what it lacks: a formal link between queen and king through marriage. It is the absence of a formal diplomatic tie through marriage that allows her to maintain her autonomy and no doubt contributes to her favorable depiction.[12]

These anonymous women are not identified by proper name but by professional role (wise woman, medium, queen) and place names (Tekoa, Abel, Endor, Sheba). In all cases, their proper names are unknown not only to the reader but also apparently to the principal named characters within their respective pericopes. The absence of the proper name draws attention to their complex power relationships with the men with whom they interact and the ways in

---

[12]What is lacking in the biblical text is supplied in postbiblical Jewish and Muslim interpretation, in which 1 Kings 10 becomes a locus for discussion on gender politics. See Jacob Lassner, *Demonizing the Queen of Sheba: Boundaries of Gender and Culture in Postbiblical Judaism and Medieval Islam* (Chicago: University of Chicago Press, 1993). The only biblical hint of a sexual liaison between Solomon and Sheba is the verb בא in 10:2: "she *came* to him" (see Pritchard, *Solomon and Sheba*, 9). Nevertheless, the situation in itself, in the context of Solomon's famed harem, raises the possibility that later interpreters—among them filmmaker Cecil B. DeMille in *Solomon and Sheba*—exploit fully.

which their narrative portrayal either remains within or moves outside the boundaries of their formal roles. In two of these stories (medium of Endor and the Tekoite), anonymity also coheres with the element of secrecy their tasks require. All four women are given a positive portrayal in the text. Neither the narrator nor the other characters express surprise at their exceptional relationships with powerful men.

All four women use words in the performance of their professional or formal roles. The medium allows Saul to consult the dead Samuel (1 Sam 28: 11–14), who would otherwise be inaccessible to him. The wise woman of Tekoa speaks to David the words that Joab has put in her mouth (2 Sam 14:3, 19) "in order to change the course of affairs" (2 Sam 14:20).[13] The wise woman of Abel acts as the spokesperson for her city to avert the attack of Joab and his troops. The queen of Sheba's test of Solomon's wisdom is conducted through words.

Like anonymous servants and messengers, these women function as agents not only in the social world implied in the text but also in plot development and characterization. The medium of Endor, at the request of King Saul, calls forth the dead Samuel, who advises Saul of his imminent demise (1 Sam 28:19). The wise woman of Tekoa convinces King David to allow his banished son Absalom back into the kingdom (2 Sam 14:21). Her Abelite counterpart averts the conquest of Abel by handing over to Joab, David's general, the head of his enemy Sheba son of Bichri (2 Sam 20:22). These events mark important turning points in the saga of monarchy and military adventure, which is the subject matter of 1 and 2 Samuel. The queen of Sheba's encounter with Solomon does not further the plot as such but it does contribute significantly to his characterization as wise. Saul's encounter with the medium of Endor shows him to be a desperate man who must break the laws that he himself promulgated in order to obtain the information that his usual sources—the Lord, the Urim, or the prophets (1 Sam 28:6)—have denied him. David's discussion with the wise woman of Tekoa demonstrates his ability to listen and to change his mind, even once he has penetrated her ruse (2 Sam 14:19). Joab's willingness to accept the bargain suggested by the wise woman of Abel shows that he is not interested in conquest for its own sake.

The roles played by these women point to particular moral and/or theological problems. Saul's recourse to the witch of Endor brings home to the reader his utter desperation, which causes him to violate his own legislation, and his utter rejection by God, indicated by the failure of more conventional means of oracular communication (1 Sam 28:6). The Tekoite woman's dramatization of David's plight provides insight into the complexity of David's feelings toward Absalom and the tangled relationship between personal emotion and

---

[13]The *NJPSV* translation here is "to conceal the real purpose of the matter." Literally: in order to change the face of the matter.

political behavior. The pragmatic attitude of the wise woman of Abel and her cold-blooded solution to the security problems faced by her city touch on the issue of the rights of the individual versus the rights of the community in matters of life and death. The contrast between the queen of Sheba and Solomon's foreign wives highlights the manner in which Solomon is the architect of his own downfall.

The fact that these four autonomous characters are women is not incidental to their narrative portrayal. Their gender is not an explicit issue but comes into play as they execute the social roles by which they are designated and also affects the ways in which readers interpret their behavior. The Tekoite plays out the role of a distressed mother. In the military context of 2 Samuel, the offer of Sheba's head is shocking only because it comes from a woman. The stereotype of the nurturing (and/or murdering) woman comes into play in our reading of the hospitality that the medium of Endor provides for Saul. Finally, the fact that it is a queen and not a king who tests Solomon's wisdom lends an under-tone of sexuality to their encounter.

In conclusion, these four women are portrayed solely in terms of their formal designations as autonomous functionaries and professionals. Very few personal details are conveyed. Nevertheless, the actions and words with which they perform their formal duties in themselves bespeak their personal identities and character traits. At the same time as they contribute to the characterization of other figures, such as David, Joab, Saul and Solomon, and, to a greater or lesser extent, to the plot development, they, too, are in the spotlight.

UNWORTHY LEVITES

In contrast to the wise women, the two Levites we turn to now do not fare well under the narrator's attention. Both fall short of their expected roles. This neg-ative depiction suggests that they may be a vehicle for the narrator's critique of the levitical priesthood in the period of the Judges.

Biblical narrative refers to two priestly groups: priests (כהנים) and the Levites (לויים). Both of these groups engaged in Israel's cultic service of Yahweh, par-ticularly in the performance of sacrifices and related rituals. These two groups appear distinct, particularly in Deuteronomy.[14] Some differentiation of function is implied. For example, Moses enjoins the people Israel to rejoice with the Levite when he goes to the "place that the LORD your God will choose" (Deut 12:11, 18) and to support the Levites because they have no portion in the land (Deut 12:12). Sometimes the two designations are combined. Levitical priests

---

[14]Levites are mentioned in 12:12, 18–19; 14:27–29; 16:11, 13–14; 18:6–7; 26:11–12; and per-haps 10:9. Levitical priests are mentioned in 17:9, 18; 18:1–8; 24:8; 27:9.

(כהנים לויים) provide legal decisions (Deut 17:8–9) and are in charge of the Torah (17:18).[15]

Occasional brief references to unnamed priests may be found. David's sons are described as priests (כהנים) in 2 Sam 8:18. An unnamed priest (כהן) determines the appropriate place from which Saul should inquire of God as to battle with the Philistines (1 Sam 14:36); 1 Sam 6:2 refers to foreign priests and diviners who are asked by the Philistines for advice on what to do with the ark of the Lord. There are no stories, however, in which an unnamed priest is prominent.

Levites were separated from among the other Israelites and dedicated to the service of the Lord, in place of all the firstborn of Israel (Num 8:5–26). They comprised a number of groups, each claiming descent from a different leader, and had a complex history integrally related to the political fortunes of Israel.[16] Unlike the other tribes, Levites were not allotted a portion of the land of Israel but were permitted to live in particular cities (Josh 14:3–4; 21:1–42). Their role included responsibility for the ark of the covenant (Josh 3:3; 8:30–35) and serving in its presence (Deut 10:7–8; 31:9, 25), consulting the Urim and Thummin (Deut 17:9, 12; 19:17), offering and receiving sacrifices (Deut 26:4) and reading and teaching the law (Deut 17:18; 27:9–10, 14; 31:9–14). The Levites were therefore deeply entrenched in the cultic life of Israel. Because their powers of divination were often needed by kings at war, Levites were also involved in Israel's political life. The designation Levite itself therefore contains two aspects: a tribal affiliation and a formal religious-political function. The two Levites of Judges 17–21 can be measured by the integrity with which they perform these tasks.

The Levite of Micah and the Danites (Judges 17–18)

An anonymous Levite from the clan of Judah in Bethlehem comes upon the house of Micah in his wanderings and lets it be known that he is ready to take up residence where he can find employment (17:7–8).[17] Micah, who has a shrine,

---

[15]For detailed discussion of the Levites and the sacrificial system, see Menahem Haran, *Temples and Temple Service in Ancient Israel: An Inquiry into the Character of Cult Phenomena and the Historical Setting of the Priestly School* (Oxford: Clarendon, 1978).

[16]See Haran, *Temples*, passim.

[17]Robert C. Boling (*Judges* [AB 6A; New York: Doubleday, 1975], 258–59) argues that this section was added by a redactor who had been profoundly influenced by the destruction of the northern kingdom in 721. C. F. Burney (*The Book of Judges* [London: Rivingtons, 1918], 409–10) suggests that this passage combines two accounts of the appearance of the Levite on the scene; in v. 7 he is introduced as a נער who happened to be sojourning there; in v. 8 he is termed האיש.

complete with ephod and teraphim, has installed one of his sons as priest (לכהן; 17:5).[18] He offers the Levite room, board, and wages if he will "Stay with me, and be to me a father and a priest" (17:10). The purpose is clear: to induce the Lord to prosper him (17:13). Micah congratulates himself on having obtained the services of a Levite, clearly superior to those that his own non-Levitical son can perform.

The scene now shifts to the political fortunes of the Danite tribe (18:1). After reminding the reader of the political chaos of this period (a common refrain throughout the book of Judges),[19] the narrator recounts the efforts of Dan to seek its own territory. Five "valiant" men (אנשים בני חיל) of Dan, sent to spy out the land, arrive at Micah's house.[20] Recognizing the voice of the young Levite, they inquire about his presence there. The Levite answers their questions and provides them with an oracle for the success of their mission.[21] His readiness to divine on their behalf indicates that he did not view his relationship with Micah as an exclusive one.

The five men continue on their reconnaissance mission and bring back a positive report to their kin (18:7–10). The Danites send warriors, who, informed by the five spies about Micah's ephod, teraphim and idol, come to the house of the young Levite. As six hundred armed Danites stand by the entrance, the five spies enter and take these ritual items. The Levite is partially kidnapped, partially cajoled, into leaving Micah and going with the Danites to be their father and priest (18:19). After a token protest, he succumbs to the lure of a better career opportunity: "Is it better for you to be priest to the house of one person, or to be priest to a tribe and clan in Israel?" (18:19). Micah pursues them but is daunted by their strength and soon returns home (18:25). The Danites, having taken Micah's objects and his priest, conquer Laish, rebuild the city, and name it Dan.

At the very end of the scene, the Levite's name is divulged as Jonathan son of Gershom, son of Moses; it is noted that his family became a dynasty that served the tribe of Danites until the captivity.[22] The Danites maintained

---

[18]John L. McKenzie (*The World of the Judges* [Englewood Cliffs, N.J.: Prentice-Hall, 1966], 160) notes that the fact that Micah's son was functioning as priest indicates that, in the absence of a Levite, any person available could function as such.

[19]Cf. 19:1; the chaos is explicitly connected to Israel's idolatry, which led God to give them over to the hands of their enemies (e.g., 2:11; 3:7, 12; 4:1; 6:1; 10:6; 13:1).

[20]Compare the similar reconnaissance missions on behalf of the Israelites as a whole (Numbers 13; Joshua 2).

[21]Boling (*Judges*, 262) suggests that he did not even utilize his divinatory equipment.

[22]On the meaning of the name and its textual variants, see Burney, *Judges*, 422; Boling, *Judges*, 266; and J. Alberto Soggin, *Judges: A Commentary* (OTL; Philadelphia: Westminster, 1981), 270.

Micah's idol "as long as the house of God was at Shiloh" (18:31). These details indicate the narrator's retrospective position with respect to the events he is recounting.[23]

This story is unusual in that the Levite's anonymity is reversed at the very end of a lengthy narrative. This reversal allows us to consider how the picture built up in a sequential reading of the story is affected by the divulging of the proper name at the end. The proper name is but the last of several identifiers supplied for the Levite by the narrator. The man is introduced in 17:7 as a young man (נער) from Bethlehem, a Judahite and a Levite. In 17:8, the same character is referred to as "the man" (האיש). The man then introduces himself to Micah as a Levite (לוי; 17:9). This variation sets the stage for the complex role he takes on within Micah's own household.

That the controlling designation is that of Levite is suggested by the cultic functions he performs. Revell points out that "Levite" is used in this story, as in Judges 19, as an epithet of occupation rather than of tribal affiliation. The term signifies primarily that the person so designated is trained to serve at a shrine.[24] Boling comments that this social-occupational designation provides adequate explanation of his movements in search of employment (18:9).[25]

The other two designations are not irrelevant, however. "Young man" and "man" are generally age-related designations, though the exact age at which a person changes from the former to the latter is not specified. Their application to the Levite establishes that he is younger than Micah but already an adult. These inconsistent age references reflect the Levite's paradoxical role in Micah's household. Micah hires the Levite to be "father" and "priest" (והיה־לי לאב ולכהן; 17:10). The title *father* emphasizes the priest's role as cultic diviner who is responsible for oracular advice (as in 18:4–6).[26] Micah offers the young man a living and bestows upon him the title *father* in order to have control of him and his divinatory skills.[27] But although Micah asks the Levite to be as a father

---

[23]The temple at Shiloh was no longer in use at the time of narration. References to the abandonment of Shiloh are found in Jer 7:12–14; 26:6–9; cf. Ps 78:60. On the priesthood at Shiloh, see Martin A. Cohen, "The Role of the Shilonite Priesthood in the United Monarchy of Ancient Israel," *HUCA* 36 (1965): 59–98.

[24]*Designation*, 41.

[25]Boling, *Judges*, 257; Soggin, *Judges*, 270; Revell, *Designation*, 41.

[26]Boling (*Judges*, 257) points out that the title *father* and the oracular responsibility transferred to prophets during the monarchy (2 Kgs 6:21; 8:9; 13:14). According to BDB (ad loc), however, the title can simply be a term of respect and honor, applied here to the priest, in 2 Kgs 5:13 by a servant to his master, and in 2 Kgs 2:12; 6:21; 13:14; and 8:9 to a prophet.

[27]Boling ("Judges," *HCSB*, 399) comments that "the title 'father' implies a priestly role as diviner (see 18:4–6)." The latter verse, however, while emphasizing the Levite's role as diviner, does not use the term *father*.

to him, the young man (נער) becomes as a son to Micah (כאחד מבניו; 17:11). The Levite becomes Micah's son by contractual arrangement.[28] The unnamed Levite thereby effectively replaces Micah's unnamed biological son, who disappears from the story as he did from the priestly role. In this manner, the Levite recalls the unnamed servant of Abraham who stood in for Abraham's son Isaac.

The story conveys two contradictory impressions. On the one hand, it apparently provides an etiology for the priests of the Danite tribe and in that vein may celebrate the success of the Danite emissaries in acquiring the progenitor of their Levitical line. On the other hand, the story exposes the Levite as a mercenary character who fulfills a semblance of the typified priestly role but in a manner that seems oddly misdirected and oblivious to the central covenantal imperative to which the priest was to contribute. The Levite thus provides the reader with anecdotal evidence for the words of Ezekiel, who excoriates the Levites who forsook the Lord when Israel went astray and calls them to bear the shame of the abominations that they committed (Ezek 44:10–14).[29] The Levite's initial anonymity allows readers to play the variety of designations and other narrative information against one another. The man's emergence from anonymity is also a taking on of personal identity. He not only performs a formal role but also acts out of self-interest, shows himself to be opportunistic, and succeeds in achieving high status within his professional role.

His initial anonymity focuses attention on his typified role as Levite, whose main duties are to provide oracles and protection for the family and its ritual objects, such as the idol, the ephod, and the teraphim.[30] In his contacts with Micah and the Danites, he emerges as opportunistic, easily bought, virtually unfettered by personal loyalty, and very willing to serve at temples containing idols. The story of the Levite's defection to the Danites marks his gradual emergence from anonymity; at the same time it raises questions about his personal and professional integrity. His behavior indicates his willingness to give up his place in Micah's household and shrine for a better offer. The fact that the five Danite reconnaissance men recognize his voice suggests that he is not entirely

---

[28]Boling, *Judges*, 256–57; cf. also Gen 45:8, in which Joseph is described as the "father" to Pharaoh.

[29]According to Ezekiel, only the sons of Zadok did not behave in this manner (44:15–31). Walther Eichrodt (*Ezekiel: A Commentary*, trans. Cosslett Quin [OTL; Philadelphia: Westminster, 1970], 565) suggests that the praise of the sons of Zadok is "unimaginable from the mouth of Ezekiel" and hence must have been added by someone from among the Zion priesthood, which claimed descent from the Zadok who served under David.

[30]It is possible that the Levite also would have conducted sacrifices, though these are not discussed in this section. It is clear, however, that the sanctuary and mode of worship alluded to in the story involved idols and hence were not strictly monotheistic.

unknown or perhaps not even anonymous to them, though it is not explained how they knew his voice.[31] His status as the Danites' Levite is confirmed by the reversal of his anonymity in 18:30. The presence of a proper name and illustrious lineage may provide the Levite and his family with some legitimacy, particularly if the Moses in his lineage is indeed the Moses of the Pentateuch.[32] If so, the progression from anonymity to named status may signify the Levite's personal development from an itinerant mercenary to a respected and well-established Danite functionary. Local respectability does not erase his earlier negative portrayal, however.

The Levite and his Concubine (Judges 19–21)

Another problematic Levite follows hard on the heels of the Danites' Levite. All characters in this section are anonymous; our focus here is on the anonymous Levite. This tale is told retrospectively, looking back at "those days, when there was no king in Israel" (19:1), and, like Judges 18, is set in part in the land of Ephraim. As the story begins, his Bethlehemite concubine (פלגשׁ) returns to her father's house. After some time, the man journeys to Bethlehem to bring her back (19:3). After a sojourn with her father, the man and woman embark on the return journey (19:10). They are taken in for the night by a man in Gibeah (19:20–21) in the territory of Benjamin. But when the host's neighbors clamor for his male guest, the host offers them instead the Levite's concubine, as well as his own daughter (19:22–26). The concubine is taken out of the house and given to the crowd; the daughter receives no further mention. In the morning, the Levite discovers her on the doorstep, puts her on his donkey, and rides home with her (19:27–28). At home, he cuts her body into twelve pieces, which he sends around to the tribes (19:29–30) of Israel, along with his account of the event. As a result, marriage between Benjaminite men and Israelite women is banned. The hardship caused thereby requires that a way around the ban be found (Judges 20–21).

As in Judges 17, this character is designated both as a Levite and as a man. These terms point to two aspects of his identity: his cultic role as Levite and his gendered role as a man in relationship with a woman. Whereas Judges 17–18 portrayed a Levite entirely in his professional aspect, Judges 19–21 portrays this man almost entirely in terms of his personal relationship with the concu-

---

[31]Whether they knew him personally, as Burney (*Judges*, 424) argues, or whether they simply recognized his accent or dialect (as suggested by James D. Martin, *The Book of Judges* [Cambridge: Cambridge University Press, 1975], 189) is impossible to determine.

[32]Boling, *Judges*, 266. In the MT, a *nun* (נ) has been superscribed between the first and second letters of the name Moses (משׁה) transforming it into Manasseh (מנשׁה), apparently to eliminate the reference to Moses. This change implies that the Masoretes did not particularly welcome the Levite as a descendant of Moses.

bine. He is called a Levite only twice (19:1; 21:4); otherwise, he is designated most often as "the man" (הָאִישׁ). No motivation is given for the Levite's decision to bring the woman back from her father's home. A charitable reading would impute to the Levite a desire for reconciliation. But his subsequent behavior, including his failure to object to her ejection, his callous attempts to rouse her the following morning,[33] and his final act of dismemberment undo any initial charitable assessment.

Nor does his own retelling of the events (Judg 20:4–6) prompt a revision of this negative construction. Beginning with the words he sent along with the dead woman's body parts, he broadcasts the message that the Benjaminites, among whom the town of Gibeah was located, are responsible for this terrible act (19:30; 20:4–6). This edition of the story absolves him of responsibility and stands at odds with the narrator's early version. And indeed, this may be the ultimate outrage:[34] By omitting his own role in the situation, he lies by omission to protect himself.

The plot of the story therefore emphasizes his gendered role and his own failure to protect the woman. But the Levitical designation is not irrelevant, for it labels his dismemberment of her body as a cultic act. As the sacrifice of a human body, this act perverts the notion of proper sacrifice, in which the Levites are supposed to engage.[35] The uncertainty of the status of the woman at the time of dismemberment adds further to the ambiguity and potential for negative evaluation of this act. Bal comments, "Is she alive? Then he slaughters her, but not for Yahweh. Is she dead? Then he, a Levite, should not touch her. Not only does the Levite, a priest, handle the defiling body; but also instead of offering the pieces to Yahweh, he sends them to his brothers."[36]

The anonymity of this Levite man therefore focuses attention on the dissonance between his double designations, as man and as Levite, and his behavior, which perverts the typified role associated with these designations. The two Levites of Judges 17–21 are linked not only by narrative proximity and geographical associations with Bethlehem and Ephraim but also by their anonymity. The combination of anonymity and their behavior, which contravenes norms of sacrifice and devotion required of Levites, expresses the narrator's negative value judgment. In their context at the end of Judges, these stories illustrate the progressive deterioration of Israelite society before the institution of the monarchy.

---

[33]According to Stuart Lasine, ("Guest and Host in Judges 19: Lot's Hospitality in an Inverted World," *JSOT* 29 [1984] :45), the man's lack of emotional response to this tragic situation turns the story into black humor.

[34]Lasine, "Guest," 49–50.

[35]E.g., Lev 1:6–10. For detailed summary of the biblical laws on sacrifice, see *ABD* 5: 870–86.

[36]*Death and Dissymmetry: The Politics of Coherence in the Book of Judges* (Chicago: University of Chicago Press, 1988), 98–99.

The first Levite's idolatry and opportunism, negative as they are, pale before this latter Levite's sacrifice of his woman. The perversity of their story world emerges even more closely when compared with other biblical passages. The Gibeahite's Levite-guest, who stands by as his host offers two women to the hordes outside, contrasts with Lot's angelic guests, who prevent the violation of the two daughters that Lot has offered to the men of Sodom (Gen 19:10–11). The Levite's dismemberment of his concubine both recalls and contrasts with Saul's act of dismembering the oxen in the face of the Ammonite threat to the residents of Jabesh-gilead. But whereas the Levite's act offends the sensibilities, Saul's act was an expression of righteous anger associated with the spirit of the Lord (1 Sam 11:6–7).[37]

Anonymity thus becomes a vehicle for the narrator's judgment not only of these men but also of the political chaos in the context of which their actions took place. Their anonymity also foreshadows the eventual disappearance of this political system, a process that begins in the biblical book that follows (cf. 1 Samuel 8).

In contrast to the unnamed servants and messengers considered earlier, the women and men considered here are not eclipsed but rather receive the full attention of the narrator within their respective pericopes. Their anonymity directs us to their role designations and the ways in which their behavior fulfills or, in the case of the Levites, fails to measure up to the demands inherent in their professional designations. To a greater or lesser extent, the personal identities of these figures overflow their role designations; their formal identification does not account for all aspects of their narrative portrayal. Their narrative portrayal allows us to see them as individuals whose personalities are not bound up solely by the specific terms that the narrator uses to identify them.

Anonymity also contributes to the way in which the narrator guides us to evaluate these figures. The women are wise and skilled; none comes in for narrative disapprobation. Not so the Levites. If the Danites revered their Levite, we readers see him in an equivocal light, as a mercenary whose main concern is his own well-being rather than service to God. The Levite of Judges 19 shocks with his callous treatment of his concubine and the offensive ways in which he tries to redeem himself.

[37]Lasine, "Guest," 37.

5

❖   ❖   ❖

Wayward Wives, Multifarious Mothers and Doomed Daughters

A LTHOUGH THE WIFE OF LOT and the mother of Rebecca are best defined as bit players, a significant number of other wives and mothers—as well as daughters—have starring roles in their respective pericopes. What separates these women from the anonymous bit players is the quantity and quality of narrative attention they receive. Their anonymity draws attention not only to their role designations but also to the interplay between these designations and the behavior attributed to them within their stories. This chapter looks first at a number of anonymous wives, specifically those women who are portrayed as having a significant relationship with a male figure other than a husband. Most of these wives are not literally wayward; only Potiphar's wife attempts a sexual encounter with her "other" man. Nevertheless, sexual undertones lurk just under the surface of their narrative accounts. Second, we turn to women in the role of mother. The ways in which such women approach the task of nurturing their children provide a perspective from which to view the biblical construction of the maternal role. Finally, we look at the daughters who, trapped by competing demands, are prevented from moving smoothly into the role of wife and mother, which represents the ideal life as inscribed in the biblical text.

WAYWARD WIVES

Hebrew has no specific word for *wife*. Wives are designated as the *women* of particular men. Abram's wife is Abram's woman (אשׁת אברם; Gen 12:17),

Judah's wife is Judah's woman (אשת־יהודה; Gen 38:12). A possessive suffix is frequently used (אשתו [his woman], e.g., Gen 12:11; אשתך [your woman], Gen 12:18), with the context supplying the antecedent for the pronoun and hence the identity of the husband.

Similarly, a husband may be designated as the *man* of a particular woman. Elimelech is identified as the man of Naomi (איש נעמי; Ruth 1:3); Leah refers to Jacob as "my man" (אישי; Gen 30:20). The most prevalent term for a husband, however, is בעל, meaning "master." This term implies a hierarchical relationship between wife and husband in which the wife is in the subordinate position. It is overly simplistic to conclude from this designation that men had absolute control over their wives.[1] For example, many stories, including a number of those that we consider in this chapter, portray situations in which men do the bidding of their wives. When Abraham, for example, balks at expelling Hagar and Ishmael from his household, as his wife, Sarah, has demanded, God tells him, "whatever Sarah says to you, do as she tells you" (Gen 21:12).

Nevertheless, the fundamentally hierarchical nature of the marital relationship is patent. The biblical law on vows, for example, stipulates that the vows of a married woman may be annulled by her husband, whether she wishes them annulled or not (Num 30:6–15). This law places the wife in the same position of dependency as a daughter, whose vows may be annulled by her father at his discretion (Num 30:3–5).

Central to the biblical narratives about husbands and wives are sexuality and procreation. Although husbands do not own their wives in the same way that they own the cattle and other livestock over which they are masters, they do have exclusive sexual rights to their wives.[2] A wife is expected to be monogamous, though similar fidelity is not required of her husband, who could take a second wife (as did Abraham, Jacob, David, Solomon, and others) or a concubine (Abraham, Jacob). The fact that some wives, such as Sarah (or wife-equivalents, in the case of Tamar in Genesis 38),[3] transgress or come close to transgressing this point does not call its centrality into question. The necessity for female monogamy that emerges from the narrative material is echoed in and reinforced by the laws against adultery (defined as intercourse with a married, or equivalent to married, woman) in Exod 20:14, Lev 19:20 and Deut 22:22.

---

[1] Carol Meyers, *Discovering Eve: Ancient Israelite Women in Context* (New York: Oxford University Press, 1988), 187.

[2] Meyers, *Discovering Eve*, 165–88.

[3] Tamar is not married to Selah, but, according to the laws of levirate marriage, she should have been and hence was still considered to be a married woman. Cf. Sarna, *JPS Genesis*, 267–69.

The connection between sexuality and procreation is axiomatic. Certainly, there are biblical husbands such as Elkanah who love their wives despite the absence of children (1 Sam 1:8). Nevertheless, the charge that Isaac gave to his son Jacob, that he should marry a suitable woman and be blessed with numerous offspring (Gen 28:2–3), exemplifies the inseparability of marriage and children. The desire for male offspring in particular underlies a range of biblical stories involving wives. The annunciation stories, in which the barrenness of a woman is reversed by an angel, prophet, or priest, conclude happily with the birth of a son.[4] A woman's success, or lack thereof, in bearing sons is one key to the rivalry between cowives such as Rachel and Leah (Genesis 29–30) and Hannah and Peninnah (1 Sam 1:6).[5] The commandment, or blessing, to be fruitful and multiply not only had personal, social, and communal importance[6] but also took on theological significance. Leviticus 26:9 connects this commandment specifically to the divine covenant: "I will look with favor upon you and make you fruitful and multiply you; and I will maintain my covenant with you." Hence this "divine blessing of humans par excellence" becomes "a metaphor, a formularized guarantee of divine protection, divine election, and divine covenant."[7] The emphasis on the production of male offspring both reflects and reinforces a patriarchal ideology as much as—or more than—it sheds light on the psychological nature of Israelite women.[8]

Embedded in the emphasis on sexual fidelity and bearing male children is the axiom that the most important man in a married woman's life should be her husband. This expectation is encoded in the possessive forms of her role designation and in the stated purpose of her creation: to be her man's partner (עזר כנגדו; Gen 2:18). Unnamed wives from the woman God created in Genesis 2 through to the Shunammite in 2 Kings 4 violate this principle, whether overtly, as in the case of Potiphar's wife, or subtly, as in the case of Manoah's wife. Though these wives are not sexually promiscuous in their behavior, the potential for a significant relationship outside the marital sphere is strongly implied.

Primordial Wives (Genesis 2–3)

Genesis 1–3 presents two creation stories. In the first account (Gen 1:1–2:3), God creates humankind in his image and likeness. Humankind comprises both male

---

[4]For a close analysis of the annunciation motif, see Robert Alter, "How Convention Helps Us Read: The Case of the Bible's Annunciation Type-Scene," *Prooftexts* 3 (1983): 115–30.

[5]A second focus of rivalry was the love of Jacob; cf. Gen 29:32; 30:15.

[6]See Meyers, *Discovering Eve*, 61.

[7]Jeremy Cohen, "*Be Fertile and Increase, Fill the Earth and Master It*": *The Ancient and Medieval Career of a Biblical Text* (Ithaca, N.Y.: Cornell University Press, 1989), 33.

[8]Esther Fuchs, "The Literary Characterization of Mothers and Sexual Politics in the Hebrew Bible," *Semeia* 46 (1989): 160–61.

and female; both are commanded to be fruitful and multiply, to fill the earth and subdue it (1:27–28).[9] The narrative makes no mention of male and female as husband and wife or of how the commandment to be fruitful and multiply is to be carried out. This account implies a non-hierarchical relationship between male and female; their creation is simultaneous; each is equally addressed by God's command; each is equally in the divine image.

A contrary portrait of male and female can be constructed from the second account in 2:7–25. Here the male is created first. Only afterward does God perceive the male's need for a helpmeet. For this purpose, he creates the female from the body of the man. The man expresses his satisfaction and names her "woman" (אשה). For this reason, says the narrator, "a man leaves his father and his mother and clings to his wife, and they become one flesh" (2:24). Both were naked and not ashamed.

The idyll in the garden is disrupted with the arrival of the "other" male, a serpent who persuades the woman to eat the fruit of the tree of knowledge of good and evil. This is the only fruit which God had forbidden to the man (2: 17); the woman understands it as being prohibited to her as well (3:3). The woman and man both eat; all three, including the serpent, are summarily cursed for disobedience (3:14–19). The serpent is condemned to crawl on its belly and eat dust; the humans are given lives of toil and mortality and are cast out of the garden (3:23).

This story is not only an etiology for humankind and the natural world. As Gen 2:24 indicates, the story also sets the paradigm for the primary social unit, the marital couple. From the very beginning, this relationship is a hierarchical one, in which the woman occupies the subordinate position. The relative status of man and woman is indicated in the very fact of her creation, which was prompted by God's wish to create a partner for (עזר כנגדו) and ease the loneliness of the man; in God's opinion, "It is not good that the man should be alone" (2:18). Although the notion of partnership may suggest equality, her role is defined in terms of the man's need rather than a common task. This role definition is reinforced by the man's own reference to her as the woman whom God had given to be with him (3:12).

The hierarchy, though incipiently present, remains fluid for the time being. Indeed, it is implicitly overturned by the woman's encounter with the serpent. Although the woman is defined in terms of her relationship to the man, her encounter with the serpent is an autonomous act, the first she experiences. He persuades her to eat of the fruit of the forbidden tree by convincing her that, contrary to God's declaration, she will not die, "for God knows that when you

---

[9]For detailed discussion of the male and female aspects of "the man," see Phyllis A. Bird, "Male and Female He Created Them: Gen 1:27b in the Context of the Priestly Account of Creation," *HTR* 74 (1981): 129–60.

eat of it your eyes will be opened, and you will be like God, knowing good and evil" (3:5). The woman judges the tree to be good for food, pleasing to the eye and desirable as a path to wisdom (3:6).

This section undermines the hierarchical relationship between man and woman by portraying the woman as active and autonomous. The man, though present, is passive and simply does her bidding (3:6). She is portrayed as a seeker after wisdom and knowledge (3:6) and, through the gift of the fruit, as the one who mediates wisdom to the man.

In reversing their positions, however, the encounter sets up a parallel hierarchy between the serpent and the woman; in this relationship, the serpent wields the power of persuasion and the woman is in the subordinate role once again. Viewed in this way, the serpent becomes the "other man" in her life. He affects her life more dramatically than her human partner has done thus far. His power to persuade launches a chain of events that introduce her to the life of sexuality, maternity, and mortality that defines woman's existence thereafter.

Eating the fruit reveals their nakedness to them. To cover their nakedness, they sew themselves loincloths of fig leaves. The curses God showers upon them include the pain of childbirth or, alternatively, the labor of many pregnancies, and the relentlessness of her sexual desire for her husband, who will rule over her (3:16).[10] Although sexuality is not explicitly mentioned, its presence and their awareness of it are intimated. The events set off by the serpent lock the woman firmly into the hierarchical relationship with her husband, for which purpose she had been created. The serpent, too, becomes fixed in the subordinate position in a hierarchical relationship in which humans, who walk on their feet, have power over snakes, which crawl on their bellies.[11]

These two sets of differences—between serpent and human, man and woman—are sealed by an act of naming. In the case of the serpent, the absence of a proper name is significant; it underscores the differentiation between him and the female human, who acquires a proper name at this point. In the human realm, the man names his wife Eve (חוה; Gen 3:20), embodying the role she is about to take on as "mother of all living."

The timing of this naming act is crucial, as it comes after the curse, in which women's role as childbearer is introduced and emphasized, and before the conception and birth of the first child (Cain; 4:1). This naming, as the

---

[10]For comparison of translations and detailed arguments for the latter translation, see Meyers, *Discovering Eve*, 95–121.

[11]An implicit area of differentiation is speech: humans speak with words, and animals do not, except on rare occasions when God gives them the power to speak (cf. Numbers 22).

etymology provided for her proper name stresses, is the prelude to the creation of more human beings, from whom the woman as well as her mate will have to be distinguished. The birth of children situates woman in yet another hierarchical relationship, that of mother and child. In this bond, it is the woman who is in the dominant position, at least during the child's infancy and youth. Her power is symbolized in her role as the one who names. Eve names her first and third children.[12] In ascribing these acts of naming to Eve, the story emphasizes her role in procreation, the power of woman as creator of human beings, and her ability to discern the essence of her children, just as the man did with respect to the animal world in 2:19.[13]

The initial anonymity of the first man and woman suggests that their relationship, from the time of creation to the time of expulsion from the garden, is both universal and normative. The woman symbolizes all women.[14] In this sense, she has no unique identity, for her traits are shared by all women. Her encounter with the snake not only marks the beginning of the end of her sojourn in the garden but also begins her journey toward personal identity and proper name. The reversal of the woman's anonymity marks a transition point in her characterization.[15] The name fixes her personal identity in terms of her maternal role. Moreover, it concretizes her status relative to that of her husband; his ability to name her, as he has named the animals, symbolizes his dominant position in their hierarchical relationship.

According to Mieke Bal, the introduction of the proper name causes the reader to reorganize all the data that apparently pertain to the woman under the category of Eve, thus falling into what Bal terms the "retrospective fallacy." Bal sees this move as a circular reading strategy in which the reader projects "an accomplished and singular named character onto previous textual elements that lead to the construction of that character."[16]

That this reading strategy is retrospective is clear; the reader learns of the proper name only at the end and then uses it as a sign under which the woman's attributes can be gathered to construct a unified character. Whether it is also a fallacy is open to question. Reader-response theorist Wolfgang Iser notes that the "activity of reading can be characterized as a sort of kaleidoscope of perspectives, preintentions, recollections," although "the process of antici-

---

[12]The naming formula as in Gen 4:1 is not always used; sometimes the name is simply conveyed by the narrator, as is the case with Abel (Gen 4:2).

[13]For detailed discussion, see Pardes, *Countertraditions*, 39–59.

[14]*Discovering Eve*, 3.

[15]The question of whether the man is named or anonymous in Genesis 1–3 is much less clear. See chapter 6.

[16]*Lethal Love: Feminist Literary Readings of Biblical Love Stories* (Bloomington: Indiana University Press, 1987), 108.

pation and retrospection itself does not by any means develop in a smooth flow."[17] It is this process, however smooth or rough, that results in the transformation of the text into an experience for the reader.[18] Hence the act of retrojecting "Eve" back into the various descriptions of *woman* in Genesis 1–3 may not be a fallacy at all but simply a part of the natural reading process.[19] Nevertheless, the retrojection of the proper name can mask the effect of her initial anonymity and the role that the giving of the proper name itself plays in attributing stable identity to her.

Anonymity therefore points to the universality and paradigmatic nature of her experience and allows the man's act of naming to function explicitly as a marker of transition into Eve's personal life story. It is her relation to the serpent that is ultimately responsible for Eve's entrenchment in the role of wife and mother. As the "other man" in her early existence, the serpent seduces her through words to taste sexuality and to embark on a life marked by the knowledge of good and evil. No sexual act between them is depicted, though R. Johanan is quoted as saying that the serpent copulated with Eve and infused her (and humankind) with lust.[20] But sexual symbolism abounds, for example, in the phallic form of the serpent, the fruit the woman gives to her husband (cf. Song 4:13, 16), and the sexual connotations of the verb "to know" (ידע, in the sense of "to know a person carnally"),[21] which appear in the very name of the tree itself ("tree of the knowledge of good and evil"; עץ הדעת טוב ורע). In giving the woman the fruit, the serpent is initiating her into a life of sexuality, to which maternity is closely bound. The snake's banishment from the world of the upright is God's attempt to eliminate the "other man" from the life experience of the woman, whose desire shall henceforth be for her husband alone.

Potiphar's wife (Gen 39:7–20)

If the snake was successfully banished from the life of the first woman, the concept of the "other man" lived on. Whereas Genesis 3 describes a male, if serpentine, figure who successfully entices a woman, Gen 39:7–20 portrays a

[17]*The Implied Reader: Patterns of Communication in Prose Fiction from Bunyan to Beckett* (Baltimore: Johns Hopkins University Press, 1974), 279.

[18]Iser, *Implied Reader*, 281.

[19]This point is also raised by Pardes, *Countertraditions*, 32.

[20]b. Yebamot 103a. This tradition is alluded to in b. Avodah Zarah 22b, b. Shabbat 146a, 2 Enoch 31:6, and perhaps also in 2 Tim 2:13–14. For discussion, see Jouette Bassler, "Adam, Eve, and the Pastor: The Use of Genesis 2–3 in the Pastoral Epistles," in *Genesis 1–3 in the History of Exegesis: Intrigue in the Garden*, ed. Gregory Allen Robbins (Lewiston, N.Y.: Edwin Mellen Press, 1988), 43–66.

[21]BDB, ad loc.

woman who unsuccessfully attempts to entice a man. Genesis 39 begins by briefly describing Joseph's career in the household of Potiphar, the Egyptian Pharaoh's chief steward. Potiphar had bought Joseph from the Ishmaelites (or Midianites), who, in turn, had purchased him from his brothers and brought him down to Egypt (Gen 37:28, 36; 39:1). Joseph's success in all his endeavors was due, so the narrator avers repeatedly (37:2, 3, 5), to the Lord's help. As a result, his master (אדניו) "made him overseer of his house and put him in charge of all that he had" (Gen 39:4) and gave Joseph access to everything except his food (39:6).

Joseph was not only successful but also "handsome and good-looking" (יפה־ תאר ויפה מראה Gen 39:6b). Such were his physical attractions that, "after a time his master's wife (אשת אדניו) cast her eyes on Joseph and said, 'Lie with me'" (39:7). Joseph refused: How could he offend his master? How could he sin before God? (39:8-9). She persisted daily, to no avail (39:10). At the story's climax (or anticlimax, from the woman's perspective), she caught hold of his garment and cried yet again, "Lie with me!" (39:12). Joseph left his garment in her hand and fled rather than give in to her passion. Furious, she called her servants and told them that Joseph tried to rape her and fled when she screamed. When "his master," her husband, returned, she repeated the story to him. Potiphar imprisoned Joseph as punishment (39:20). Her wanton behavior and subsequent framing of Joseph move the plot of the Joseph saga forward. Joseph's imprisonment, though unwarranted from the narrator's perspective, nevertheless launches the events that later place him in a position of high power and result in his reconciliation with his family.[22]

One consequence of the woman's anonymity is that attention is drawn to the dissonance between her explicit designation as אשת אדניו—literally, the wife of his (i.e., Joseph's) master—and her unwifely lustful advances toward Joseph. This discord conveys the narrator's negative judgment upon her as a woman who fails to direct her sexuality only toward her husband, as a proper wife should do. It also contributes to the characterization of Joseph. The narrator uses the woman's behavior to demonstrate Joseph's righteousness and piety. She pursues Joseph and then lies about it; Joseph upholds all standards of chastity and acts in consideration of and obedience to his master. She tries to lead Joseph astray; Joseph exhibits admirable self-control.[23] Of course, his

[22]This story may also be compared to other stories from ancient Near Eastern literature. See Susan Tower Hollis, "The Woman in Ancient Examples of the Potiphar's Wife Motif, K2111," in *Gender and Difference in Ancient Israel*, ed. Peggy L. Day (Minneapolis: Fortress, 1989), 28–42.

[23]James L. Kugel, *In Potiphar's House: The Interpretive Life of Biblical Texts* (San Francisco: Harper, 1990), 21–22.

determination not to violate his master's trust may also hint at his political ambition, which could potentially be jeopardized by such a liaison.

This summary views these events from Joseph's point of view.[24] For the narrator, allied with Joseph, the woman is both a seductress and a liar. The narrator leaves enough traces of her story and her point of view, however, to allow readers to resist his perspective. We can do so in two ways. First, we may accept the narrator's story but view her seduction of Joseph sympathetically. Second, we may give some credence to her story.

The former approach is taken by Alice Bach. She reconstructs the woman's story by drawing on the Testament of Joseph, Joseph and Asenath, Midrash Rabbah, and other postbiblical readings of the episode. Bach's story tells of the woman's love and desire, which stemmed from her first glimpse of him in the marketplace. It is she who urges her husband to buy Joseph from the Ishmaelites in the first place; despite her responsibility for his imprisonment, she exhibits an intense desire to free him from jail. In Bach's hands, the woman's story becomes a romance of unrequited love.[25]

In contrast to Bach, Laura Donaldson justifies the woman's pursuit of Joseph on strategic grounds. Donaldson argues that the woman's aim is to assert her right as heir to the household. To do this, she must prevent the household's passing from Potiphar to Joseph. Donaldson suggests:

> By asserting herself sexually, she can potentially gain some leverage with the man who has so abruptly invaded her daily world. When that strategy fails, Potiphar's wife hurriedly devises another ruse: a self-serving explanation of the incident that convinces her husband and effects the very removal of Joseph she so desperately desires.[26]

According to Donaldson, the woman's designation as Potiphar's wife signifies her inability to own her own body. Donaldson conjectures that the woman "becomes Potiphar's possession in order to claim the second meaning of 'proprius' [the Latin root of 'proper']: the potential for having property. And it is precisely this potential in the form of controlling the houshold of her husband that Joseph threatens."[27]

The statement that Potiphar's wife is, in fact, interested in asserting or in-

---

[24]Scholars often assume the narrator in this story to be reliable and hence take his point of view to be "true"; see, for example, Speiser, *Genesis*, 366.

[25]"Breaking Free of the Biblical Frame-up: Uncovering the Woman in Genesis 39," in *A Feminist Companion to Genesis*, ed. Athalya Brenner (Sheffield: Sheffield Academic Press, 1993), 318–42.

[26]"Cyborgs, Ciphers, and Sexuality: Re-theorizing Literary and Biblical Character," in *Characterization in Biblical Literature*, ed. Adele Berlin and Elizabeth Struthers Malbon, *Semeia* 63 (1993): 90–92.

[27]"Cyborgs, Ciphers, and Sexuality," 91.

heriting control over her husband's household, while not impossible, is difficult to support from the (admittedly one-sided) narration of the story. Nevertheless, Donaldson's reading draws attention to the political and economic undertones to the story. The woman's designation as "his master's wife" emphasizes that Joseph would risk his status with Potiphar by entering into a sexual liaison with Potiphar's wife. Such a liaison could lead to Joseph's death or banishment and hence his removal as a rival, as Donaldson suggests. If kept secret from her husband, it could put Joseph under the woman's sway; he would thus become a pawn in her power struggle with her husband. These possibilities highlight the issues of formal and informal, primary and derived authority, that are at stake in the relationship between Joseph and Potiphar and that will become even more central in the partnership between Joseph and the Pharaoh.

Yet another reading would suggest that the woman contrived this story not so much as revenge on Joseph or as a stepping-stone to economic power but as a weapon against her husband. The woman blames Potiphar for bringing Joseph into the household, much as she accuses Joseph of taking advantage of a situation in which he is alone with a desirable woman. To her servants, she calls out that her husband has brought a Hebrew among them to insult them. This Hebrew "came in to me to lie with me"; when she cried out, he left his garment beside her and fled outside (39:14–15). The story she tells her husband is edited slightly. She refers to her husband's introduction of the Hebrew into the household and to the Hebrew's insulting behavior, implying but not stating that the latter was Potiphar's intention. This version of her story is also less explicit about the Hebrew's behavior and omits reference to his "coming in to her to lie with her." Nevertheless, the implications are clear. Her husband has endangered her honor and safety; Joseph is a scoundrel.

The text reveals nothing directly concerning the relationship between the woman and her husband. The attempt to imagine her husband from the wife's perspective yields three questions. First, why, indeed, did Potiphar introduce this foreign man into the household? The narrator assures us that Potiphar permitted Joseph access to everything in his household except "the food [literally, bread, לחם] that he ate" (39:6): Joseph apparently understands this stipulation euphemistically as a reference to Potiphar's wife herself (39:9).[28] Even so, it may be surprising that Potiphar allowed this extraordinarily attractive young man to spend so much time with his wife in his house. Under these circumstances, the woman's accusation that her husband had brought the Hebrew among them for a less than honorable purpose is not surprising.

Second, what significance is to be attached to the punishment meted out by Potiphar to Joseph? On the one hand, the fact that Potiphar sent Joseph to

---

[28]Rashi (ad loc) and Gen. Rab. 86:6 understand "bread" here as a euphemism for "wife."

jail might indicate that he took his wife's accusation seriously.[29] Sending Joseph to prison both punished him and removed him firmly from Potiphar's house, just as God's curse on the serpent removed him from the woman's purview. On the other hand, imprisonment may have been too lenient a penalty for the crime of rape. Potiphar's response may suggest that he did not, in fact, give much credence to his wife's story; had he really suspected Joseph of rape, Potiphar would have had him summarily executed.[30]

Third, what can be said about the sexual relationship between Potiphar and his wife? This question is raised by the identification of Potiphar as סריס פרעה. This designation is translated in the NRSV as "an officer of Pharaoh" and in the NJPSV as "a courtier of Pharaoh." The primary meaning of סריס, however, is "eunuch."[31] If this meaning is adopted, we may surmise the absence of a sexual relationship between the woman and her husband, making her interest in the attractive Israelite man all the more understandable. Genesis Rabbah suggests that the woman was not the only one in Potiphar's household who found Joseph attractive. To the anonymous commentator on this phrase, the designation סריס פרעה "intimates that he was castrated, thus teaching that he [Potiphar] purchased him [Joseph] for the purposes of sodomy, whereupon the Holy One, blessed be He, emasculated him [Potiphar]."[32]

The narrator's controlling voice therefore does not rule out the possibility of a variety of counterreadings based on hints within the narrative itself, as well as on postbiblical retellings of the story. These alternative stories accept the biblical story's portrayal of the woman's desire for Joseph, but they account for it on the basis of love, desire for power, or marital difficulties. None of these readings takes the second option available to the resistant reader, which is to give full credence to her charge of sexual assault. The silence of the commentators testifies to the difficulty of following this second path. The notion that Joseph attempted to rape this woman can be supported only by disregarding completely the narrator's depiction of the woman's persistent and blatant demand, "Lie with me" (39:7, 10, 12).

The fact that Joseph was close enough for her to clutch and remove his garment, however, leaves open the possibility that her interest was not entirely unrequited. According to Genesis Rabbah, the notion that Joseph was quite willing to respond to Potiphar's wife is present in the first part of Gen 39:11: "One day, however, when he went into the house to do his work, and while no one else was in the house." The phrase "to do his work" is taken literally— that is, with reference to sexual activity—whereas the phrase "no one else was

---

[29]Nelly Furman, "His Story versus Her Story: Male Genealogy and Female Strategy in the Jacob Cycle, *Semeia* 46 (1989): 149.

[30]Bach, "Frame-up," 333.

[31]BDB, ad loc.

[32]Gen. Rab. 86:3.

in the house" means that "on examination he did not find himself a man, for R. Samuel said: The bow was drawn but it relaxed."[33]

The woman's anonymity therefore draws attention to the dissonance between her identification as the wife of Joseph's master, Potiphar, and her sexual interest in Joseph. The narrator's version of the tale castigates her for directing her sexual attentions at a man other than her husband. The story is a vehicle through which the narrator both supports the biblical view that a wife should be sexually available to her husband only and expresses the stereotype of the wicked and seductive foreign woman.[34] The counterreadings inquire into the reasons for her behavior and, in doing so, resist the narrator's labeling of the foreign woman as wanton.

Women and Prophets (1 Kgs 17:12–13; 2 Kgs 4:1–7, 4:8–37)

The books of Kings portray three unnamed women whose primary narrative relationship is not with their spouses but with the prophets Elijah or Elisha. The widow of Zarephah is appointed by God to take care of the prophet Elijah. She herself is in danger of starving, as is her son (1 Kgs 17:12–13). Although she does not directly ask Elijah for help, he prevents their death by means of a multiplication miracle: "The jar of meal was not emptied, neither did the jug of oil fail, according to the word of the LORD that he spoke by Elijah" (17:16). This reprieve is only temporary, however; some time later the son falls mortally ill.[35] The widow accuses Elijah of causing his death: "What have you against me, O man of God? You have come to me to bring my sin to remembrance, and to cause the death of my son!" (17:18). She does not ask him directly for a miracle, although her accusatory tone may be read as implying such a demand. Elijah responds by petitioning God on her behalf (17:20). The miracle is performed out of sight of the mother, but, upon seeing her child alive, she acknowledges Elijah as a man of God, who has the word of the Lord in his mouth (17.24). No sexual relationship is depicted or implied, but it is clear that the widow and Elijah depend on one another for material support, as husband and wife would have, and are united in their efforts to sustain the son, as parents would have been.

Similar stories are told with respect to Elijah's successor, the prophet Elisha. In 2 Kgs 4:1–7, the widowed wife of a son of the prophets (בני הנביאים) calls out to Elisha for help: Her children are to be taken as slaves in repayment of

---

[33]Gen. Rab. 87:7.

[34]Cf. Prov 2:16–19, which warns against the foreign or strange woman who beguiles with smooth words and forsakes the partner of her youth. Though these words may be taken metaphorically or symbolically, they express a stereotypical view of the foreign woman as wanton.

[35]Gray (*I and II Kings*, 382) argues that the child did not, in fact, die. Whether he did or did not reach the point of death, the emphasis is clearly on the prophet's ability to bring him back to life.

debts. Like his mentor Elijah, Elisha responds with a multiplication miracle, providing her and her children with enough oil to repay their debts and support themselves thereafter. Unlike her counterpart in 1 Kings 17, this woman is not portrayed as praising Elisha. The narrative is sufficiently unambiguous to allow the readers to draw their own conclusions regarding the prophet's miraculous abilities.

The anonymity of the women draws attention to their widowed state. In the absence of a husband to support them, they turn to the prophet, who fulfills this role through miraculous means. Because the women are widows, the prophets' substitution for the husband in the role of provider creates no conflict.

More complex is the lengthy story of the Shunammite woman (2 Kgs 4:8–37). In contrast to the two widows just mentioned, the Shunammite is wealthy and, at her own initiative, provides room and board for the prophet (2 Kgs 4: 8). Elisha plays another role, however, that is normally associated with a husband, as the one who is responsible for the conception and survival of her child.

The woman's story begins with a variation on the annunciation scene. In thanks for providing him with food and shelter, Elisha promises her a son, despite her barrenness and her age. Not having asked for such reward, she is skeptical: "No, my lord, O man of God; do not deceive your servant" (4:16). She does conceive, however, and bears a son within the year (4:17).[36] Some time later, this son dies.[37] She puts him on Elisha's bed and goes out in search of the prophet. Upon finding him, she clasps his feet, revealing to Elisha her great distress—and the (to him) disconcerting fact that the Lord had not made this event known to him (4:27).

The Shunammite woman holds the prophet responsible for her suffering at the death of her son: "Did I ask my lord for a son? Did not I say, 'Do not mislead me'?" (2 Kgs 4:28). Like Elijah, Elisha performs the miracle by resurrecting the son. His power is recognized by the woman, who again, this time in praise, "fell at his feet, bowing to the ground" (4:37). Although the story glorifies the prophet's abilities as wonder-worker, it also, through the voice of the woman, implies the limitations to his prowess. The woman is transformed by the threat to the life of her son into an assertive, angry woman accusing the prophet, to whom she is indebted for earlier favors, of contributing to the death of her son. At each point, the prophet responds satisfactorily, thereby reinstating

[36]On the effect on the reader of the fact that the conception and birth of this son were not at the woman's request, see Burke O. Long, "A Figure at the Gate: Readers, Reading, and Biblical Theologians," in *Canon, Theology, and Old Testament Interpretation: Essays in Honor of Brevard S. Childs,* ed. D. L. Peterson, et al. (Philadelphia: Fortress Press, 1988), 171; and Sternberg, *Poetics,* 310.

[37]Gray (*I and II Kings,* 499) suggests that popular tradition may have exaggerated the unconsciousness of the boy. This interpretation assumes that the story is historically true but ignores the role that the death and resurrection play in the Elisha cycle.

himself in her confidence. Nevertheless, the reader is left with a hint of narrative ambivalence.[38]

All the characters in this passage, aside from the prophet Elisha and his aide Gehazi, are anonymous; of these, the woman designated as the mother is most important. The husband is a minor figure. He is defined only in relation to his wife and son, reversing the usual mode of designation, according to which wives are identified in relation to their husbands. He appears briefly three times. In the first appearance, he is identified as her man (אישה). He listens silently to her plan to provide the prophet Elisha with room and board (4:9). In the second, he is designated as the child's father (אביו). He plays no role in the nurturing of the child and, indeed, seems disconnected from him. When the child comes to him complaining of a headache, he tells the servant to carry the child to his mother (4:18). In the third, he is identified again as the Shunammite's husband (אישה). She orders him to send her a servant and donkey so that she might find Elisha in the hope that he will cure the child. He tries to talk her out of this plan, but she prevails (4:22–23). Most significant, perhaps, is the absence of any reference to a sexual encounter between him and his wife as a prelude to the conception of this son (4:17). These elements imply a distance between husband and wife, as well as between father and son.

The disconnection between husband and wife is also conveyed through the designations of the woman. She is never designated as a wife but solely as the Shunammite (השונמית; 4:12, 25; "that Shunammite," 4:37), the boy's mother (אמו; 4:20) or the woman (האישה; 4:17). Elisha—and not her husband—is the significant man in her life. The narrative makes it clear that there is no sexual contact between them. The woman stands at the door while Elisha announces the impending conception and birth of her son (4:15) and frequently communicates with Elisha through Gehazi (4:13, 26). Nevertheless, it is Elisha who provides her with a son and who exerts great effort to bring him to life again.

Unlike Potiphar's wife, the Shunammite does not cross the bounds of sexual propriety. She is unfailingly courteous to her husband (4:9), and, although she does not always accept his counsel, she is polite in her refusal (4:23). The ways in which she is identified in the absence of her proper name, however, do seem to imply a dissonance between her formal role as a man's wife and her strong connection to the prophet Elisha, who is ultimately responsible for her designation as mother.

Manoah's Wife (Judges 13)

Unlike the story of the Shunammite woman, in which the annunciation motif is sketched briefly, Judges 13 draws out the motif more fully than any other biblical example. Two of its protagonists, Manoah and Samson, are named; the

[38]Alexander Rofé, "The Classification of the Prophetical Stories," *JBL* 89 (1970): 433–34, and Long, "Figure," 174.

other two, the woman and the angel, are not. Here we focus on the woman's portrayal.[39] The angel appears to the woman and announces that she will give birth to a son, who will be a Nazirite from birth. Even during pregnancy, she must avoid wine, strong drink, and unclean foods; after his birth, his hair is not to be cut (13:3–5). The woman tells this story to her husband, who entreats God to allow the visitor to appear to them again. The angel does appear again, but to the woman alone in a field. The woman runs to get her husband. Manoah inquires as to the child's "rule of life" (13:12). The angel remarks that this information has already been made known to the woman but repeats the instructions concerning her diet during pregnancy (13:14). Manoah offers hospitality to the angel. The angel declines but suggests that a burnt offering would be appropriate (13:16). Manoah then asks the angel's name, "so that we may honor you when your words come true" (13:17). The angel says only that his name is "wonderful." Manoah offers up the sacrifice; the angel ascends in the flame, and Manoah, who finally realizes the man's angelic identity, fears for his life. His wife assures him that they are not in danger because the prophecy must still be fulfilled. The woman bears a son, who is named Samson and blessed by the Lord (13:24).

The absence of her proper name draws our attention to the specific designations used to describe and refer to the woman in this story. According to Exum, the narrator's suppression of her name underscores neither her centrality nor her relationship to the angel but her role as a mother. For Exum, "her importance lies in her fulfillment of a role, and thus she is not even given a name."[40] On the surface, Exum's interpretation is consistent with the general observation that anonymity draws attention from the character's personal identity to her typified role(s). In fact, this woman is never explicitly designated "mother." The woman is introduced as Manoah's wife (אשתו; 13:2), a designation used also in 13:11a, 20–23. Elsewhere, she is referred to by the narrator (13:3, 6, 10, 24), by the angel (13:13), and even by her husband (13:11b) as "the woman" (האשה). By the end of the story, she has become a mother, though this designation does not appear until the next chapter (14:2).

This set of designations hints at the possible dissonance between her typified role as wife and her narrative independence from her husband. We are not given any direct insight into the nature of the marital relationship between the woman and her husband, as we are in the annunciation stories of Rachel and Hannah.[41] To her husband, she behaves like a dutiful wife, who reports the two appearances of the man of God to her human man and tactfully refrains from

[39]The depiction of the angel is treated in chapter 7.

[40]*Fragmented Women. Feminist (Sub)versions of Biblical Narratives* (Valley Forge, Pa.: Trinity Press International, 1993), 67.

[41]See Gen 30:2, 1 Sam 1:8.

interfering or interrupting during Manoah's encounter with the angel. These qualities may have led Crenshaw and others to conclude that she represents the "ideal Israelite woman,"[42] the "model of Israelite womanhood,"[43] in contrast to the other women in Samson's life.[44]

These apparently flattering descriptions do not do her justice. Indeed, the narrative both explicitly and implicitly sets her apart from her named husband. Her demure and deferential behavior does not conceal, from the reader or from the angel, the fact that she surpasses her husband in her perception of the significance of these events and of the identity of her divine visitor. Her superior understanding is evident in her first impression of the "man of God" and his angelic appearance, which led to her restraint in questioning him, and is also clear in her interpretation of the burnt offering by which the angel arose to heaven. As she observes, "If the LORD had meant to kill us, he would not have accepted a burnt offering and a grain offering at our hands, or shown us all these things, or now announced to us such things as these" (13:23). Boling considers her to possess a "plodding confidence" that everything will turn out for the best,[45] but her reassurances to her husband in 13:23 could just as easily be read as patient tolerance of the obtuseness and unnecessary fear exhibited by her husband following the angel's extraordinary ascent.

Although she is patently superior to her husband in insight and understanding, Manoah's wife does not overtly challenge her husband's authority. Nevertheless, the parameters of their relationship are called into question by the other male protagonist of the story. As in the stories of the Shunammite and Potiphar's wife, the center of her attention within the narrative is not her husband but another "man"—namely, the angel.

The connection is implied by the similarities between them. Not only are they anonymous but also they share both prophetic knowledge and ability. The angel prophesies the birth, lifestyle, and mission of the child. The woman's prophetic abilities are subtler but are implied by the changes that she makes to the angel's initial message to her in 13:3–5. The angel has informed the woman that the lad would be a Nazirite of God "from birth" and would begin to save Israel from the Philistines (13:5). Upon reporting these promises to Manoah, the woman alters the angel's wording to say that he would be a Nazirite of God from the womb "to the day of his death" (עד יום מותו; 13:7).[46] The woman has

---

[42]James L. Crenshaw, *Samson: A Secret Betrayed, a Vow Ignored* (Atlanta: John Knox Press, 1978), 70.

[43]Lillian R. Klein, *The Triumph of Irony in the Book of Judges* (Sheffield: Almond Press, 1988), 120.

[44]Soggin, *Judges*, 236.

[45]*Judges*, 226.

[46]See Alter, *Art*, 101.

therefore revised the angel's message in two ways: first, by omitting the child's role in Israel's ongoing struggle with the Philistines,[47] and second, by introducing a reference to her son's death. This latter indicates that the son will be a Nazirite for his entire life, a rather unusual condition, because most people took on Nazirite vows for a specified period of time only.[48] Further, although the phrase "from birth to the day of his death" denotes "all his life," it subtly introduces an ominous note, which mars the otherwise joyous and hopeful mood of her report.[49]

Mieke Bal sees the woman's words "to the day of his death" in a more sinister light, suggesting that this phrase will ultimately condemn Samson.[50] She argues that the woman's knowledge not only predicts Samson's fate but also produces his death.[51] Therefore, like Judith, Samson's mother kills through a speech act, an act she has committed autonomously by altering the angel's predictions.[52] It may be overinterpretation to argue that the woman kills her future son with her words. What is striking, however, is that the woman takes on the predictive or prophetic role of the angel by extending the Nazirite vow to encompass her son's entire life. In doing so, she implies that his death will in some way be caused by his breaking of the vow. Just as the angel's annunciation prophecy is fulfilled, so are the woman's amendment and its implication fulfilled through his fatal haircut at the hands of Delilah (16:19). In this way, the woman shares not only the anonymity of the angel but also another important element of his identity, namely, his role as prophet. The woman has unusual and considerable foreknowledge concerning her son: She knows of his future birth, his Nazirite way of life, his role in the life of Israel and his death.[53]

There is an undercurrent of intimacy in the narrative portrayal of their encounters. The angel appears twice to the woman alone, despite the explicit request of the husband; his initial message regarding the child is reserved for her ears alone. But what is the extent and nature of their connection? Josephus saw Manoah as being inordinately jealous and suspicious of this man, whom his wife met so mysteriously while alone. In *Ant.* 5.276–80, Josephus notes that Manoah was "madly enamoured of his wife and hence inordinately jealous." In response to the woman's description of her visitor, Manoah "in his jealousy

---

[47]As Alter (*Art*, 101) notes, this omission leaves the way open for Manoah's question in 13:8.

[48]Num 6:13–21.

[49]Alter, *Art*, 101.

[50]*Death*, 31.

[51]Bal, *Death*, 74.

[52]Bal, *Death*, 75, 146.

[53]Samson's mother is only one of several women who strongly influence the course of Judges 13–16. The ironic dimensions of the role of women in the Samson saga are discussed by many authors, including Bal, *Death*, 202, and Klein, *Irony*, 120.

was driven . . . to distraction and to conceive the suspicions that such passion arouses." These suspicions were not allayed even after Manoah had seen the angel face to face (*Ant.* 5:280).

Though Josephus implies that Manoah's jealousy was unfounded, a less chaste reading is also possible. Suspicions of personal intimacy between the woman and the angel are based on a number of hints in the text. In the first place, there is no positive indication in Judges 13 that Samson is the natural son of Manoah. No doubt it is reasonable to deduce from the fact that the woman is called Manoah's wife that they were therefore the natural parents of Samson who are mentioned in the remainder of the Samson saga (e.g., 14:2–6). Nevertheless, Judges 13 does not refer to Manoah as Samson's father; Manoah does not refer to his future child as his son but only as "the boy" (הנער; 13:8, 12).

Another clue to a more intimate relationship between the angel and the woman is in his initial prophecy to the woman in 13:3–5. In 13:3, the angel reminds the woman that she is barren and has not borne a child, and he promises that she will conceive and bear a son. The verb "you will conceive" (הרית) conveys a future sense and is consistent with the prophetic tone of the passage. In 13:5, the prophecy is repeated. This time, however, the verb is perfect (הרה), which, if taken literally, would mean that conception has already occurred. Now, it is possible that we should not make too much of this difference and decide, along with most translators, that a future sense is intended here as well.[54] Or we could join some exegetes in labeling this verse as an intrusive, later addition to the story[55] because it repeats the information given in 13:3.[56] Then again, it is possible to take the change in verb tense seriously. Lillian Klein suggests that the perfect form of the verb (13:5) indicates that the woman became pregnant during the encounter with the angel, just as, according to Klein, Sarah had done during the visit of the divine messenger.[57] This suspicion is reinforced by the fact that 13:24 notes neither a sexual encounter with her husband nor the conception of Samson. While we may supply these without too much imagination, the omission leaves open the playful possibility that he was conceived during her encounter with the angel.[58]

---

[54]NRSV, RSV, and *NJPSV* translate this verb as a future tense. Boling (*Judges*, 220) translates: "Actually, you are already pregnant and bearing a son." He notes that the shift in verb forms is in order, following the double asseverative כי הנך (literally, "for behold"). Other examples of this pattern may be found in Gen 16:11 and Isa 7:14.

[55]James L. Crenshaw, "The Samson Saga: Filial Devotion or Erotic Attachment?" *ZAW* 86 (1974): 475.

[56]James A. Wharton, "The Secret of Yahweh: Story and Affirmation in Judges 13–16," *Int* 27 (1973): 59.

[57]*Irony*, 111.

[58]Contra Adrien Janis Bledstein ("Is Judges a Woman's Satire of Men Who Play God?" in *Feminist Companion to Judges*, ed. Brenner, 49), who says that the narrator stresses that there is no divine-mortal hanky-panky.

Bal, too, sees a sexual undercurrent to these twin predicates. In keeping with her speech-act analysis of the passage, Bal suggests that, for the biblical narrator, word and deed are the same; the promise of fertility is at the same time the act of fertilizing.[59] According to Klein, the suggestion of a sexual relationship between the angel and the woman is strengthened by her report in 13:6 that the angel "came to me" (בא אלי).[60] Although this verb can have a simple literary meaning, it can also mean "he came in unto me," a common biblical way of referring to sexual intercourse.[61] This wording is especially noteworthy in the absence of any reference that Manoah "came in unto" his wife, although it must be noted that the explicit reference to sexual intercourse is occasionally absent from other annunciation stories as well (Gen 21:2; 2 Kgs 4:17).

Finally, hints of sexual intimacy between the woman and the angel are to be found in the narrator's brief words about the circumstances in which he "came to her" the second time. Here we are told, apparently gratuitously, that he came to her sitting in a field, without her husband. Although this reference to the field may foreshadow future developments in the Samson saga,[62] it could easily call to the mind of a reader familiar with the legal texts in Deuteronomy the various cases regarding extramarital sexual encounters. Deuteronomy 22:25 stipulates that women who engage in sexual encounters in fields could not be punished because their cries of protest would have gone unheard. This is not to suggest that Manoah's wife was raped by the angel, but the simple fact that they spent time alone together in a field raises the suspicion that there was more to their encounter than talk.

The paternity of Samson and the precise nature of the relationship between the woman and the angel ultimately remain ambiguous. What emerges is the closeness, perhaps even intimacy, of the relationship between these two characters. Their encounter, even if consisting solely of words (or speech-acts), is the only fully harmonious one in the story: The angel comes to ameliorate a situation that was likely of some concern to the woman[63]; she accepts his words without pressing him for extra information. He trusts her to comply with his instructions and would not have brought Manoah into the picture at all but for the latter's insistence. She, in turn, intuits the identity that the angel will show himself reluctant to divulge to Manoah. In addition, the narrative implies some similarities between the angel and the woman: They both have foreknowledge

---

[59]*Death*, 26.

[60]Klein, *Irony*, 114.

[61]E.g., Gen 16:4 (Abraham and Hagar) and Gen 29:23, 30; 30:16 (Jacob and his wives).

[62]Crenshaw, "Saga," 475. However, the term *field* (שדה) does not appear again in the saga, though 15:5 describes Samson's destruction of wheat fields and olive orchards.

[63]See Crenshaw, "Saga," 474, who pleads that we allow ourselves to feel the anguish of the barren woman.

of the child's birth, lifestyle, and public role and understand the nature of God's plan.

In the light of these connections, the fact that they are both unnamed within the narrative symbolizes their connection and leads the reader to ponder the nature of their relationship. As a being sent by God, the angel's name cannot be divulged (13:18). Though the woman herself is not divine, she has encounters with and knowledge of a divine being, contacts that exceed in quantity and quality those between the angel and her named and very human spouse. Her son, too, though named by the woman and divinely promised, demonstrates his all-too-human failings in the rest of the Samson saga and therefore does not live up to expectations in his role as judge and potential savior of Israel from Philistine control.

These comments suggest that it is her very namelessness that points to and reinforces the woman's central role in this story. Anonymity does not obscure her personal identity but highlights and gives depth both to her role and to her character. In doing so, her anonymity contributes to a playful ambiguity surrounding the relationship between them and the precise nature of the angel's involvement in Samson's conception.

The anonymity of these wives draws attention to the dissonance between their formal roles and their behavior. Although identified as the woman or wife of a man, they all have significant relationships with other male figures. These figures stand in for their husbands as (potential) sexual partners, material providers, or fathers of their children, narratively speaking if not biologically so. All aid in plot development and in the characterization of major male figures such as Joseph, Elisha, and Samson. Potiphar's wife provides occasion for the narrator to express his views on marital infidelity and the wantonness of foreign women. The other three stories keep their sexual nuances under wraps, though these undertones are readily available for readers who wish to acknowledge them. With the exception of Potiphar's wife, who is molded to the stereotype of the foreign woman, these women support the close tie between wifehood and maternity. Their "wayward" behavior ultimately contributes to, or serves the interests of, their maternal roles as mothers. The narrator initially holds out the possibility of relationship between a woman and an "other man," but the relationship itself consigns these women to sexual fidelity and the maternal role.

MULTIFARIOUS MOTHERS

The desire for children is exemplified in the stories of Rachel and Leah, who compete for the attention of Jacob. Particularly poignant is Rachel's plea to her husband, "Give me children, or I shall die!" (Gen 30:1). Whereas Rachel's longing for offspring is not overtly gender-specific,[64] Hannah's tearful entreaty to God is for a son (1 Sam 1:11). Indeed, with the exception of Rebecca's mother, mothers are virtually always portrayed in relationship with sons and not with daughters.[65] Further, upon becoming mothers, women are depicted with respect to infant sons and adult sons but rarely in relation to growing children.

Once a child is born, the mother's main role is to nurture and protect the infant, just as Hagar, for example, attempted to protect Ishmael from expiring in the desert (Gen 21:15–19). Often this protection extends to protecting their economic and political interests. For example, Sarah is driven to cast Hagar and Ishmael out of her household by her determination that "the son of this slave woman shall not inherit along with my son Isaac" (Gen 21:10). Bathsheba presents her son Solomon to David as his successor, both to provide him with a political future and to spare his life and her own (1 Kgs 1:15–21).

Unnamed mothers abound. As in the case of unnamed wives, the anonymity of these mothers allows the reader to evaluate the degree to which they fulfill, define, or negate the role by which they are formally defined. Like many named mothers, unnamed mothers are portrayed solely in relation to male offspring, whether as children or as adults.[66] Their portrayal centers on the role of mother as one who nurtures, or fails to nurture, her infant or as one who admires her adult son to excess. Some of the stories also challenge aspects of the stereotypical maternal picture and pass judgment on the ways in which specific women execute their roles. Throughout, the mothers' personal identities are both subsumed by and expressed in their maternal roles. In this section we observe a range of mothers, from the women who collude to ensure the infant Moses' survival (Exod 2:1–10), to the mothers who contract to kill and eat their children during the Aramean siege of Samaria (2 Kgs 6:26–32) and the mothers of two adult sons, Micah (Judg 17:1–4) and Sisera (5:28–30).

The Mothers of Moses (Exod 2:1–10)

The book of Exodus begins with a brief description of the hardships faced by the Israelites in Egypt under the new Pharaoh "who did not know Joseph" (Exod 1:8), the delightful story of the two midwives who resisted the Pharaoh's order to kill newborn Hebrew boys (1:15–21), and Pharaoh's command to throw every Israelite boy into the Nile (1:22).

Exodus 2:1–10 tells the story of one boy who was placed in the Nile, though not in the manner or with the results anticipated by the Pharaoh. The passage presents us initially with five anonymous characters: the Levite man, his Levite wife, their infant son, his sister, and the Pharaoh's daughter. Four

---

[64]The plural form בנים can mean "sons" or "children."

[65]The prime exception is the relationship between Ruth and Naomi.

[66]The exception is the mother of Rebecca, who is mentioned in Gen 24:53, 55.

remain anonymous within this pericope, though the parents and sister are named in later passages[67]; the fifth, Moses, is named at the end. The man and woman of the Levite tribe are introduced in the first verse, but already in the second verse the attention shifts to the woman. Here she is not called a wife or mother of anyone but simply "the woman" (הָאִשָּׁה). In short order she conceives, gives birth to a son, and, seeing that he is "good," hides him for three months. This sequence of events, implying a period of a full year, is summarized in one verse solely from the woman's perspective, detailing her actions and her impressions.

The term "saw that he was good" (כִּי־טוֹב הוּא)[68] is strongly reminiscent of the creation narrative, in which God evaluates the creation of each day with similar phrases (Gen 1:4, 10, 18, 21, 25, 31). In Exodus 2, the anonymous woman, designated only by tribal origin, creates by conceiving and giving birth, judges her creation, and bases subsequent actions on that judgment. As the creator of new life, the woman is simply fulfilling the mandate given to woman in Gen 3: 16. That she judges her creation to be good and therefore maintains its life implies the question: what would she have done had her son not been "good"? Hence her portrayal stresses that she had power not only in the fact of the child's birth but also over his very life, just as God does over his creation. Finally, her depiction leaves virtually no part for her husband, though ancient commentators saw fit to remedy this situation.[69]

The focus on the woman and her actions continues in Exod 2:3. She decides that she can no longer hide him, makes an ark (תבה) for him, waterproofs it, places the child inside, and puts it in the river. This detail recalls the flood story, in which God, through the agency of Noah, saves living creatures from the destructive forces of water by placing them in a waterproofed ark (תבה; Genesis 6–9). In carrying out this plan, the woman technically fulfills Pharaoh's command that every Israelite boy should be thrown into the Nile but, in fact, assures his short-term survival.

Now a new character, the infant's sister, appears on the scene and stakes out an observation point by the river (2:4).[70] The presence of an older sister is

---

[67]The parents are identified as Amram and Jochebed in Exod 6:20; the sister is called Miriam in Exod 15:20, Num 26:59.

[68]NRSV: "saw that he was a fine baby."

[69]E.g., Philo, *De Vita Mosis.* 1.10; Josephus, *Ant.* 2.10–23; BibAnt 9:3–16.

[70]For a recent attempt to recover Miriam from the biblical text, see Phyllis Trible, "Subversive Justice: Tracing the Miriam Traditions," in *Justice and the Holy: Essays in Honor of Walter Harrelson*, ed. Douglas A. Knight and Peter J. Paris (Atlanta: Scholars Press, 1989), 99–109; and "Bringing Miriam out of the Shadows," *Bib Rev* 5 (1989): 14–25, 34. For a survey of the treatment of Miriam in postbiblical sources, see Eileen Schuller, "Women of the Exodus in Biblical Retellings of the Second Temple Period," in *Gender and Difference in Ancient Israel*, ed. Peggy L. Day (Minneapolis: Fortress, 1989), 178–94.

somewhat surprising because her existence is not even alluded to in the short recitation of the marriage of the Levite couple and the conception and birth of her infant brother. Her presence, however, provides some reassurance that events are not entirely out of control.

The Pharaoh's daughter and her unnamed attendants enter in 2:5; Pharaoh's daughter discovers the child and has pity on him (2:6). The unnamed sister suggests that the Pharaoh's daughter hire a wetnurse. It is difficult to determine whether the Egyptian woman's decision to keep the child is first made when she takes pity upon him or whether it is suggested to her by the sister's offer to find a wetnurse. The Pharaoh's daughter directs the sister to find a wetnurse, who, as the reader but not the Egyptian woman knows, is the boy's biological mother (2:8). After weaning, the child is brought back to the Pharaoh's household and is named Moses by his daughter (2:10), probably—though we are not told—replacing the name he had been given by his birth parents.[71] This act of naming asserts the claim of Pharaoh's daughter on this child and represents the transfer of the maternal role from his biological mother to his adoptive one.

It may be said that the anonymity of these women (as well as of the Levite man) eclipses their personal identities and focuses attention on the infant object of their efforts, who, though passive and ill-defined in this story, will eventually lead the Israelites out of Egypt.[72] This interpretation is supported by the basic plot of the story, which begins with his birth and ends with his naming. The first-time reader of this story who does not have prior knowledge of the centrality of Moses to the history of Israel as recounted in the Pentateuch would nevertheless understand from the structure of the story that this child is to be an important personage.

In addition, however, the anonymity of the three active characters both highlights and subverts their typified roles. The biological mother of Moses, introduced to us as the Levite woman who marries the Levite man, is never referred to as his wife. And only once (2:8b) is she identified explicitly as the boy's mother, though 2:2 leaves no doubt that she is. Otherwise, the narrator refers to her exclusively as "the woman." Though married, her depiction does not relate to the role of wife at all. Aside from the fact of conception, no relationship with a man is portrayed, nor are issues of obedience and submission

---

[71]The rabbis (Leviticus Rabbah 1:3) suggest that Moses had ten names in infancy and early childhood (though only six are enumerated): "Ten names were applied: Jered, Heber, Jekuthiel, Abi Gedor, Abi Soco, Abi Zanoah. R. Judah B. Ila'i said: Also Tobiah was his name [based on the presence of טוב (*tov*; good) in Exod 2:2.] . . . Also Shemaiah was his name. . . ." Cf. also Exodus Rabbah. 1:26.

[72]J. Cheryl Exum, " 'You Shall Let Every Daughter Live:' A Study of Exodus 1:8–2: 10," *Semeia* 28 (1983): 75. Reprinted in *A Feminist Companion to Exodus to Deuteronomy*, ed. Athalya Brenner (Sheffield: Sheffield University Press, 1994), 52.

addressed. Then again, although the term *mother* is used only once, the woman not only fulfills but also elevates or intensifies the typified role of mother. She creates and evaluates this child as God did the world; she preserves him from destruction by water, as God had preserved created beings from the flood; she nurses him through early childhood, as Israelite mothers should do. Like Hannah (1 Samuel 1), she does not raise her son beyond this point but gives him over to the Pharaoh's daughter, presumably to be raised in the palace. The biblical text skips right over his childhood in the palace, though postbiblical sources and film directors fill the gap in fulsome detail.[73]

The sister is one of the few anonymous women designated as *sister*.[74] Her wisdom in standing watch at the water's edge and her presence of mind upon observing the Pharaoh's daughter are impressive. Her mediation allows both of the other women to mother the infant child.

The portrayal of the anonymous daughter of Pharaoh subtly casts aspersions on her dutiful fulfillment of that typified role and transforms her into the mother of an Israelite. Whether this woman had a husband is not revealed. The absence of a spouse from the narrative, coupled with her anonymity, allows us to construct her character on the basis of her dual role of daughter and mother.[75] Less compliant, more famous, and more sympathetic than the Pharaonic daughter who is Solomon's consort (1 Kgs 3:1), she is drawn briefly but compellingly. Her relationship to her father is not portrayed directly; she is shown primarily in her contact with the mother and sister of the infant and in her role as the one who saves him from death. In light of the decree of death that Pharaoh had placed on all Israelite boys and the responsibility of "all his people" (כל עמו) to drown newborn Hebrew boys in the Nile (1:22), her adoption of the Hebrew infant calls into question her role as the Pharaoh's daughter. Rescuing the infant from the Nile is precisely the opposite of what a loyal subject of Pharaoh, let alone his daughter, should do. This act of salvation is cemented by her collusion with the boy's Hebrew mother and sister to ensure his survival.

Although she is described as Pharaoh's daughter, she is, in fact, allied with those whom the Pharaoh has defined as his enemies; she is engaging in acts

---

[73]Cf. *Ant.* 2.232–37; Louis Ginzberg, *Legends of the Jews*, vol. 2 (Philadelphia: Jewish Publication Society, 1910), 271–76; and Cecil B. DeMille's epic film, *The Ten Commandments* (1956).

[74]Two other anonymous sisters are the sister of Samson's Timnite wife (Judg 15:2) and the sister of the Pharaoh's wife, Queen Tahpenes, who married Hadad the Edomite (1 Kgs 11:19–20).

[75]First Chronicles 4:18 makes brief reference to another Pharaoh's daughter, Bityah. Some later Jewish commentators identified this Bityah with Pharaoh's daughter of Exod 2:1–10. Cf. Ex. Rab. 1:26, 1:30, 18:3. Josephus (*Ant.* 2.232) refers to the Pharaonic daughter of Exod. 2:5 as Thermutis.

that go against his directives, subvert his authority, and tend to the survival of the person through whom Pharaoh's fears will be realized.[76] The absence of the proper name intensifies the focus on her typified role as daughter and emphasizes the good that an atypical, contrary daughter—a daughter who defies the typical filial relationship—can do for Israel. It also allies her explicitly with Moses' biological mother, who is also identified as a daughter (daughter of Levi, בת־לוי; Exod 2:1).

The Pharaoh's daughter is therefore the mirror of the boy's mother. Both women take on some motherly aspects vis-à-vis the child: One gives birth and nurses; the other names and adopts. The sister mediates the relationship between these two mothers; the cooperation of these three unnamed women ensures the survival of the child.

The anonymity of the women draws attention to their typified roles. The mother of Moses, though designated as *woman*, plays the creative and nurturing role of mother in a powerful and decisive way; she is ready to relinquish the child and hence efface her role as his mother in order to ensure his survival. Similarly, the sister takes her place in the drama by watching over the child and solving the problem of how the Pharaoh's daughter will care for (and hide?) the child. The anomalous figure is the Pharaoh's daughter, the boy's adoptive mother, who simultaneously defies her father's order and demonstrates that maternity is not simply a biological process. This passage therefore stretches the definition of *mother* to include all women who nurture children and to acknowledge the power of mothers over the lives of their offspring.

Jeroboam's Wife (1 Kings 14:1–18)

Like the tales of the Zarephath widow, the widow of the son of the prophets, and the Shunammite woman previously considered, this passage also depicts an encounter between an unnamed woman and a named prophet. The woman is the wife of King Jeroboam of Israel, who is sent by her husband to inquire of the prophet Ahijah concerning the fate of their ill child, Abijah (14:2–3). Though in disguise, as her husband had demanded, and pretending to be another, she is recognized by the prophet, who had been informed of her identity and mission by God (14:5). Ahijah gives her a message to take back to Jeroboam: The king has acted wickedly, and his dynasty will be destroyed. As soon as she returns to her city, Ahijah pronounces, the son will die, yet this fate is preferable to that which awaits the rest of Jeroboam's family; the son, at least, will be buried (14:6–16). The death and burial of the son mark the fulfillment of this prophecy (14:17–18).

---

[76]J. C. Siebert-Hommes, "Twelve Women in Exodus 1 and 2: The Role of Daughters and Sons in the Stories concerning Moses," *Amsterdamse Cahiers voor Exegeses en Bijbelse Theologie* 9 (1988): 52.

Although she is portrayed as the mother of Abijah, this woman is formally designated solely as Jeroboam's wife (14:2, 4, 5, 6, 17). Her trip to the prophet is in obedience to her husband's command, as is her disguise. While it is her role as wife that guides her behavior, it is her role as mother that delivers the emotional impact of the story. The designation *mother* is never explicitly applied. The child is referred to by name (Abijah; 14:1), as "the boy" (הנער; 14:3) and as the "son of Jeroboam" (בן־ירבעם; 14:1) but only once as "her son" (בנה), in the words by which the Lord prepares the prophet for her visit (14:5). This pattern foreshadows his demise and thereby the end of her active role as his mother.

The emotional power of the story stems from the dissonance between her role as wife, which is her formal role designation and informs the overt behavior attributed to her in the story, and her role as a mother, about which so little is said. The absence of the term *mother,* her anonymity, her silence, and her passivity, far from effacing her maternal role, in fact, accentuate it. They invite the reader to provide the horrified emotions about which the story is silent. Just as her disguise does not hide her identity as Jeroboam's wife from the prophet,[77] neither do her anonymity and silence hide her identity as a mother from the reader. Whereas she remains Jeroboam's wife, the death of the child, in which she played a role, removes from her the role of mother.

This passage differs from the other mother-meets-prophet stories in a number of ways. The other sons survive, but hers does not. Whereas the women in the other stories act autonomously, this woman acts as an agent of her husband. Whereas they actively, even aggressively, petition the prophet or maneuver and collude to save the child, she is completely silent and passive, obedient to her husband's demand that she veil her identity through disguise and pretense. Any clues as to her state of mind are withheld, though one might well imagine her distress. She does not beg the prophet for her son's life but merely discovers his fate.[78] Yet presumably the blind prophet, who with God's help was able to perceive the woman's identity, could also, with God's help, have saved her child.

The woman's passivity is most poignant in the description of her return to the city, which according to the prophecy is the moment of her child's death. Although the child's fate has been preordained, she determines when this fate will be carried out. A different woman might have vowed never to return to Tirzah again; this woman however accepts both the authority of the male figures in the story and the immutability of the decree. Finally, her story differs with respect to narrative context. With the exception of Exod 2:1–10, the stories of anonymous mothers are disconnected from the political framework of the nar-

[77]See Richard Coggins, "On Kings and Disguises," *JSOT* 50 (1991): 59–60.
[78]Cf. Robert L. Cohn, "Convention and Creativity in the Book of Kings: The Case of the Dying Monarch," *CBQ* 47 (1985): 606–8.

rative plot as a whole. This story, however, is tied into the main plot of 1 Kings by the content of Ahijah's prophecy and the fate of the son. Whereas the other stories focus directly on the power of the prophets and their interactions with the various women, this tale stresses the judgment of the prophet against Jeroboam, the husband of the woman and the father of the sick child.

The death of Jeroboam's son Abijah invites a comparison with the death of another king's son, the first child of David and Bathsheba (2 Samuel 12). This death, too, is prophesied by a prophet, Nathan, as a punishment for the father, David (2 Sam 12:14). The differences between the two stories, however, are as instructive as the similarities. Whereas David implores God directly for the life of his child (2 Sam 12:16), Jeroboam sends his wife in disguise only to ask the prophet Ahijah about his son's fate. The death of David's child atones for David's sin; his next child with Bathsheba, Solomon, is favored by God and inherits his kingdom (2 Sam 12:24). The death and burial of Jeroboam's son, however, functions as a mark of Jeroboam's disfavor, as the death of this child marks the end of his dynasty.

Anonymity draws attention to the conflict between the woman's role as *wife*, which is her formal identification, and her portrayal as mother, which is the source of the story's pathos. Her personal identity is revealed precisely by the passivity with which she obeys both men. Though her son is doomed by his father's wrongdoing and sentenced by God through the blind prophet, she makes no attempt to reverse his fate. In her submissiveness, she upholds God's judgment upon her husband and accepts the loss of her child.

Prostitute-Mothers (1 Kgs 3:16–28)

The survival of children is also at stake for unnamed women who turn to a king for conflict resolution. In 1 Kgs 3:16–28, Solomon adjudicates a dispute between two prostitutes. The case is presented in great detail by one of the harlots (3:17–21). Both harlots had given birth to infants. According to the plaintiff, her housemate accidentally killed her own newborn and then switched the babies to make it appear that it was the speaker's child who had died. The defendant argues the reverse. The women argue until Solomon interrupts by summarizing the case: "The one says, 'This is my son that is alive, and your son is dead;' while the other says, 'Not so! Your son is dead, and my son is the living one' " (3:23). Solomon's risky suggestion to slice the living child in half reveals the true mother, who would rather give up the child to the other than have him die (3:26–27). The narrator views this case as a prime example of the king's wisdom (3:28).

This story expresses the narrator's positive assessment of King Solomon's wisdom. By portraying at length and in detail the dilemma before the king, the narrator allows the reader, along with "all Israel" (3:28), to marvel at the wisdom of the Solomonic solution. This wisdom consists not only in devising a trick that would expose the real mother but also in being able to see beyond the stereotype of the harlot to the identity of these women as mothers.[79]

Yet in the course of describing the dilemma, the narrator creates a second riddle, to which no solution is provided.[80] Which speaker is the woman to whom the king presented the child? It may be natural to assume that the speaker in 3:17–21 is the woman referred to as the mother in 3:26.[81] This identification is not made at all clear in 3:26–27, however, which connects the identity of the real mother to her response to Solomon's offer to divide the child in two. The reader, while privy to the words of the two women, is not given access to the visual and other identifying details that Solomon would have used to distinguish the speakers. Proper names would have placed the reader on an equal footing with Solomon. In the absence of names, the two women's identities are indistinguishable until Solomon has rendered his decision.[82]

The riddle that is therefore asked of the reader is: Who is the woman whose son was the live one (3:26)? This, in turn, raises a more abstract question: By what criteria does one define her as the real mother? It may be natural to assume that the real mother was the child's biological mother,[83] but it is not the only possibility allowed by the story. This story may be read not only as a challenge to the stereotypical view of prostitutes but also as a revision of motherhood as necessarily a biological category. Solomon awards the child to the woman who displays greater veneration for the life of the child. One may imagine that she would also be the one better able to raise the child. Solomon's judgment endorses the concept of motherhood as a social rather than a biological institution, and perhaps Solomon's wisdom lies here. Solomon provides symbolic paternity by giving one of them a living child to raise.[84] In this sense, he plays a role in

[79]See Phyllis Bird, "The Harlot as Heroine: Narrative Art and Social Presupposition in Three Old Testament Texts," *Semeia* 46 (1989): 119–39, and W. A. M. Beuken, "No Wise King without a Wise Woman (I Kings III 16–28)," in *New Avenues in the Study of the Old Testament: A Collection of Old Testament Studies Published on the Occasion of the Fiftieth Anniversary of the Oudtestamentisch Werkgezelschap and the Retirement of Prof. Dr. M. J. Mulder,* ed. A. S. van der Woude (Leiden: Brill, 1989), 6–7.

[80]See Stuart Lasine, "The Riddle of Solomon's Judgment and the Riddle of Human Nature in the Hebrew Bible," *JSOT* 45 (1989), 61–86.

[81]As does, for example, James A. Montgomery, *A Critical and Exegetical Commentary on the Books of Kings* (New York: Scribner's, 1951), 110.

[82]As Beuken ("Wise King," 6) notes, the two women are differentiated only at the point of their response to Solomon's proposal to divide the child. See also K. A. Deurloo, "The King's Wisdom in Judgement: Narration as Example (I Kings iii)," in *New Avenues in the Study of the Old Testament,* 11–21.

[83]See Burke O. Long, *1 Kings* (The Forms of the Old Testament Literature 9; Grand Rapids: Eerdmans, 1984), 68.

[84]This point is hinted at in Carole Fontaine, "The Bearing of Wisdom on the Shape of 2 Samuel 11–12 and 1 Kings 3," *JSOT* 34 (1986): 68.

the life of this prostitute that is like the role of the prophets and the angel who aid in the conception or survival of the children of the widow of Zarephath, the Shunammite woman, and Manoah's wife.

The theme of social motherhood is mirrored by the specific role designations attached to the two disputing mothers. Though introduced as "prostitutes" (נשים זנות) in the first verse of the story (3:16), this designation does not appear a second time. The women refer to themselves and to one another as "woman" (3:17, 18, 19, 22, 26). Though the plot revolves around their maternal roles, the designation *mother* appears only when Solomon awards the baby to one of the women, declaring, "She is his mother" (3:27).

Cannibal Mothers (2 Kgs 6:26–30)

The callousness shown by the woman who is ready to have Solomon divide the baby in two is mirrored in the second story in 2 Kgs 6:26–30.[85] This story, too, focuses on a dispute between two women over the life of a child. Here the king who is asked to adjudicate the dispute is not named within the pericope, but the context identifies him as King Joram (also known as Jehoram) of Israel (2 Kgs 3:1; 8:16). The scene takes place during the famine in Samaria, which had resulted from the siege of King Ben-hadad of Aram (6:24). Unlike the plaintiff in 1 Kings 3, the woman calling for the king's help is not claiming a child but complaining of breach of contract: A second woman has failed to fulfill a prior agreement by refusing to give up her child for food, as the speaker had done with her own.

Like 1 Kgs 3:16–28, this story overturns the assumptions and expectations of the reader. In this case, however, the result is negative and shocking. In the content of her complaint, the woman—never designated as *mother*—is admitting to cannibalism of the worst possible sort. It is no wonder that the king has no wisdom to offer and can only react in grief at the depths to which his besieged subjects have sunk. What the Solomonic solution to this dilemma would have been it is difficult to imagine. Solomon's wise judgment and the veneration of human life that he and the prostitute-mother display in 1 Kings 3 stand in contrast to the despair of King Joram and the disturbing inhumanity of the mother in 2 Kings 6. The sequence and specific narrative contexts of these stories illustrate the narrator's views concerning the progressive deterioration of the monarchy and the material and moral situation of the people.

Despair and destruction pervade this story. The story illustrates that the consequences of disobedience as set out in Deut 28:56–57, the worst of which is maternal cannibalism, have, indeed, come to pass. In this way, the story

---

[85]See Stuart Lasine, "Jehoram and the Cannibal Mothers (2 Kings 6:24–33): Solomon's Judgment in an Inverted World," *JSOT* 50 (1991): 27–53, and Burke O. Long, *2 Kings* (The Forms of the Old Testament Literature 10; Grand Rapids: Eerdmans, 1991), 92–99.

describes the divine judgment against the people Israel. The anonymity of these women draws attention to the typified role of the mother, well fulfilled by the "winning" prostitute in 1 Kgs 3:16–28 and so terribly betrayed by the plaintiff in 2 Kgs 6:26–30.

Micah's Mother (Judg 17:1–4)

The story of Micah's mother begins with the confession of Micah that he was the one responsible for the theft of eleven hundred shekels of silver from his mother, as a consequence of which she had uttered an imprecation. Upon hearing this confession, she utters a blessing instead ("May my son be blessed by the LORD!"; 17:2), thereby nullifying the curse. After he returns the silver, she immediately consecrates the silver to the Lord and returns the silver to her son so that he might make a "sculptured image and a molten image." She then takes two hundred shekels of the silver and gives it to a smith, who makes the idol, which is kept in Micah's house.

This episode introduces the lengthy and complex story of the unnamed Levite hired to be the priest in Micah's shrine (see chapter 4). Despite its brevity, the episode also permits a relatively detailed portrait of Micah's mother. She is a wealthy woman, as evidenced by the large sum stolen from her; she is also pious but in a rather misguided way, as indicated by her reliance on curses and her eagerness to make images. This expression of piety, while in accordance with what may have been common in the story world implied in the book of Judges, is clearly in contravention of the Mosaic commandments (Exod 20:4). It is also condemned by the narrator, as indicated by the chain of events set off by the creation of these images.

Similarly misguided is her devotion to her son. Although it may have been noble of him to confess the theft to her, her response does not take him to task for the theft but rather returns to him that which he had stolen from her. A particularly puzzling gap is the question of what became of the other nine hundred shekels, after only two hundred were used for the two images.[86] This portrayal therefore exemplifies, and also exaggerates, the devotion of a mother to her child, which renders her blind to his wrongdoings.

Sisera's Mother (Judg 5:28–30)

Utter devotion and blindness are also attributed to the mother of Sisera. Unlike most of the stories we have looked at, the references to Sisera's mother appear

---

[86]Boling (*Judges*, 254) notes that the introduction to Micah through his mother forms a calculated contrast to Samson and his mother, showing Micah as a cultic opportunist in contrast to Samson, who is portrayed as a rebellious ingrate. Boling (*Judges*, 256) also suggests that the purpose of this passage is, in fact, to make the reader question the fate of the remaining nine hundred shekels of silver.

secondhand, as it were, in the words of another character as reported by the narrator. Sisera's mother appears nowhere in the biblical narrative in which her son is featured (Judges 4) and is known only through the poetic recasting of that narrative in the song of Deborah (5:28–30).

The references to Sisera's mother come after Deborah's recitation of the death of Sisera at the hands of Jael. The drama of this death and the speaker's exultation are conveyed as the scene shifts abruptly to the window behind which Sisera's mother waits for him—in vain, as Deborah's readers know.[87] She asks: "Why is his chariot so long in coming? Why tarry the hoofbeats of his chariots?" (5:28). To these questions her wisest lady and she herself provide the answer: "Are they not finding and dividing the spoil?—A girl or two for every man; spoil of dyed stuffs for Sisera, spoil of dyed stuffs embroidered, two pieces of dyed work embroidered for my neck as spoil?" (5:30).

This poetic depiction plays on two opposing stereotypes. On the one hand, the poem attributes to Sisera's mother an emotion typical to mothers: anxiety for the welfare of their offspring, fueled in this case by his failure to return home when expected. Her attempts at self-assurance—that is, the fabrication of reasons for his unexplained delay—are also familiar.[88] On the other hand, this woman is not just any mother but the mother of the archenemy of Israel, whose slaying is celebrated in Deborah's poem. As such, she, too, is the enemy; her sorrow is Deborah's triumph. This is encoded in the poem's irony. The audience knows what she does not: Sisera is not merely delayed but will never appear; far from gathering embroidered cloths for every neck, he lies dead at the feet of Jael. This irony is enhanced by the poem's schematic arrangement, which serves to distance Sisera's mother from a reader's sympathy.[89] As William Urbrock notes, this anonymous woman is:

> literally hedged about in the poem by the name of her vanquished son, which appears in vv. 20 and 26 before she is introduced and again after we have met her, in v. 30. Furthermore, known only by her epithet "mother of Sisera" a title, after all, that in other circumstances might be designed to bring honor to a childbearing woman, she is the polar opposite to Deborah, "mother in Israel."[90]

[87]On the poetic function of this abrupt transition, see Alan J. Hauser, "Judges 5: Parataxis in Hebrew Poetry," *JBL* 99 (1980): 23–41.

[88]Hauser ("Judges 5," 39) points out that the double usage of "why" (מדוע) heightens the audience's sense of her fear and uncertainty, as does the parallel form of her questions.

[89]William J. Urbrock, "Sisera's Mother in Judges 5 and Haim Gouri's Immo," *HAR* 11 (1987): 423.

[90]"Sisera's Mother," 425. Gouri's poem and Urbrock's analysis of Judges 5 represent an interesting attempt to read against the text by describing her sympathetically, and by drawing out the similarities between her and Jephthah's daughter.

Hence her anonymity obscures her individuality and draws our attention to her son, his fate, and its significance for Israel.

In contrast to other categories, the explicit role designations by which these unnamed women are known do not always circumscribe their narrative roles but identify only one, often minor aspect of the role. Though frequently designated as *women* or *wives*, their identities as mothers are apparent from the content and structure of the stories in which they appear and from the specific acts attributed to them. The role of mother was so deeply embedded in the social structure reflected or created in the biblical text that the specific designation is not required to identify a woman as such.

Anonymity highlights the degree to which the behavior of these women corresponds to their roles as wives and mothers. It is in the correlation, or lack thereof, between role and behavior that their individuality emerges. Their personal identities, in turn, fulfill, offend, stretch, or redefine the boundaries set by their role designations.

The anonymous women we have examined in this section have at least two identities. Their stories identify them as both wives and mothers, testifying to the inseparability of these two roles in the social world implied by the narrative. Although we have divided them into wayward wives and multifarious mothers, other groupings suggest themselves. A number of the women we looked at in their roles as mothers could just as easily have been included with the wayward wives, for they, too, have "other" men, be they prophets or kings, in their lives. The stories of the Zarephath widow, the Shunammite woman, and the wife of Jeroboam portray anonymous mothers in contact with prophets over the survival of their children. The Shunammite woman and the wife of Manoah receive children in the context of an annunciation event. Sexuality is explicitly featured in the stories of the primordial woman and Potiphar's wife, though in different ways. The mothers of Moses, the two prostitutes of Solomon's reign, and the cannibal mothers of King Joram's time illustrate different ways in which women collude or compete over the lives of children. For most of these women, the dual roles of wife and mother pose no conflict. For the wife of Jeroboam, however, the tension seems unbearable. Her marriage to an evil king renders her powerless to save her son, who must die to punish his father. In a cruel twist, she herself determines the time of her child's death.

DOOMED DAUGHTERS

Role conflict appears more pervasively in the stories of unnamed daughters who are not only defined but also trapped by the multiple roles they enact. In drawing attention to their multiple roles, anonymity allows the reader to perceive the fates of these women as the consequences of the competing demands of these roles.

The Timnite Daughter (Judg 14:1–15:8)

The competing demands of the roles of daughter and wife emerge forcefully and poignantly in the story of the Timnite woman. This woman is identified primarily as Samson's wife (אשׁת שׁמשׁון; 14:15, 16, 20; 15:1, 6). Her role as a daughter is denoted not by her designation as such—the term בת does not appear in the story—but by the strong narrative presence of a man identified solely as "her father" (אביה; 15:1, 6).

The story begins when Samson goes down to Timnah and espies a Philistine woman (14:1). Upon his return, he demands that his parents acquire her for him as a wife (14:2). Their response anticipates the perennial objection of Jewish parents to the impending exogamous marriage of their children: "Is there not a woman among your kin, or among all our people, that you must go to take a wife from the uncircumcised Philistines?" (14:3).[91] The narrator justifies Samson's interest in the Timnite woman as the pretext he had been seeking to act against the Philistines (14:4). This rationale reminds the reader of the mission the angel had set out for Samson before his birth: to begin the deliverance of Israel from the hand of the Philistines (13:5).

Samson and his parents travel twice to Timnah: first to arrange the marriage and then to celebrate the wedding. On the first trip, Samson tears apart a young lion that has roared at him. On his way to the wedding, he sees that the carcass of the lion is filled with bees and honey, which he scrapes out, eats, and shares with his parents, without divulging its source (14:8–9).

Though a wedding feast takes place, the actual marriage and its consummation are not described or even mentioned. Instead, the narrator recounts a riddle scene. Samson challenges the thirty Philistine "companions" (שׁלשׁים מרעים), who were provided for him by some unspecified party (14:11), to solve this riddle: "Out of the eater came something to eat. Out of the strong came something sweet" (14:14).[92] The riddle is to be solved before the end of the seven-day wedding feast. The loser is to provide the winner with thirty linen garments and thirty festal garments (14:12–13).

After three days of unsuccessful attempts to decipher the riddle, the young men make Samson's wife an offer she dare not refuse: either she coaxes Sam-

[91]Crenshaw ("Saga," 481) argues against the view that this passage may include an attack on the patrilocal marriage in which the wife remains with her parents and receives periodic visits from her husband. Cf. Bal, *Death*, 88.

[92]On this riddle see Greenstein, "Riddle"; Bal, *Lethal Love*, 46; Claudia V. Camp and Carole R. Fontaine, "The Words of the Wise and Their Riddles," in *Text and Tradition: The Hebrew Bible and Folklore*, ed. Susan Niditch (Atlanta: Scholars Press, 1990), 127–51.

son's secret from him, or she and her father's house will be set on fire (14:15). In an attempt to comply with the young men's demands, she weeps before Samson and complains: "You hate me; you do not really love me. You have asked a riddle of my people, but you have not explained it to me" (14:16a). His response raises anew the issue of conflicting allegiances: he has not told his parents, so why should he tell her? (14:16b). After days of nagging, however, he divulges the answer, which she promptly conveys to her countrymen (14:17). At the last possible moment, just before sundown on the seventh day, the men of the town present Samson with the riddle's solution. Enraged, Samson accuses them of manipulating his wife; he kills thirty men and gives their festal garments to those who had explained the riddle, thereby fulfilling his promise yet giving vent to his hot anger.[93] The episode closes with Samson's return to his father's house, and—as a surprising aside—his wife's (re)marriage to Samson's Philistine companion (מרעהו; 14:19–20).

Whether Samson and the Timnite woman consummated their marriage is not clear. The status of their relationship is interpreted by Samson and her father in two different ways. By marrying his daughter off to another man, the Timnite man erases, invalidates, or ignores her marriage to Samson and diminishes Samson's status. That Samson, by contrast, considers himself married to the Timnite woman is indicated by his return to Timnah. He brings gifts for her and fully expects to "go into [his] wife's room" (15:1). Her father prevents him, saying, "I was sure that you had rejected her; so I gave her to your companion." The father then offers Samson his younger, prettier daughter in her stead (15:2).

Samson's revenge is violent and extreme. He ties torches to the tails of three hundred foxes and then turns them loose on the fields, vineyards, and storage rooms of the Philistines. In this way, he single-handedly inflicts considerable damage. The Philistines, understanding his motivations full well (15:6), retaliate by burning the Timnite woman and her father.[94] Samson responds with mass murder and so the cycle of violence continues (15:9).

The tension inherent in the woman's dual identity as her father's daughter and Samson's wife is thus resolved in favor of her role as daughter. Her fate is determined by her father's continued control of her sexuality despite her marriage to Samson. By giving her to another man, he also exercises power over Samson, to whom he denies the sexual access to which his marriage had entitled him. The daughter continues to belong to her father even after her second

---

[93]On the theme of Samson as wild man, see Susan Niditch, "Samson as Culture Hero, Trickster, and Bandit: The Empowerment of the Weak," *CBQ* 52 (1990): 608–24.

[94]Some manuscripts have "her father's house," obviously the basis for Crenshaw's assumption that the younger Timnite daughter was burned as well. See Crenshaw, "Saga," 485.

marriage, as indicated by the fact that she perishes along with him in his house. The conclusion of the story ties it into both the social and the political dimensions of the Samson saga. On the social plane, the story is concerned with endogamy and exogamy. Both the woman and Samson are torn between the competing claims of his filial and spousal relationships.

The anonymity of the Timnite woman may be seen in a number of different ways. First, it coheres with her passivity, the invalidation of her marriage and her death by fire, which erase her from Samson's life, as well as from his narrative. In this respect, her anonymity aligns her with all the other characters in this story, who are also unnamed. Their anonymity allows the narrative focus to remain on Samson as the sole named character.

Second, it allows the reader to contrast her life story with that of a number of named biblical brides. Samson's betrothal and erstwhile marriage to the Timnite evokes, if only by contrast, the biblical romances of Isaac, Jacob, and Moses. Like Leah, the Timnite woman has a younger, more attractive sister, who is passively involved in their father's deceitful act toward the bridegroom. Like Jacob, Samson is deceived by his father-in-law, though, in contrast to Jacob, he desires the older rather than the younger daughter. In contrast to Isaac's proxy, to Jacob, and to Moses, who meet and speak with the future brides beside a well and then are invited to their fathers' homes, Samson is impressed only with the sight of this Timnite woman[95] and returns home to speak with his parents instead of meeting immediately with his future in-laws. Moreover, the betrothals and subsequent marriages of Isaac, Jacob, and Moses with the women encountered at the well produced alliances within, or at least supportive of, the people Israel. The absence of these central elements from the Timnite's tale foreshadows the calamities to which the marriage itself will lead.[96]

Third, the absence of a proper name draws the reader's attention to the Timnite's typified roles. The narrator depicts an ironic contrast between her formal role designation as Samson's wife and the role she acts out as her father's daughter. Though the narrator designates her consistently as Samson's wife, this designation is called into question by her deception of Samson, her subsequent marriage to another man, and her father's continued control over her sexuality. Her role as daughter determines her fate. Not only is she subject to her father's power but also she remains with him throughout, not parting from him even in death.

[95]The meaning of "she pleases me" (14:4) is unclear. Yakov Thompson ("Samson in Timnah: Judges 14–15: Form and Function," *Dor le Dor* 15 [1986–87]: 251) argues that this expression here does not allude to Samson's physical attraction to her but rather signifies that she was, in his eyes, the right one through whom to fulfill his purpose. In my view, this imputes more spiritual insight to Samson than his portrayal in the Samson saga as a whole would warrant.

[96]Alter (*Art*, 61–62) suggests that Judges 14 plays on the betrothal type scene by omitting it.

Trapped as she is between two men who struggle for power over her, it is nevertheless the young men of her town who exert the greatest force upon her. Their demands lead her to deceive her husband and betray his secrets. Samson's retort, "If you had not plowed with my heifer, you would not have found out my riddle" (14:18), has sexual undertones. A graphic visual image is conjured by the accusation; the use of the word *heifer* as a reference to his wife debases her.

In the dramatic words of Crenshaw, this woman is a pitiful figure who "walks slowly but surely into a flaming death. Faced with a choice between kinship and the novelty of wedded bliss, and hastened to a decision by a terrifying threat, she makes the inevitable move toward deception of the only one who could extricate her from the power of destiny."[97] The Timnite's anonymity points to the web of roles in which she is entangled. All of these roles have implications regarding her sexuality, and in all of them she is the passive victim. As the subordinate partner in multiple sets of hierarchical relationships, there is no resolution possible other than her death. The woman's anonymity intimates the ultimate effacement of her narrative identity, accomplished with her immolation. Her disappearance achieves the polemical/homiletical goals of the narrator, as an example of the dangers of exogamy. Her story also provides opportunity for Samson to show his violent and impulsive nature.

Though consumed by fire and the agenda of the narrator, this woman and her identity are not completely subsumed by her typified portrayal as a forbidden, foreign woman and a seductive temptress; this woman indeed coaxes Samson, in a way that, as Bal notes, conforms to stereotypical female behavior.[98]

Finally, the anonymity of the woman both fits into the overall goals of the narrator by focusing our attention on her typified role as foreign wife and provides a parody of the role of wife by reversing the typical betrothal of the hero scene.

Jephthah's Daughter (Judg 11:34–40)

Whereas the Timnite is not permitted to live with her husband as his wife, Jephthah's daughter does not live long enough to be married at all. The context of her story is the war between the Israelites and the Ammonites, the descendants of Lot's younger daughter (19:38). In the lengthy story of Jephthah, only Jephthah and his father, Gilead, are given proper names, though the latter name may refer to the location (as in 11:7) and not the father (11:1–2).[99] Jephthah's mother, his brothers, the elders of Gilead, and the young women are all anonymous.

---

[97]"Saga," 484.

[98]The imperative פתי (Judg 14:15) could mean coax, persuade and/or seduce. On this range of meanings, see Camp and Fontaine, "Words," 147; and Bal, *Love*, 43.

[99]Trible, *Texts of Terror*, 94.

The story begins with the appointment of the warrior Jephthah as chief of the Gileadite forces against the Ammonites. After diplomatic attempts to settle the conflict fail, "the spirit of the LORD came upon Jephthah" (11:29). On the eve of battle, Jephthah made a vow to the Lord: "If you will give the Ammonites into my hands, then whoever comes out of the doors of my house to meet me, when I return victorious from the Ammonites, shall be the LORD's, to be offered up by me as a burnt offering" (11:30–31).

Victory was his. On arriving home, however, it was his daughter who came out to meet him, "with timbrels and with dancing," as Israelite women have often celebrated military victory (11:34).[100] Neither he nor his daughter apparently considers ways in which the vow might be rescinded or annulled; instead, he bewails his fate, and she accepts hers. She asks only for permission to spend two months with her friends upon the hills "and bewail my virginity" (בתולי; 11:37). He agrees and she departs. Upon her return, he "did with her according to the vow he had made" (11:39). In the aftermath, the narrator notes, "there arose an Israelite custom that for four days every year the daughters of Israel would go out to lament the daughter of Jephthah the Gileadite" (Judg 11:39–40).

The anonymity of Jephthah's daughter is noted and commented on by many scholars. Lillian Klein, for example, perceives a contradiction between her anonymity and the dignity with which she meets her fate, a view that presumes that anonymity in and of itself denotes a lack of dignity.[101] Many commentators understand her anonymity to be symbolic of her fate[102] and note the narrative irony in the fact that, though nameless, she is memorialized in an annual women's ritual. As Bal notes, "Although she can only be remembered as what she never was allowed to become, as Bath-Jephthah, it is she and not the man who does have a proper name who is remembered."[103]

The anonymity of this character focuses our attention on her typified filial role. Esther Fuchs comments that 11:34, in which the girl is described as the only child of Jephthah,[104] "establishes the fundamental rules that will un-

[100]Cf. the Song of Miriam, Exod 15:20.

[101]"A Spectrum of Female Characters," in *A Feminist Companion to Judges*, ed. Athalya Brenner (Sheffield: JSOT Press, 1993), 26.

[102]See, for example, Bal, *Death*, 43; J. Cheryl Exum, *Fragmented Women: Feminist (Sub)versions of Biblical Narratives* (Valley Forge, Pa.: Trinity Press International, 1993), 16; Esther Fuchs, "Marginalization, Ambiguity, Silencing: the Story of Jephthah's Daughter," in *A Feminist Companion to Judges*, 117. A thematic role is also given to other aspects of her portrayal, including the fact that the words of the song with which she greeted her father are not noted. See Athalya Brenner and Fokkelien van Dijk-Hemmes, *On Gendering Texts: Female and Male Voices in the Hebrew Bible* (Brill: Leiden, 1993), 37.

[103]*Death*, 68.

[104]The phrasing of 11:34c is reminiscent of the Akedah story, though the contrasts between the two stories are significant. See Trible, *Texts of Terror*, 101.

dergird the daughter's presentation henceforth: she is nameless, she is identified and defined by her filial relationship with Jephthah and it is this relationship that underlies her characterization and determines her significance in
the story."[105]

The story portrays—nay, requires—the daughter's submissiveness. Just as
Jephthah does not attempt to alter the turn of events,[106] neither does his daughter—his victim—challenge the vow, beg him to annul it, or resist it. In this
sense, she typifies the obedience expected of daughters, even, as it turns out,
unto death. More than this, however, she appears not only to be willing to obey
her father but also to justify him. As Fuchs notes, "The narrator could not be
more effective in constructing the perfect filial role model. Jephthah's daughter
is the supreme image of the perfect daughter, whose loyalty and submissiveness
to her father knows no limits."[107] That is, she accepts the constraints of the
situation as he has laid them out.

J. Cheryl Exum sees this story as a justification and celebration of the value
of submission to patriarchal authority:

> You may have to sacrifice your autonomy; you may lose your life, and even
> your name, but your sacrifice will be remembered, indeed celebrated, for gen-
> erations to come. Herein lies, I believe, the reason Jephthah's daughter's name
> is not preserved: because she is commemorated not for herself but *as a daugh-
> ter*.[108]

These commentators assume that her filial designation and her submission
to its constraints subsume or efface this daughter's personhood. But at the same
time as she typifies, in a tragically extreme way, the filial obedience girls owe
to their fathers, her last request is also a fundamental challenge to this stereotypical role. Although she ultimately affirms patriarchy and the role of the father
and daughter within it,[109] her final words to him subtly—perhaps too subtly[110]—
interrupt or break the patriarchal bond. Jephthah's first speech upon being

---

[105]"Marginalization," 119.

[106]Rabbinic texts raise the question of why Jephthah did not seek the annulment of
the vow by the high priest (Midrash Tanhuma, end of Lev) or comment that the vow,
in fact, did not have to be annulled or fulfilled (Gen. Rab. 60:3). For discussion, see
Daniel Landes, "A Vow of Death," in *Confronting Omnicide: Jewish Reflections on Weapons of Mass Destruction*, ed. Daniel Landes (Northvale, N.J.: Jason Aronson, 1991), 7–9.

[107]"Marginalization," 126. Cf. Exum, *Fragmented*, 28.

[108]"On Judges 11," 139.

[109]Lynda E. Boose, "The Father's House and the Daughter in It: The Structures of
Western Culture's Daughter-Father Relationship," in *Daughters and Fathers*, ed. Lynda
E. Boose and Betty S. Flowers (Baltimore: Johns Hopkins University Press, 1989), 40.

[110]Fuchs ("Marginalization," 126) says that the daughter's calm response and subsequent silence permit the reader to remain focused on the father's grief. I would argue
that, on the contrary, this silence serves only to accentuate the anger, shock, and dismay
of the reader.

greeted by his daughter attempts to shift blame to her: "Alas, my daughter! You have brought me very low; you have become the cause of great trouble to me" (11:35a). His own role, however, is not obliterated: "For I have opened my mouth to the LORD, and I cannot take back my vow" (11:35b). Even as she acknowledges—whether correctly or not—the inevitability of her fate in light of Jephthah's military victory, the daughter's response ignores the first part of his statement and places the responsibility for the vow and its consequences on his shoulders: "My father, if you have opened your mouth to the LORD, do to me according to what has gone out of your mouth" (11:36).

This response articulates her submission to her filial role, her capitulation to paternal power. And her loss is also his. Her emergence from the house assures the demise not only of his posterity but also of his paternal identity. This loss of identity may be sealed only at the moment of her death, but it is anticipated and enacted at the moment that he grants her request to absent herself for a two-month period. While her fate ultimately affirms patriarchy and the role of father and daughter within it, her final request—which he dare not refuse—interrupts or breaks the patriarchal bond.

Hence this vow is a tragedy not only for her but also for him, for by keeping to the vow[111] he also ensures his own barrenness and the end of his line.[112] Jephthah and his daughter first construct and then destroy one another. If she is defined in relationship to Jephthah, so is Jephthah as father defined in relationship to her. "She was his only child; he had no son or daughter except her" (11:34). The threefold reference to the girl as his daughter (11:34, 35, 40) is balanced by a threefold reference to Jephthah as her father (11:36, 37, 39); indeed, Jephthah is mentioned by name only in the introductory and concluding verses to this narrative segment (11:34, 40).

Jephthah's daughter responds to her father's self-interested lament by affirming the need to uphold the vow. In doing so, she accepts the premise that failure to fulfill the vow will jeopardize this or future victory.[113] Along with this submission, however, her words accomplish one important goal. She identifies her father as the one who is ultimately responsible for her fate; it is he who uttered the vow to the Lord and who will do to her as he had vowed (11:36).[114] The fulfillment of the vow will not only end her life but also sever the patriarchal relationship.

[111]This leaves aside the difficult question of whether he should have made the vow in the first place.

[112]See Exum, *Fragmented*, 21. Fuchs ("Marginalization," 116 and passim), however, suggests that to see this as Jephthah's tragedy is to comply with the viewpoint of the narrator.

[113]This premise is apparently held by the father, too.

[114]Also noted by Exum, *Fragmented*, 40.

In her subsequent request, Jephthah's daughter takes the first step in this direction by severing the relationship herself. Although she allows him to destroy her life, she in turn puts an end to his role as a father by spending her last two months outside the domestic space in which he—and patriarchy—reign supreme. In postponing her loss of life and future, she carries out his loss of paternal relationship and identity as a father, effective immediately. Hence this woman does more than make some motions toward self-assertion, as Exum claims,[115] but rather, as Bal intimates, she exploits the (limited) possibility left open to her[116] by dealing the death blow to Jephthah's paternity.

Anonymity focuses attention on her stage of life and the concept of loss: loss of life, loss of posterity. The specific object of her lament is her *bethulim* (בתולים). Although English versions often translate this word as "virginity," the term may refer to a stage like adolescence, denoting a female who has reached puberty but has not yet given birth to her first child.[117] Her role as sacrificial victim may have required virginity as a token of purity.[118] But the narrative emphasis on her virginity is equivocal. On the one hand, it amounts to a reduction of her personhood to the sexual and reproductive functions she might someday have performed for a man. On the other hand, it is a lament for her premature death at the hands of the man who would otherwise have guided her transition from virginity to conjugal life.

The designation of this woman as her father's daughter focuses the reader's attention both on the nature of that relationship and on the degree to which this story subverts or undermines the stereotypical image. Just as Jephthah violates his daughter by his vow, so does she violate the terms of patriarchy by her departure from her father's house. In doing so, she also establishes her primary relationship as being with other women (רעות).[119] This kinship is strengthened by the narrator's reference to the practice of the daughters of Israel (בנות ישראל) to spend four days a year away from their fathers' domains, in her memory.

Whether this passage provides hints of an ancient women's ritual and what this ritual might have entailed have been the subject of much speculation. Boling considers it doubtful that this is an etiological tale because there is no other trace of such a ritual.[120] Feminist scholars, however, take the narrator's reference

---

[115]*Fragmented*, 38.

[116]*Death*, 68.

[117]See Peggy L. Day, "From the Child Is Born the Woman: The Story of Jephthah's Daughter," in *Gender and Difference in Ancient Israel*, ed. Peggy L. Day (Minneapolis: Fortress, 1989), 58–74. This view is also held by Bal, *Death*, 48, and Exum, *Fragmented*, 39.

[118]Exum, *Fragmented*, 31.

[119]BDB, ad loc.

[120]*Judges*, 209–10.

to this forgotten ritual more seriously. Bal suggests that the ritual marks the stage at which the ripeness of the young women will be distributed by their fathers, a process in which they themselves have power only over the ritual that prepares them.[121] Peggy Day imagines an annual ceremony at which young women were socially recognized as having left childhood behind and entered physical maturity. This ceremony may have included a ritual lament which acknowledged the "death" of one stage in life in preparation for entry into a new stage.[122] Exum argues that the usage of the verb *lament* (בכה, cf. 11:37) suggests, on analogy with Judg 5:11, that the women recited the story of Jephthah's daughter during this ritual.[123] The absence of corroborating evidence does not mean that the ritual did not take place (pace Boling); it does, however, impede our ability to construct it with confidence.

The reference to the ritual injects a subtle note of irony. The veil over her personal identity, as implied by her anonymity, is lifted not only by her autonomous behavior but also through the ritual by which she is memorialized. Like her name, the details of this ritual are not divulged,[124] but its presence in the text, like hers, marks her spot and testifies to her personhood.

This unnamed daughter, the only child of her father, recalls another child who faced the sacrifical knife. The contrasts between the daughter of Jephthah and the son of Abraham outweigh their similarity, however. Whereas she is unnamed and without posterity, Isaac is named and becomes a patriarch of Israel. Whereas there is no mention of an emotional tie between the girl and Jephthah, Isaac is explicitly called Abraham's beloved son (Gen 22:2). And whereas her sacrifice came about through her father's unnecessary vow, Isaac's near sacrifice is mandated and then annulled by God himself. Most important, Jepthath's daughter resists her father's act to the extent and in the way that she is able to. Whereas Isaac passively acquiesces to his father's act, Jephthah's daughter severs the father-child bond herself.

The Levite's Concubine (Judg 19:1–20:7)

One woman who seems initially to have made the transition between the roles of daughter and wife is the Levite's concubine. As noted earlier, all characters in this story are anonymous. The present discussion focuses primarily on the woman, identified as the Levite's concubine (פלגש), but also briefly considers the depiction of the unnamed men in the story.

Like the story of the Timnite woman, this episode is replete with ambiguities which impinge upon our construction of the anonymous characters. The

---

[121]*Death*, 49.

[122]"From the Child," 60.

[123]*Fragmented*, 35.

[124]Lori Lefkowitz, personal communication, December 1996.

most striking of these relates to the status and behavior of the woman. What is her relationship to the Levite, and, more pressing, what precipitates her return to her father's house?

The woman is introduced as the Levite's concubine from Bethlehem in Judah (19:1). The term פלגש designates a wife who is of servant status (2 Sam 5: 13; 19:6; 1 Kgs 11:3).[125] Whether this Levite had other wives is not known. The designation פלגש places her under the Levite's authority as a wife but also implies that in some sense her status falls short of the typified role of wife.[126] Adding to this ambiguity in her marital status is the uncertainty with respect to her moral status. Immediately after being identified as the Levite's concubine, she is said to have חזנה עליו and left him to return to her father's house in Bethlehem.

The primary meaning of the verb זנה is "to commit fornication, be a harlot."[127] Taken literally, then, Judg 19:2 asserts that the woman was guilty of promiscuity. In the words of the King James Version, the Levite's concubine "played the whore against him." Following this literal line of interpretation, the story conveys a subtle sense that the victim is to blame for her own fate. Perhaps, indeed, gang rape and its consequences are fitting payment for a "concubine" who "played the harlot." As Exum suggests, this reading predisposes readers to view the rape of this namelesss Levite's concubine less sympathetically than they might view the rape of a lawful wife.[128]

A less literal interpretation is implied by the NJPSV translation: "she deserted him." Although this term, too, has negative connotations, they do not necessarily imply sexual promiscuity but indicate her return to her father's house. That the Hebrew phrase can refer to divorce is suggested by Jer 3:1: "If a man divorces his wife and she goes from him and becomes another man's wife, will he return to her? . . . You have played the whore (זנית) with many lovers; and would you return to me? says the LORD." On the basis of this verse, Zakovitch suggests that women who dared to leave their husbands were frequently taken to be guilty of immoral behavior, hence the application of the verb זנה ("to play the harlot") to such actions.[129] This parallel suggests that the narrator's use of this verb is not necessarily an objective description of the woman as a prostitute or whore; it could be a pejorative expression for and negative value judgment on women who dare to leave their husbands. In Bal's view, this woman is considered faithless by both her father and her husband; the father considers her going to live with her husband to be unfaithfulness to

---

[125]Revell, *Designation*, 36.

[126]Zakovitch, "The Woman's Rights in the Biblical Law of Divorce," *The Jewish Law Annual* 4 (1981): 38.

[127]BDB, ad loc.

[128]*Fragmented*, 177.

[129]"Divorce," 39. See also Boling, *Judges*, 274.

him; the husband considers her return to her father to be unfaithfulness against himself.[130] Against Bal's interpretation, it must be said that no direct indication of this negative judgment is present in the story. The relations of the father toward his daughter are not depicted except indirectly in his apparent acceptance of her return to his house, nor is it apparent in the encounter between the two men, which is portrayed only in terms of the guest-host relationship.

Yet another possibility emerges from Alexandrian text of the Septuagint, in which the key phrase, ὡργίςθη αὐτῷ, is translated as "became angry with" in the NRSV. As Boling notes, "it is strange that the woman would become a prostitute and then run home." That her departure was caused by anger also makes sense of the next verse, in which the Levite journeys forth "to speak tenderly to her and bring her back" (19:3). There is no indication that he suspects her of sexual promiscuity and wishes to punish her for it. This translation is based on the *qere* (the way in which the word is usually read), which is להשיבה "to make her return." But Zakovitch argues that the *ketib* (written form) in 19: 3, namely, להשיבו ("to let him return to her"), in fact, preserves the original reading here. The *ketib* implies the woman's right to decide whether she will let her huband take her again.[131]

Finally, according to the MT, the woman herself brings the Levite to her father's house, as indicated by the verb ותביאהו ("she brought him"; 19:3b). Other versions indicate simply that he arrived there (ויבא "he came"), presumably unheralded until he actually appeared at the door.[132] Although most commentaries pay scant attention to the MT reading, it has significance for the reader's impression of the relationship between the Levite and the woman and, indirectly, of that between the father and his daughter as well. The MT implies her willingness to return to the Levite and her readiness to leave her father's house. In this case, her father's emphatic hospitality seems merely an exaggerated act. The *BHS* reading, "he came," provides no basis on which to assess the woman's views. She becomes inscrutable and passive, as she is in the aftermath of her departure.

In sum, different readings of the early part of the story can be constructed, depending on whether the literal or the figurative meaning is to be assigned to the verb "to play the harlot" and from the variant readings of the verbs in 19:3. Whether she is of questionable moral character or an aggrieved wife and whether she brought him to her father's house or dreaded his arrival cannot be determined. What is clear, however, is that her fate is decided by other men:

---

[130]*Death*, 88.

[131]"Divorce," 39.

[132]Boling (*Judges*, 274) reads "when he came," along with the Septuagint and some manuscripts, noting that the "MT requires that we presuppose that upon arrival the concubine met him and 'brought him' to her father's house. The difference may go back to oral variants."

her father, who warmly receives the Levite and extends (or, from the Levite's point of view, overextends) gracious hospitality toward him[133]; the Levite, who decides when and where they will spend the night; the old host, who offers his own daughter as well as the concubine to the men outside his house and thereby demonstrates that the protection entailed in hospitality is the privilege of male guests only.[134]

The anonymity of this woman can be seen as symbolic of her silence, the progressive passivity attributed to her, and the tragic fate with which the story culminates. These features combine to efface her identity and her very existence. That this woman is silenced, denied subjectivity, erased, and scattered, both by the men in the story and by the storyteller, is clear. At the very least, anonymity symbolizes this denial of her identity and personhood. But, her anonymity does more than efface her identity. It highlights her typified role. Like the Timnite, she is caught among a number of men who trade in her sexuality. As the Levite's concubine, she is under his authority. Whatever her motivations for leaving, her return to her father defies the Levite's authority. This physical return to her father's domain is also a return to his protection, to a state of subservience to his power and to his control over her sexuality. In this light, the days that the Levite spends in her father's home also imply the subservience of guest to host. His departure along with his concubine signifies his triumph in an implicit power struggle with the father and the return of the woman to his power, if not, as circumstances show, to his protection.

The woman is caught in yet a third power structure, that of guest in the Gibeahite man's house. This man, too, is unnamed. But like the Timnite's compatriots, he has the power of life and death over her. In consigning her to the men outside, he decides her fate and demonstrates profound disregard for her worthiness, safety, and very humanity. For this woman, too, the only way out of the web in which she is caught is death.

Finally, some broader conclusions can be drawn from the general anonymity in this passage. The absence of all personal names lends this section a legendary, paradigmatic quality. This quality endows the characters and the events in which they participate with a significance that is unrelated to their individuality. This reading is supported by several features of Judges 19–21. As we have already seen, the story is set in the larger context of the kingless nation. As the final episode of the book of Judges, this episode acts as a bridge to, and justification for, the institution of the monarchy, which will be the subject of the subsequent works in the Deuteronomic history. The fate of the concubine has a tremendous impact on the entire nation, which receives the twelve pieces of

---

[133]The father's motivations are unclear. Cf. the parallel to Genesis 24, in which Rebecca's parents were anxious to keep their daughter (and their guest) from leaving so soon.

[134]See Trible, *Texts of Terror*, 75.

her body with the words: "Has such a thing ever happened since the day that the Israelites came up from the land of Egypt until this day?" (19:30). The battles and other measures taken in response to this act occupy the last two chapters of the book and lead the narrator to conclude this story in a way that recalls its beginning: "In those days there was no king in Israel; all the people did what was right in their own eyes" (21:25). This *inclusio* indicates the general anarchy of the time and implies that these bizarre events would not have occurred in a monarchy.[135] The general anonymity suggests that the individual identities of these figures are not as important as the fact that the events in which they participate occurred in a kingless nation.

The Daughters of Lot (Gen 19)

Like the Levite's concubine, the daughters of Lot are offered by a man in their household for the sexual enjoyment of men outside their door; like the Pharaoh's daughter (Exod 2:1–10), they challenge the normative life path by becoming mothers without becoming wives.

Two angels have come to Lot, who lives in the doomed city of Sodom, to warn him to flee before the city is destroyed. Lot urges hospitality upon them, and, after initial reluctance, they accept. The men of Sodom surround the house and demand that Lot allow them access to his guests, "that we may know them" (19:5). Lot offers his two daughters "who have not known a man." "Let me bring them out to you," he urges, "and do to them as you please; only do nothing to these men, for they have come under the shelter of my roof" (Gen 19:8). The crowds refuse the offer; the situation is redeemed by the angels, who bring Lot inside, shut the door, and strike the men outside with blindness (19:9–11).

The angels advise Lot and his family to leave Sodom immediately. Lot's two sons-in-law are skeptical and refuse to leave. The following morning the angels drag Lot, his wife, and his daughters out of the house and order them to flee to the hills without looking back. Lot asks to be allowed to flee to Zoar instead. Lot's wife looks back and turns into a pillar of salt as Sodom and Gomorrah are destroyed. Lot and his daughters settle into a cave in the hills outside Zoar. Some unspecified period of time elapses, until the father has grown old (Gen 19:31). Believing that "there is not a man on earth to come in to us after the manner of all the world" (19:31),[136] the elder daughter proposes

---

[135]See Boling, *Judges*, 63, 294.

[136]Their sense that there are no men with whom to consort is somewhat puzzling. It implies either that having spent so long in the cave they simply are not aware of the existence of men other than their father or that for some reason the men that they might meet—a meeting which would likely require that they emerge from the cave—are unacceptable for some reason not made known to the reader.

that they make Lot drunk and lie with him. The purpose of this plan is to "preserve offspring" through their father (19:32). The desired result is achieved: Both daughters conceive and give birth to sons, whom they name Moab and Ben-ammi.

All the actors in this story are unnamed, save Lot. A number of them, such as the sons-in-law and Lot's wife, are characterized only briefly. The principal foci are the angels and the relationship between Lot and the daughters "who have not known a man" (אשר לא־ידעו איש; 19:8). These two women are designated exclusively as his daughters (cf. 19:15, 19, 30, 36). This designation emphasizes that their primary relationship is with their father; the mother is absent from the narrative. The two young women are differentiated as elder and younger only when they develop their plan. It would seem that the girls are betrothed but not yet married.[137]

The anonymity of the daughters initially effaces their personal identity and allows us to glimpse them as Lot must have done at the moment of his offer: as objects for the sexual enjoyment of the men outside his door. In the second place, however, the anonymity of these women allows us to focus on their identities as Lot's daughters. This identification, according to their typified roles as daughters, stands in stark contrast to their sexual objectification; the responsibility of the father is to protect the virginity of his daughters, not offer them up for gang rape. Hence the main effect of their anonymity is to bring readers face to face with the way in which this offer overturns the typified role of daughters and acts as a basis for reevaluating the character of Lot.

Lot is caught between two roles. As a father, he should do all he can to ensure that his daughters remain virgins until marriage. In biblical law, a daughter is to remain a virgin until marriage, at which time a bride-price (מהר) is paid to the father.[138] If she is raped or seduced before betrothal or marriage, the man responsible must pay the equivalent of the bride-price to her father anyway, even if marriage does not result (Exod 22:15–16). This payment presumably compensates for her loss in value.[139] Although these laws may have

---

[137]Speiser (*Genesis*, 140) suggests that Lot had two older daughters, married to the sons-in-law mentioned in 19:14, though he does not see as impossible the alternative suggestion, that the two daughters whom Lot offers to the crowd were betrothed to but not yet married to the sons-in-law. Other scholars, such as Von Rad (*Genesis*, 219) and Sarna (*JPS Genesis*, 136), hold the latter view.

[138]On practices related to the bride-price and dowry, see Raymond Westbrook, *Property and the Family in Biblical Law* (JSOTSup 113; Sheffield: JSOT Press, 1991), 142–64.

[139]The father's right of determination is seen by some to be weaker in the Deuteronomic laws than in the Covenant code of Exodus. Cf. Deut 22:28–29, in which the guilty man must marry the girl he violates. Apparently rape was not considered a violation of the daughter so much as a theft of property that deprived her father and necessitated compensation to him. See Boose, "Father's House," 45.

postdated the composition of Genesis 19, they nevertheless would have formed the background against which readers of the text in its current form judge Lot's actions. As a host, Lot is impelled to do all in his power to maintain the well-being and safety of his guests. Had Lot's offer been taken up by the crowd, his daughters' monetary value and marriageable status would have been greatly diminished, if not completely destroyed.

These competing demands generate different evaluations of his character. John Skinner exonerates Lot by suggesting that his readiness to sacrifice the honor of his daughters, while abhorrent to Hebrew morality, nevertheless shows Lot as a courageous champion of the obligations of hospitality in a situation of extreme embarrassment.[140] Speiser refers to this act only obliquely and offers hospitality as a mild excuse: "true to the unwritten code, Lot will stop at nothing in his effort to protect his guests."[141] Von Rad grapples more seriously with the issue of the reader's assessment of Lot's character:

> The surprising offer of his daughters must not be judged simply by our Western ideas. That Lot intends under no circumstances to violate his hospitality, that his guests were for him more untouchable than his own daughters, must have gripped the ancient reader, who knew whom Lot intended to protect in this way. But on the other hand, this procedure to which Lot resorted scarcely suited the sensibility of the ancient Israelite. Our narrator would be misunderstood if we did not give him credit for expecting his readers to judge a very complicated situation.[142]

Jeansonne, however, sees hospitality as a thin and ultimately untenable excuse for Lot's behavior.[143] Turner argues that the positive impression made by Lot's hospitality toward his two visitors is quickly dispelled by his wicked offer of his virgin daughters to the angry crowd.[144] On analogy to the fate of the Levite's concubine in Judges 19, the rape of these women may have endangered not only their honor but also their very lives.

In this pericope, the father's actions and words render the father-daughter relationship problematic. In the aftermath of their escape from Sodom (Gen 19: 30–38), his act is matched by the behavior of the daughters, which similarly

---

[140]*A Critical and Exegetical Commentary on Genesis* (Edinburgh: T and T Clark, 1930), 307.

[141]Speiser, *Genesis*, 143. In the final analysis, however, Speiser describes Lot as undecided, flustered, ineffectual, and incoherent.

[142]*Genesis*, 218.

[143]"The Characterization of Lot in Genesis," *BTB* 18/4 (1988): 126.

[144]"Lot as Jekyll and Hyde: A Reading of Genesis 18–19," in *The Bible in Three Dimensions: Essays in Celebration of Forty Years of Biblical Studies in the University of Sheffield*, ed. David J. A. Clines, et al. (JSOTSup 87; Sheffield: JSOT Press, 1990), 94–95.

violates the norms of the father-daughter relationship. The destruction of Sodom also means the demise of Lot's future sons-in-law, who remained behind. Their isolation in a cave outside Zoar leads the daughters to believe that, indeed, there are no men left alive except their aging father (19:31). Their earlier reprieve from sexual violation, therefore, does not result in a conventional pattern of marriage and maternity. Because marriage seems unattainable, the daughters aim for maternity.

The daughters' plan for parenthood shocks, for it entails the premeditated deception of Lot and not one but two acts of incestuous intercouse. Their remedy serves as the counterpart to Lot's earlier, odious proposal for resolving the dilemma in which he was placed by the Sodomite townspeople.[145] Nevertheless, there is a qualitative difference between the two. On the one hand, Lot's proposal, had it been acted upon, would have resulted in the gang rape and possible death of his daughters, a gruesome fulfillment of the normal consortium that they later find lacking.[146] The daughters' scheme, on the other hand, implies full recognition of its deviance from the norm and their desperate motivation.

Perhaps for this reason, the narrator expresses no explicit negative judgment on the daughters. An implicit judgment, however, may be discerned in his telling of the etiological aspect of the story. The older daughter becomes the matriarch of the Moabites and the younger of the Ammonites, both sometime enemies of the Israelite nation,[147] though Moab is the eventual source of King David's lineage.[148]

In the earlier narrative segment, the anonymity of the daughters symbolizes the silence and passivity implied in the absence of a record of their reaction to or protest against their father's offer. The concluding segment, by contrast, portrays the women as daughters who plan and successfully carry out an unusual course of action. Their act transforms their father not only into their sexual partner, in violation of incest taboos, but also into the father of his own grandchildren. Further, it differentiates the sisters, using the adjectives "elder" and "younger" (19:31–35). This minimal differentiation facilitates recording their communication with each other over their plan and yet does not obscure the agreement and harmony between them. In this respect, they are unique among

---

[145]Von Rad (*Genesis*, 219), for example, sees the double incest as the nemesis that Lot's daughters bring upon him for offering them to the crowd.

[146]The possibility of a fatal outcome is suggested by the parallel in Judges 19.

[147]Von Rad (*Genesis*, 223–24) suggests that this pericope may contain traditional segments, such as an original Moabite tradition in which the wild determination of both ancestral mothers was glorified, but "without doubt the narrative now contains indirectly a severe judgment on the incest in Lot's house, and Lot's life becomes inwardly and outwardly bankrupt."

[148]Cf. Ruth 4:18–22.

biblical sisters and cowives, who often display a high degree of jealousy and competition over the sexual favors of their shared mates and over their respective procreative abilities.[149]

In highlighting their designations as daughters, the anonymity of these women underlines their deviation from the stereotypical role of daughter and their atypical path to motherhood. As daughters, they differ from the norm in two ways. First, they are offered up by their father for the sexual enjoyment of a crowd of men. Second, they themselves reverse the normal power structure by taking control of their father's sexuality and giving birth to his sons. The irony lies in their misperception of the availability of men to father their children. This illusion bespeaks the narrowing of their lives to the boundaries of their cave, the domestic space they share with their father. Domestic space— whether house or cave—is an equivocal symbol. Their father's house is safe for these women as long as they remain inside; danger comes when the father himself forces them outside. The cave, however, is an unusual domestic space. It signifies both their isolation from human society and the reversal of hierarchical norms. Normally, it is the role of the father to control the daughter's sexuality and control her progress along the path to marriage and eventual maternity; the inhabitants of this cave have reversed these roles.

The anonymous daughters also contribute to the characterization of Lot. Lot stands out as the only named character in this pericope. But the questions that his behavior raises regarding his moral character recall Abraham's impassioned plea that God save the righteous residents of Sodom (18:23–32). Is Lot a righteous man worth saving? The narrative appears ambivalent. That Lot's life is, indeed, saved implies his worthiness, but the subsequent narrowing of its boundaries to the cave and the company of his daughters qualifies this judgment.

The anonymity of the daughters is one of several factors linking them to the Levite's concubine. Although it is difficult to determine whether one story was used explicitly in the telling of the other, the thematic similarities are clear.[150] Both illustrate the power of men over women and the effacement of personhood that the exertion of such power inevitably entails. Lot's daughters are trapped not between the competing demands of two roles but in the role of daughter itself because of their circumstances as well as their (mis)perceptions of their social situation. Unlike the women of Judges 14 and 19, they extract themselves from their dilemma by taking matters in hand. Like the mothers of Moses, their cooperation and collusion bind them together in common purpose and apparently without jealousy.

---

[149]E.g., Rachel and Leah (Genesis 30), Hannah and Peninah (1 Samuel 1).

[150]On the literary relationship between Genesis 19 and Judges 19, see Boling, *Judges*, 176.

These anonymous daughters invite comparison. First, they express in bold and stark terms the typified filial relationship of obedience. All the fathers have control of the daughters' sexuality; the daughters' obedience is stated or assumed. Lot's offer of his daughters to the violent crowd outside his door in Sodom presumes his power to offer them and the unlikelihood of their resistance. Jephthah's daughter does not question or flee from the death decree brought upon her by her father's vow. The Levite's concubine is silent as she is passed from her father back to the Levite and then out the door of her host's home in Gibeah. Similarly, no protest is recorded on the part of the Timnite woman as she is given by her father in marriage to Samson and then again to another man.

Second, all of the daughters are blocked from moving successfully to the stage of wife and mother—that is, to pass from the control of fathers to the control of husbands. Samson's Timnite wife remains with her father despite her marriages. The Levite's concubine reverses the normative progression through the stages of female identity by leaving the Levite to return to her father and then tragically retraces her steps by leaving her father's house to return with the Levite. The marriage plans of Lot's daughters, begun before the angels' visit, are cut short by the destruction of Sodom and the refusal of Lot's sons-in-law to flee with them. The narrative's lament for the virginity of Jephthah's daughter emphasizes that she, too, will never be married.

Third, all stories reflect on the relationship—positive or negative—between a daughter's safety and the domestic space that she shares with her father. Intuitively, it would seem that the domestic space in which they dwell together should be safe for the daughter. And indeed, all of the daughters experience a measure of safety within their father's house. Leaving that domain or, as in the case of the Timnite, introducing another man into that domain invites danger, however. The Timnite woman's troubles begin when she marries outside her father's constellation. The Levite's concubine is safe until she leaves her father's home in the company of the Levite and again within the home of their host in Gibeah until she is pushed out into the violent crowd. Similarly, Lot's daughters are safe in Lot's house until he himself offers to turn them out to the men of Sodom; that they remain safe is due entirely to the efforts of Lot's angelic guests. Somewhat ironically, the cave—an incomplete, rudimentary, and unconstructed shelter—they inhabit with their father after their departure from Sodom may be seen as symbolic of their exclusion from normative domestic life. Hence the cave is an appropriate locus for the reversal of the normative father-daughter relationship, which occurs when they take control of their father's sexuality.

In each case, it is the girl's erstwhile protector—her father—himself who is implicated, to a greater or lesser extent, in the danger experienced with respect to the domestic domain. The concubine's father enthusiastically greets the Levite whom his daughter had left, though his attempts to press his hospitality may be read as an attempt to delay his daughter's departure from his protective sphere. Lot threatens his daughters' safety by offering to send them out of the house to face the certain and violent loss of their virginity and perhaps their lives. In marrying Samson's Timnite wife off to another man, the woman's father sets off a chain of events which culminates in her death and his own. Jephthah's daughter, too, would have been safe in her father's house; it is the conjunction between Jephthah's vow and her ill-timed emergence from domestic space that sentences her to death.[151] Jephthah's daughter requests and receives a period of time when she is outside domestic space altogether. Her sojourn on the mountains is a time of safety and reprieve, spent with her female friends outside the boundaries of domestic space and the patriarchal relationships that define it. Nevertheless, this brief period of autonomy is limited by its terminal conclusion and overshadowed by girls' weeping. The time of freedom from domestic space is spent in lamenting the fact that Jephthah's daughter will not live to inhabit domestic space with future husband and potential child.

The ambiguous relationship between a daughter's safety and the paternal domain carries over into the fourth motif, the role of daughters in the construction or, perhaps better, the destruction of paternal identity. This motif is present most drastically in the story of the Timnite woman, whose father perishes along with her as a consequence of her unsuccessful transition to wifehood. This fate is perhaps not undeserved because his actions are to blame. Just as Lot violated the premises of paternal responsibility by offering his daughters to the Sodomite crowd, so, too, do his daughters violate the boundaries of the father-daughter relationship by initiating sexual intercourse with him when he is drunk. In doing so, they first revoke and then re-create his paternal identity by providing him with newborn sons. Jephthah's daughter undoes her father's paternal role at the moment she leaves for the mountains. By implication, the concubine's death also spells the loss of paternity for her father and mirrors the physical distance created when she departs from his home in the Levite's company.

Finally and perhaps most chilling, where are the mothers of these anonymous daughters?[152] Why do they not protect their daughters from their fathers' actions? Only the mother of Lot's daughter figures in any way. Her absence from the incest scene could not be helped, of course. But where was she when

[151]Although he did not coerce her emergence, the wording of his vow leaves open the possibility that he may have foreseen it. Trible, *Texts of Terror*, 97, 112 note 27.

[152]This absence also fits into a narrative pattern according to which mothers are generally absent from scenes of confrontation between fathers and daughters. The exception is Rebecca's mother, who is present, though silent, for the discussion of the marriage of Rebecca (Gen 24:55). By contrast, mothers are often present to mediate the relationship between fathers and sons. In Genesis 21, Sarah and Hagar mediate the relationship between Abraham and his sons; in Genesis 27, Rebecca mediates the relationship of Isaac with his sons. Note, however, the absence of Sarah from Genesis 22.

her husband was offering her daughters up as virgins to the Sodomite crowd outside the door? The text draws no attention to these mothers, not even to note their absence, so preoccupied is it with the dynamics of the father-daughter relationship.[153]

As with other anonymous characters, the anonymity of these daughters highlights their role designations and draws us to compare one with another. Personal identity emerges in the ways in which their behavior conforms to or challenges the expectations of this role and, in particular, the hierarchical relationship between fathers and daughters.

---

[153]The same question may be asked of mothers of named daughters, such as Dinah and Tamar, daughter of David.

PART III

ANONYMITY AND THE
BOUNDARIES OF
PERSONAL IDENTITY

6

◈　◈　◈

The Convergence of Characters

T HE EXISTENCE OF CLEAR BOUNDARIES between one person and another underlies the very notion of personal identity. Although the absence of the proper name does not rule out the presence of individuality, it potentially blurs the lines between characters upon which construction of identity depends. One example that we have already encountered concerns the identities of the prostitute-mothers in 1 Kings 3. Their anonymity prevents the reader from determining whether the living child is awarded to the plaintiff or to the defendant. The ambiguity created by the blurring of distinct identity creates uncertainty and challenges the reader's tendency to impute stable character to biblical figures. Although uncertainty may create confusion, it may also be a valuable vantage point from which to interpret the story.

Narrative context often provides the information necessary to distinguish one character from another. Biblical narrative presents two sorts of situations, however, in which the lines of demarcation remain murky. In some cases, it can be difficult to determine whether a proper name is in fact provided in the narrative. This situation challenges the notion of a fixed boundary between the properly named and the anonymous. In other cases, personal pronouns make it hard to distinguish between two or more anonymous characters within one story, particularly when both are identified by the same role designations. This chapter looks at examples of these two situations and considers the impact of boundary blurring on the construction of character and interpretation of narrative.

Named or Unnamed?

Bath Shua and Bathsheba

For the most part, it is not very difficult to differentiate between named and unnamed characters. Occasionally, however, this determination requires the reader to exercise some judgment. In Gen 38:2, Judah espies "the daughter of a certain Canaanite whose name was Shua." Within the space of four verses (38:2–5), Judah and the daughter of Shua marry, conceive, and bear three sons. No further mention is made of her until 38:12, which, in recording her death, refers to her as Bath Shua (בת־שוע). This character fits well into the category that we have termed the bit players (see chapter 1). The unnamed daughter of Shua appears only briefly and unremarkably in the story and contributes to the plot by bearing the sons who will marry or be betrothed to Tamar.

Initially it would seem that the daughter of Sheba (בת־שבע; Bathsheba; 2 Sam 11) similarly lacks a proper name and is called only by the name of a male ancestor and not by her own. Such effacement of her personhood would cohere with David's illicit appropriation of her body and with the effacement of her will throughout the early stages of their relationship; David sees her, summons her, has intercourse with her, seeks to erase the paternity of the child she carries, and makes her a widow, with nary a word from her except for the announcement of her pregnancy (2 Sam 11:5).

That "Bathsheba" is a proper name, however, is suggested by a number of factors. First, in contrast to the daughter of Shua, the patronymic in her designation does not refer to her father, whose name is Eliam (11:3). Second, she is introduced at length as "Bathsheba daughter of Eliam, the wife of Uriah the Hittite" (2 Sam 11:3). This statement of identification parallels closely the formula used to introduce named biblical figures. Dozens of male characters are introduced by name and patronymic, such as Joab son of Zeruiah, Jehoshaphat son of Ahilud (2 Sam 8:16), Machir son of Ammiel (2 Sam 9:4), and Mephibosheth son of Jonathan son of Saul (2 Sam 9:6). These parallels suggest that "Bathsheba" is her proper name and "daughter of Eliam" her patronymic. Named female characters are often introduced by their proper names as well as their husbands', such as Deborah wife of Lappidoth (Judg 4:4) and Jael wife of Heber the Kenite (4:17). Bathsheba's introduction, which consists of her name, her father's name, and her husband's name, combines both formulations. Finally, "Bathsheba" persists as the referent for this woman not only in 2 Samuel 11–12 but also in 1 Kings 1–2 in a way that is consistent with the use of the proper name. For these reasons, this study has placed the line separating the named from the unnamed between Bathsheba and the daughter of Shua.

Pharaohs of Egypt

More difficult is the situation presented by the several biblical figures whom the narrator refers to as Pharaoh. The majority of kings, Israelite and otherwise, are designated by their proper names, as well as by their titular roles, and frequently by the land over which they rule. In his detailed study of individual designations in Judges, Samuel, and Kings, E. J. Revell discusses the conventional basis for the use of the title *king*.[1] Where the king is the "agent"—that is, portrayed in the active role—he is designated by his personal name. Where he is the "patient"—that is, portrayed as being acted upon—he is designated by title. Revell notes, however, that exceptions abound: "A ruler presented as agent may be designated as 'king' where the narrator has reason to stress his status; a ruler presented as patient may be designated by name where his status is irrelevant. The general pattern is, however, clear: an agent is designated by name and a patient by title."[2]

The title *pharaoh*, meaning literally "Great House," offends this general pattern.[3] The various pharaohs whom Joseph and Moses encounter in Genesis and Exodus are major actors in long series of pericopes, yet their proper names are never divulged. The only properly named pharaoh is the obscure Pharaoh Neco (2 Kgs 23:29–35).[4]

This pattern of reference poses a problem with respect to differentiation among the several pharaohs of 1 Kings, about whom very little is told. It is not clear whether the pharaoh whose daughter married Solomon (1 Kgs 3:1), who was victorious over Gezer (9:16), whose sister-in-law married King Hadad the

[1]*Designation*, 85.

[2]Revell, *Designation*, 89. Revell suggests that in the case of a number of anonymous foreign kings, such as the kings of the Ammonites (Judg 11:12–14; 28), Aram (1 Kgs 22:31), and Assyria (2 Kgs 18:7), the name of the ruler may have been unknown or omitted as unimportant.

[3]*Pharaoh* is an honorific title that, by metonymy, becomes a title for the king himself, just as *the White House* is used to refer to the president of the United States. Cf. Nahum Sarna, *JPS Torah Commentary: Exodus* (Philadelphia: JPS, 1991), 6, 350; Sarna, *JPS Genesis*, 95; Donald B. Redford, *Egypt, Canaan, and Israel in Ancient Times* (Princeton, N.J.: Princeton University Press, 1992), 410. The alternation of *pharaoh* and *king of Egypt* that appears in the Joseph story and, even more so, in Exodus 1–14, is not generally seen as indicative of various sources. See Redford, *A Study of the Biblical Story of Joseph* (VTSup 20; Leiden: Brill, 1970), 177 note 1; John Van Seters, *The Life of Moses: The Yahwist as Historian in Exodus-Numbers* (Louisville, Ky.: Westminster/John Knox Press, 1994), 74 note 33; J. Vergote, *Joseph en Égypte: Genèse chap. 37–50 à la lumière des études égyptologiques récentes* (Orientalia et Biblica Lovaniensia 3; Louvain: Publications Universitaires, 1959), 45–48.

[4]Scholars attempt to provide names for other pharaohs as well. For example, the pharaoh in Exodus 1–3 is generally thought to be Rameses II; Greenstein, *HCSB*, 79.

Edomite (1 Kgs 11:19), and whom the Rabshakeh describes as "that broken reed of a staff, which will pierce the hand of anyone who leans on it" (2 Kgs 18:21) are the same individual. With respect to the pharaohs of Genesis and Exodus, however, the transitions from one designee to another are clear. The pharaoh who welcomed Sarai into his harem (Gen 12:10–20) was surely not the pharaoh who decades later made Joseph his second in command (Gen 41:40). The pharaoh who feared the Israelites' fertility was a king who did not know Joseph (Exod 1:8); not he but his successor ruled Egypt at the time of the exodus itself (Exod 4:19).

The patent absence of the proper name would seem to qualify these pharaohs for a place in our study of anonymous characters, despite their ubiquity and prominence. If so, the pharaoh's anonymity would function in two ways. First, it would enforce the point of the Exodus story as a conflict between Yahweh and the pharaoh and perhaps also their competition for the loyalty of Israel. We could argue that the anonymity of the pharaoh contrasts with the named nature of God. The single designation *pharaoh* pertains to a number of human characters. The single God of Israel, by contrast, is designated by a number of titles and epithets. Second, the Pharaoh's anonymity would draw attention to the institution and political role he represents. If scholars are correct in arguing that within Egyptian religion the holder of this political role was also seen as a divine figure, then the use of the term *pharaoh* allows a critique of Egyptian religion and the institution of the divine man, without dignifying them with the word *gods*.

Nevertheless, two factors place the pharaohs just outside our purview. First, in contrast to virtually all other anonymous characters, some of the pharaohs appear in lengthy narratives that extend over a number of chapters. Except for the Shunammite woman, who appears in 2 Kgs 4:8–37 and is mentioned again briefly in 2 Kgs 8:1–6, unnamed figures are limited to a single pericope. The kings of Egypt are not at all passive; they exert their power, manipulate events, and argue with God's representatives. The pharaohs are so richly characterized that anonymity becomes only one of very many pieces of information the reader utilizes to understand them and the stories in which they play such important roles. Admittedly, this argument is circular; including the pharaohs would simply require that we stretch this general rule to allow for one major exception.

The second factor is more telling. The majority of unnamed characters are designated by role (e.g., "medium"; 1 Sam 28:7), sometimes amplified by provenance (e.g., "Endor"; 1 Sam 28:7) and, for variety, by gender ("woman"; 1 Sam 28:9) or personal pronoun ("she"; 1 Sam 28:21b). The term *pharaoh*, by contrast, appears frequently in a formulaic construction with the synonymous term, "king of Egypt" (מלך מצרים). In the phrase "Pharaoh, king of Egypt," "Pharaoh" functions as a proper name, modified by the role designation, "king of Egypt," as in Ezek 29:3, in which the prophet is told to say, "Thus says the LORD God: I am against you, Pharaoh king of Egypt." This interpretation is supported by the parallel construction in which a proper name is modified by the phrase "king of Egypt." First Kings 11:40, for example, refers to "Shishak, king of Egypt" (שׁישׁק מלך־מצרים); 2 Kgs 17:4 speaks of "So, king of Egypt" (סוא מלך־מצרים). For these reason, this study does not include pharaohs in the ranks of the anonymous.

"A Man" and "Adam" in Genesis 1–5

The primordial human is often taken to be a man named Adam. The English words *man* and *Adam* are distinct; they leave no doubt that the first is a role designation and the second a proper name. The Hebrew is far less clear. The Hebrew name "Adam" (אדם) can also mean "a man." God's decision to "make humankind [literally, *a* man] in our image, according to our likeness" (1:26) could just as easily declare his determination to create Adam. The actual account of creation contains the definite article but increases confusion by using plural pronouns to refer to this singular noun: "so God created humankind [*the* man; האדם] in his image, in the image of God he created them; male and female he created them" (1:27). The ambiguity created by plural pronouns could have been resolved had the narrator, or Elohim, provided one proper name, denoting a single character, or two proper names, which would have functioned as separate referents for the male and female that comprise the first human. The absence of proper names and, indeed, of any other linguistic markers of separation, indicates the singularity of this created being, the aspects of which are united in action as they seem to be in essence.

In this first creation narrative, the indefinite "man" whom God contemplated in 1:26 is a generic rather than a proper name, which paves the way for the specific "man" created in 1:27. The anonymity of this being implies its universality. Humankind is thereby defined as being comprised of two genders, both of which are commanded to be fruitful and multiply and be sovereign over the world (1:28). Without warning, however, we are launched into a second story in which "the man" is created seemingly anew. Genesis 2:7 specifies that God created "the man" (*ha-adam*; האדם) from the dust of the earth (*ha-adamah*; האדמה). This creation story emphasizes the likeness between the man and the earth from which he is made.[5]

Phyllis Trible has argued that, in fact, *the man* here, as in 1:27, is a generic and gender-neutral noun best translated into English as "earthling" or "earth-creature."[6] Trible's suggestion is appealing, both because it undermines the con-

[5] See Joel W. Rosenberg, "The Garden Story Forward and Backward: The Non-Narrative Dimension of Gen. 2–3," *Prooftexts* 1 (1981): 11.

[6] *God and the Rhetoric of Sexuality* (Philadelphia: Fortress, 1978), 83 and passim. Her views have been extremely influential among feminist scholars. See, for example, Meyers, *Discovering*, 78–82, and Mieke Bal, *Love*, 113. For a summary of feminist scholarship on Genesis 1–3, see Eileen Schuller, "Feminist Biblical Hermeneutics: Genesis 1–3 as a Test Case," in *Gender, Genre and Religion: Feminist Reflections*, ed. Morny Joy and Eva K. Neumaier-Dargyay, 31–46 (Waterloo, Ont.: Wilfrid Laurier Press, 1995).

ventional interpretations, which reflect and support a patriarchal understanding of gender relations, and because it acknowledges the process of differentation and human definition the passage depicts. But as Susan Lanser points out, Trible and others assume that meaning is solely a product of semantic and grammatical properties and in doing so deny a fairly standard process of inference which is at work in conventional reading processes. For example, logically *ha-adam* (the man) may not be male before the creation of the woman in Gen. 2:22–23, but ordinary readers infer the maleness of *ha-adam* because masculine pronouns are used to refer to it and a female helper is created for it.[7]

The use of masculine pronouns and the continuation of the story therefore suggest that this creature, unlike "the man" of the first creation story, is unambiguously singular and masculine.[8]

The partner that God finds for the man is made not from the earth but from the man himself. The man rejoices: "This at last is bone of my bones and flesh of my flesh" (2:23). This exclamation is not only a poetic expression of the man's sense of kinship and partnership, but also a reference to the means by which his partner was created. This declaration is followed by what most interpreters have understood as a naming formula (2:23b)[9]: "this one shall be called Woman [*ishah*; אִשָּׁה], for out of Man [*ish*, אִישׁ] this one was taken."

Remarkably, the man has responded to the creation of this creature not only by naming her, as he has done the animals (2:19–20), but also by changing his own name to one which sounds like hers and which for him symbolizes the means of her creation.[10] Yet these names, too, are generic, as indicated by the narrator's etiological comment concerning the behavior of men and women: "Therefore a man [*ish*; אִישׁ] leaves his father and his mother and clings to his wife [*ishto*; אִשְׁתּוֹ], and they become one flesh" (2:24).

The man, however, is not formally named and continues to be referred to primarily as "the man" until 5:1, at which point *adam* (אדם) clearly denotes his proper name rather than the species to which he belongs.[11] That the proper name of this man is identical with the word that has hitherto been used as the

---

[7]"(Feminist) Criticism in the Garden: Inferring Genesis 2–3," *Semeia* 41 (1988): 70–72.

[8]See Gen 2:15, which uses the masculine singular pronominal ending.

[9]This marks another point of disagreement between Trible and Lanser. Trible (*Rhetoric*, 99) argues that this verse does not contain a name-giving formula, on the grounds that the word *call* by itself does not mean naming, unless it is joined to the noun *name*. Lanser ("Criticism," 73), however, argues on the basis of speech-act theory that "the text has already generated the context in which *call* may be inferred to mean *call the name of*."

[10]This is a popular etymology based on assonance. In fact, *ishah* is not derived from *ish* but from *enosh*. See BDB at אִשָּׁה; אִישׁ.

[11]*Adam* without the definite article occurs in 2:21; 3:17, 20b. In these verses, the context supports a generic reading.

generic name, however, identifies the male perspective of the story and the male experience that defines what is normative for humankind.

The foregoing analysis of the emergence of the proper name entails a sequential reading of Genesis 1–4. It suggests that the man's proper name emerges at the point at which procreation, enjoined in 1:28, is about to be actualized, necessitating the creation of differentiation among human beings and of convenient labels with which to refer to them. The smooth progress of such a reading is challenged, as we have seen, by the presence of two creation stories, in each of which the names for God and for the first created human being function differently. A second challenge to this sequential analysis can be found in 5:1b–2: "When God created humankind [*adam*; אדם], he made them [Heb: him] in the likeness of God. Male and female he created them, and he blessed them and named them 'Humankind' when they were created." Here the definite article is absent, yet *adam* is clearly the generic term rather than the proper name for the male human. These verses emphasize God's role as Creator and Namer par excellence. They also summarize the creation episode and act as a bridge to the genealogical section, which will take the reader to the Noah story. The narrator's language in these verses is reminiscent of the creation of *ha-adam* in 1:27; *adam* is apparently understood as the generic name for the species, which has both female and male within it. The narrator therefore seems to backtrack, reverting from the use of *adam* as a proper name for the first male representative of the species to using it as the generic term for the species as a whole. This move is itself reversed in the very next verse, however, when Adam is clearly again the name of the human male progenitor (5:3).[12]

The use of *ha-adam* (the man) in these first few chapters of Genesis both calls attention to and renders problematic the presence of the proper name. Also unresolved is the relationship between the man created in 1:27 and the one formed in 2:7. Whereas proper names might be taken for granted in the everyday world, the creation stories in Genesis prevent that from being the case with respect to the first humans. In contrast to the name "Eve," bestowed and explained by the man and the narrator (2:20), the proper name "Adam" simply creeps in through the omission of the definite article.

The generic name points to the paradigmatic quality of these creation stories, which express an etiology for the physical world, mortality, sexuality, the

---

[12]These two verses may be harmonized simply by saying that *adam* is the name both for the species and for the individual first male himself. A source-critical response sees this point as a seam between E (5:2) and J (5:3) or as a redactor's attempt to tie the two together semiotically in a way that complements their juxtaposition in the first chapters of Genesis. Martin Noth (*A History of Israel* [New York: Harper and Row, 1960], 17), however, attributes these verses to P, suggesting in note 42 that P used 5:1b, 2, and 3a to bracket the subsequent material with the creation story.

marital bond, and the relationship between God and humankind. The two stories present competing paradigms of human existence. The first story portrays humankind as double-gendered; the male and the female, the plural and the singular, are bound up together in this one being created in the image of God. The second story revolves around the man as a male being, who has dominance over God's creation and for whose needs God creates woman. This man must work hard and father children. The history of humankind as a community of individuals, however, begins with the naming of the man and the woman. Just as the woman's name, "mother of all living" (חוה, 3:20), encodes the primary role to which Gen 3:16 assigns her, so does the man's proper name, "Adam," bind him to the earth, *ha-adamah*, which he must toil.

WHO IS WHO?

Uncertainties arise not only in determining whether a character is named or unnamed but also in distinguishing one unnamed figure from another. The latter confusion occurs in stories where several, or even all, characters are unnamed. Such stories create the potential for confusion that results from the use of personal pronouns without clear antecedents and the merging or converging of character identities.

"The Man" in Judg 19:25

The anonymity of both the Levite and his Gibeahite host in Judges 19 adds ambiguity to an already complex story. The difficult verse is 19:25: "So the man seized his concubine, and put her out to them." The problem is the word *man* (איש). It is impossible to identify the man of 19:25 because the term is used of both the Levite and his host. Although in some verses the former is defined as the "master" of the concubine (19:27) and the latter as the "master" of the house (19:23), the usage is inconsistent. The context usually clarifies which man is being referred to, but in this crucial verse such a determination is impossible. Even the immediate context is not of much help, for in 19:23 the word *man* is used of both guest and host.

Who, then, sent the concubine out the door? If the man of 19:25 is the Gibeahite host, he is insolent, indeed, to offer a woman who bears no relationship to him other than that of guest. If it is the Levite who seized his own concubine,[13] his act undoes any affectionate intentions that his quest of her might have implied (19:3) and exposes his later retelling of the tale—in which he admits no blame—as a whitewash (20:4–7). Neither man is blameless, but

[13]This is the view of Boling (*Judges*, 25), who does, however, note the ambiguity. Cf. also George Foot Moore, *A Critical and Exegetical Commentary on the Book of Judges* (New York: Scribner's, 1895) 419.

the precise measuring out of guilt is hampered by the absence of the clear differentiation that proper names would have provided.

The pervasive anonymity in this story not only creates ambiguity but also unites Levite and host in their indifference to the woman's personhood and links them with the Gibeahite crowd which exerts ultimate power over her sexuality and her very life. Because neither man steps in to save her from the men outside, they effectively acquiesce in her gang rape and its consequences, despite the Levite's later aggrieved assertions to the contrary (Judg 20:4–6). Anonymity links the many men against this single concubine.

Anonymity also establishes the presence of two symmetrical sets of relationships: between the Levite and the father in Judg 19:1–9 and between the Levite and the host in 19:10–26. In each case, it is the concubine who joins the two men together. Just as the father had the power to detain her at home or let her go with the Levite, so does the host have the power to offer her protection within his house or to push her outside. The host, too, is a father, though his daughter does not appear on the scene. In offering her to the crowd, he asserts the same patriarchal authority over the concubine as he holds over his own daughter.

The anonymity of Levite, father, host, and crowd does not obscure their differences, but it does link them in their behavior toward the woman. From the concubine's perspective, they are undifferentiated in terms of their unremitting power over her sexuality, safety, and life. Anonymity creates a disturbing ambiguity in the text and a corresponding ambivalence in the reader's assessment of the Levite.[14] The anonymity of the woman, by contrast, points precisely to her identity as a woman who reverses the life's journey of the ideal biblical wife by leaving the domain of her husband to return to the domain of her father. This anomalous behavior, in the eyes of the narrator, leaves her sexual integrity open to question and exposes her to the dangers that lurk when one steps outside the norm. For her, there is no escaping the power of a paternal figure, even once she has left her own father's domain.

The "Company of Prophets" in 1 Kings 20

The undifferentiated "company of prophets," featured in 1 Kings 20, also illustrates the confusion that multiple anonymity can create. The designation *company* or *sons of the prophets* (בני הנביאים) refers to a group of prophets who usually appear as a collective of anonymous men, though occasionally an individual member is singled out for narrative attention (2 Kgs 4:39). The company engages in ecstatic behavior and the inspired playing of instruments (1 Sam 10:5–13). Its members perform sacrifices (1 Kgs 18:20–40) and provide counsel to kings (1 Kgs 22:10–12).

---

[14]If the narrator were a postmodern writer, we might suggest that this was done deliberately, and perhaps, indeed, this possibility should not be ruled out.

The company seems not to have enjoyed absolute respect. In 2 Kgs 9:1–10, Elisha asks a young member (נער) of the company of prophets to act as his messenger in the anointing of Jehu as the next king of Israel. Elisha gives him very explicit instructions: to travel to Ramoth-gilead, find Jehu, get him to leave his companions, take him into an inner chamber, anoint him, pronounce the words "Thus says the LORD: I anoint you king over Israel" (9:3), and then to flee immediately without lingering. The young man, the young prophet (הנער הנער הנביא), fulfills this task, though his speech to Jehu is considerably longer and more detailed than the formula pronounced by Elisha. After the young prophet leaves, Jehu's companions inquire: "Why did that madman come to you?" (9: 11). Jehu evades the question by responding, "You know the sort and how they babble." They press him, and he confesses that the prophet had said, "Thus says the LORD: I anoint you king over Israel" (9:11), the precise words iterated by Elisha in 9:2. They immediately spread their cloaks for him to walk on, blow the trumpet, and proclaim him king (9:14). This passage provides a glimpse of other characters' perceptions of the company of prophets: as madmen, who babble and mutter, yet whose words are taken seriously as divine prophecy.

The company of prophets is under the authority of a central prophet, who supports them materially. In 2 Kgs 4:38, the company of prophets is sitting before Elisha at a time of famine. Elisha orders his servant to make stew for the company. One of their number puts some wild gourds into the pot of stew; those who eat the stew cry out, "O man of God, there is death in the pot." Elisha puts flour into the pot, and all is well. Not only food but also shelter was provided by the prophet. In 2 Kgs 6:1–7, the company of prophets asks Elisha for permission to go to Jordan, collect logs, and build homes because the place where they were living under his charge was too small. As one was felling a log, his ax head fell into the water; he was alarmed because it did not belong to him but was borrowed. Elisha made the iron float so the man could pick it up.

Tensions between the company and Elisha are present in the transition between the leadership of Elijah and Elisha (2 Kings 2), during which the company of prophets repeatedly informs Elisha of the impending departure or death of Elijah (2 Kgs 2:3, 5) and he repeatedly silences them. Their lesser status is indicated by that fact that they remain on one side of the Jordan River when Elijah and Elisha cross over to the other side (2 Kgs 2:7–8).

The most detailed story of the company of prophets is in 1 Kings 20. The context of this story is the conflict between King Ahab of Israel and King Ben-hadad of Aram. After a verbal skirmish between the two men, a prophet approaches King Ahab and provides an unsolicited divine prediction: The army of Aram will be given into Israelite hands that very day, through the aides of the provincial governors (20:13). King Ahab will begin the battle (20:14). These events come to pass (20:15–21). The prophet returns to King Ahab and warns of an Aramean attack at the turn of the year (20:22). This prophecy, too, comes to pass (20:26). Finally, the prophet announces that the Lord will provide the Israelites with victory against the Arameans (20:28). This prophecy also is fulfilled (20:29–34). In defeat, Ben-hadad, the Aramean king, hides in the city. His servants suggest that they don sackcloth and ashes and surrender themselves to the king, as the kings of Israel have a reputation for being merciful to their defeated foes. The tactic succeeds; King Ahab concludes a treaty with Ben-hadad and dismisses him (20:30–34).

In 20:35, the story shifts abruptly. An unnamed man, identified as a "certain member of a company of prophets" (איש אחד מבני הנביאים), asks another such man, by the word of the Lord, to strike him. The other refuses. As punishment for disobedience, the first disciple prophesies his fellow's death by a lion, which comes to pass (20:36). He then approaches a second man with the same request. This second man obeys and wounds him. The wounded man then covers his eyes with a cloth and waits by the road for the king. When the king passes by, he calls out to him with the following story. In the thick of battle, he had been given the task of guarding one of the enemy. The penalty for failure or disobedience was death or financial penalty of a talent of silver. Unfortunately, the man was distracted, and his charge escaped (20:39–40). The king responds that the verdict is self-evident and has been pronounced by the man himself. At this point, the man removes his disguise and is recognized by the king as one of the prophets (מהנביאים הוא). The man concludes with a final divine word: Because the king had released "the man . . . whom I had devoted to destruction" (King Ben-hadad), he himself shall die (20:42).

Is the wounded prophet of 20:35–42 the same as the prophet of 20:13–34? The story permits no easy resolution of this question. The key verse is 20:41, which describes the king's recognition of the wounded prophet as one of the prophets. This verse may suggest that the king had recognized the wounded prophet as the one who had prophesied his victory in the earlier narrative segment. It is also possible, however, that the prophets had distinguishing features that permitted their identification as such.[15]

It is not easy to keep track of the identities of the various unnamed prophets in this story. The confusion among characters echoes the theme of disguise and deception that appears throughout the story. The king's servants disguise their identities to manipulate Ahab into a treaty with his defeated enemy; the prophet

---

[15] J. Lindblom, in *Prophecy in Ancient Israel* (Philadelphia: Fortress, 1973), 67; Gray (*I and II Kings*, 385) suggests that prophets may have had special tattoo markings. Commentators tend not to identify the two prophets, arguing that this passage is constructed from a number of different traditions regarding the company of prophets. See Gray, *I and II Kings*; Gwilyn Jones, *1 and 2 Kings* (New Century Commentary; Grand Rapids: Eerdmans, 1984), 24.

disguises himself before the king to convey his prophecy of judgment. Similarly, the reader, too, may be deceived or, at least, confounded by the multiplicity of prophets and thereby enter into the experience of the doomed Ahab.

"The Man of God" and the "Prophet" in 1 Kings 13

The converging of characters is intimately tied to the structure and themes of 1 Kings 13. This story features two anonymous prophets, one of whom is also called a man of God. Before examining this story, we look briefly at the roles associated with these designations.

The primary role of the prophet (נביא) is to convey the divine words, judgments, and predictions of God to an individual or to the people Israel as a whole. This function is mentioned explicitly in 2 Kgs 17:22–23, in which the narrator comments that the people of Israel continued in their sins "until the LORD removed Israel out of his sight, as he had foretold through all his servants the prophets." The success of the prophets in foretelling future events is illustrated by the narrative itself, which frequently portrays the events by which those prophecies come to pass. The fulfillment of Ahijah's prophecy concerning the demise of the house of Jeroboam (1 Kgs 14:10–16), for example, begins in the very next verses with the death of Jeroboam's son (1 Kgs 14:17–18). Prophets frequently express God's displeasure with the Israelite monarchy (and monarchies, after the division of the kingdom). For example, Nathan is the vehicle for God's disapprobation of David's behavior with respect to Uriah and Bathsheba (2 Kings 11–12). At the Lord's command, Elijah becomes the bane of Ahab and Jezebel's existence (1 Kings 17–21). But human interactions and personality traits have an impact on the ways in which they enact their prophetic roles. One example is the ferocious curse the prophet Elisha bestows on the young children who jeer him for his bald head (2 Kings 23–24).

Virtually synonymous with *prophet* is *man of God* (איש האלהים). This term appears as a designation for specific individuals such as Moses (Deut 33:1; Josh 14:6) and Shemaiah (1 Kgs 12:22). It is used most frequently, however, of the prophets Elijah (e.g., 1 Kgs 17:18) and Elisha (2 Kings, passim). A more general designation than *prophet*, it is used occasionally by biblical characters to convey uncertainty as to the precise role and identity of the person whom they encounter. For example, the young Saul is taken by his servant to meet a man of God—later identified as Samuel—who will help Saul find his father's donkeys (1 Sam 9:6). The wife of Manoah refers to her mysterious visitor in the field as a man of God when she recounts the incident to her husband (Judg 13:6). Similarly, the Shunammite woman tells her husband that she is sure that Elisha is a holy man of God (2 Kgs 4:9).

The functions associated with the *man of God* designation are the same as those attributed to prophets. The man of God has a special relationship to God that involves direct communication. In Josh 14:6, for example, Caleb tells

Joshua: "You know what the LORD said to Moses the man of God in Kadesh-barnea concerning you and me." Saul's servant believes that what the man of God says always comes true (1 Sam 9:6). In 1 Sam 2:27, an unnamed man of God reveals God's will to Eli the priest.

The narrative context of 1 Kings 13 is the tale of Israelite idolatry which contributes to the downfall of Jeroboam, monarch of the northern kingdom, Israel.[16] The passage introduces a man of God who utters a prophecy against the altar at Bethel concerning its destruction at the time of Josiah (13:2–3). This prophetic act is performed on the site and in the presence of King Jeroboam, who is burning incense at the altar (13:4). In angry response to the prophecy, the king stretches out his hand and cries, "Seize him!" (13:4). The king's hand withers and is paralyzed, and the altar destroyed (13:5). The king then changes his tactics and asks the prophet to ask God to restore his hand. This he does (13:6). Apparently now convinced of the man of God's authority and power, the king invites him home and promises a reward (13:7). But this invitation is rejected; the man of God explains that the Lord has forbidden him to eat food, drink water or return by the way that he had come (13:9).

The focus now shifts to a character designated as an *old prophet* (נביא אחד זקן) in Bethel, whose sons have told him of these events (13:11). The old prophet intercepts the man of God (13:14) and invites the visitor home. The prophet initially meets with the same negative response as did King Jeroboam. The old prophet then assures the visiting man of God that "I also am a prophet as you are" (13:18). He thereby both establishes his own credentials and declares he is equal in status to the Judahite man of God. He then announces a competing prophecy: "an angel spoke to me by the word of the LORD: Bring him back with you into your house so that he may eat food and drink water" (13:18).

The reader is told that the prophecy is a lie (13:18). The man of God, unaware of the deceit, is persuaded (13:19). In light of the vehement divine response to King Jeroboam, it is no surprise that the Judahite man's gullibility does not go unpunished. While sitting at the table, the Bethel prophet receives a word of God—authentic, this time—which describes and then condemns the disobedience of the Judahite man of God, to which he himself had incited him

---

[16]This passage is fraught with source-critical, structural, contextual, and exegetical difficulties. Scholars disagree on the dating and sources for this story. The anonymity of all characters, references to angels, magical remnants, and animals, and the mechanical view of prophecy and its validation lead Crenshaw to believe that the story is a late legend or midrash inserted secondarily and late into 1 Kings. See James L. Crenshaw, *Prophetic Conflict: Its Effect upon Israelite Religion* (Berlin: Walter de Gruyter, 1971), 42–43. William Foxwell Albright (*Archaeology and the Religion of Israel* [Baltimore: Johns Hopkins University Press, 1956], 156), by contrast, argues that the story is early, illustrating the hostility of the nascent prophetic movement toward the shrines of Jeroboam I.

(13:21–22). Because he has disobeyed, the man of God shall not come to his ancestral tomb (13:22). This experience authenticates the Bethel man's self-professed prophetic identity.

The rest of the story describes the means by which the prophecy is fulfilled. The man of God eats, drinks, and then departs for home on the prophet's donkey. He is met on the road by a lion who kills him. His body is thrown to the side of the road and guarded by the lion and the donkey on which he had been riding. The old prophet finds the dead man, gives him a properly mournful burial, and lays him in his (the old prophet's? and/or the Judahite's?) grave (13: 31). The old prophet laments him, calls him his brother, and charges his children to bury him in the same tomb, that their bones may lie together (13:31). Finally, the old prophet proclaims the truth of the Judahite man of God's initial prophecy against the altar at Bethel and against Samaria in general, reminding the reader of the broader political context of the scene.

With the exception of King Jeroboam, none of the characters is designated by proper name. Not only are the two principal characters anonymous but also their functional designations are virtually synonymous. Although the narrator consistently refers to the Judahite as "the man of God" and to the Bethel man as "the prophet," these terms are used more or less synonymously in biblical narrative, as we have already seen. The Bethel prophet himself confirms their equivalent status when he tells the Judahite, "I also am a prophet as you are" (13:18). The visitor's prophetic credentials are confirmed by two different acts: prophesying against the king and healing the king's hand. He appears initially as a man of integrity, obedient to the word he has received, even to the point of declining a royal invitation. The old prophet, by contrast, is initially portrayed negatively: He lies about receiving a prophecy in order to manipulate the behavior of the visiting man of God.[17] Nevertheless, his authentic prophetic identity is accepted by the narrator.

Given the similarity of their functions, the anonymity of the two men blurs or even merges their identities. This effect is enhanced by the use of personal pronouns. For example, the false prophecy in 13:18 is introduced by the words, "Then he said to him" (ויאמר לו). Only the context allows us to identify the Bethel prophet as the speaker and the Judahite man of God as the addressee. Similarly, 13:23 states: "After he had eaten food and had drunk, they saddled for him a donkey belonging to the prophet who had brought him back."[18] Again

---

[17]Lindblom (*Prophecy*, 63–64), however, suggests that the story was told to address a question that must have vexed the prophets: How can they know which prophecy is true? The answer given by the story is that one must obey the prophecy one has received oneself. It is the Judahite prophet's transgression of this principle that leads to his death.

[18]This is the literal translation; the NRSV supplies "man of God" as the antecedent of "he."

it is the context, particularly the explicit reference to the prophet, that allows the singular pronouns to be understood as referents for the Judahite. Adding to the sense of convergence between the two characters are the expanded designations used for the Bethel prophet in 13:20 and 13:26. In the former verse, the Bethel man is described as "the prophet who had brought him back" (הנביא אשר השיבו); in 13:26 this description is further amplified as: "the prophet who had brought him back from the way" (הנביא אשר השיבו מן־הדרך). The Bethel prophet is now defined with respect to his behavior in relation to the Judahite.

Whereas the momentary uncertainties caused by the liberal use of masculine pronouns are easily resolved, the merging of identities they herald is explicitly advanced in the plot segment that ensues with the Judahite's departure. Just as the old prophet initially sought to entrap the Judahite, so now he seeks his corpse in order to care for it with reverence and respect (13:29). In burying it, he also anticipates his own death, in which his bones are to rest with those of the Judahite. Adversaries at the outset, the two are now brothers, as the Bethel prophet declares (13:30). Even more, the Bethel prophet not only cares for the Judahite's corpse but also takes over his prophecy. In reaching his corpse by donkey, the Bethel prophet reenacts the last journey of his Judahite colleague. In burying him in his own grave and reiterating his prophetic words, the Bethel prophet effectively blends his identity with that of the dead prophet, an act made all the more possible, and effective, by their anonymity.

Anonymity and the resulting convergence of the two characters require readers to constantly revise their moral evaluations of the two figures. Initially, the Judahite man of God is coded "good"; he prophesies against the evil king and is careful to obey God's command. The old Bethel prophet deceives the Judahite about receiving a prophecy, manipulating the Judahite into disobeying his own mandate. This act marks the Bethelite as "bad."

No sooner are these distinctions established, however, than they are challenged. The Judahite's susceptibility casts doubt on his own prophetic abilities. The old prophet of Bethel utters an authentic prophecy that condemns the Judahite for falling into the trap set by the old prophet. This prophecy itself is problematic, for it fails to recognize the dilemma in which the Bethel prophet had placed the Judahite. Should the Judahite *not* have trusted the Bethel prophet? Is it not plausible that a recent prophecy, such as the Bethel prophet claimed to receive, could have replaced the earlier one received by the Judahite directly? In any case, the authentic prophecy labels the Judahite's behavior as disobedience, suggesting that the readers need also revise their evaluation of his character. The Judahite receives the punishment which had been prophesied to the Bethel prophet, but this divinely decreed death does not invalidate his initial prophecy, which is reiterated by his erstwhile host. Similarly, the Bethelite, who, one would think, bears some moral responsibility for the Judahite's death, subverts the initially negative evaluation through his care of the body and confirmation of the Judahite's prophecy. By the story's end, both men are morally equivocal and yet both confirm the same prophecy concerning the destruction of Jeroboam's idolatrous altar and cult at Bethel.

The instability of character is thus matched by the constant shifting of the reader's moral evaluations, but to what end? Several aspects of the passage suggest that the main point of the passage is to criticize Jeroboam's cult at Bethel. This critique is expressed by the content of the Judahite's initial prophecy (13:2), reiterated by the Bethel prophet at the end (13:32). But it also emerges more obliquely through the central role accorded to matters related to food and hospitality, which are prominent in three scenes. First, the king's invitation to the Judahite may have been innocuous, a simple invitation to the king's private home, as Uriel Simon suggests.[19] The context of the invitation and the venue of the proposed meal, however, imply a cultic or covenantal significance.[20] Walsh argues, "To break bread in Beth-El, especially with the royal patron of the doomed sanctuary, would be to condone that city's cultic abominations and to compromise the divine condemnation."[21] Second, and similarly puzzling, are the invitation extended by the Bethel prophet and his determination to see that the Judahite accepts the invitation. The Bethel prophet's invitation may be seen in light of his interest in his home sanctuary and his views on the prophecy of the Judahite man of God. Walsh views this invitation as a conscious attempt to trick the man of God into compromise and thereby to avoid the danger to the prophet's home sanctuary.[22] John Gray suggests that the invitation may be a test to determine whether he really is a man of God: "If the man of God could evade this word of God [eating, drinking, and going back] with impunity, this would reflect on the seriousness of his oracle of doom on the cult and sanctuary of Bethel, a matter in which the prophet of Bethel, both as prophet and as a member of the prophetic guild attached to the sanctuary . . . was vitally interested."[23] A third related element may be the fact that the lion refrains from eating his prey. The lion who kills and does not eat when by rights he should do so contrasts with the Judahite man of God, who dies because he ate when he should not have done so.[24]

[19]"I Kings 13: A Prophetic Sign—Denial and Persistence," *HUCA* 47 (1976): 89, note 24.

[20]Crenshaw, *Prophetic Conflict*, 44.

[21]"The Contexts of 1 Kings XIII," *VT* 39 (1989): 358.

[22]Walsh, "Contexts," 360.

[23]*I and II Kings*, 322.

[24]Simon, "I Kings 13," 96. Gray (*I and II Kings*, 331) notes that lions of a small breed were known in Palestine in the biblical period, but that the presentation here reflects the didactic nature of the passage and, like the Balaam story, probably borrowed folkloric motifs.

While these points are open to multiple interpretations, their shared focus on food returns our attention to the cultic activities of Jeroboam, which apparently involved eating and drinking, as well as sacrificing to golden calves (12:32). These activities are roundly condemned by the narrator in the pericope preceding this story (12:25–33). They also come to the fore in a later passage, 2 Kgs 23:16–18, in which the Judahite man of God is mentioned again. In the latter passage, set some three hundred years after 1 Kings 13,[25] King Josiah destroys the tombs and altars related to the reign of Jeroboam, except for "the tomb of the man of God who came from Judah and predicted these things that you have done against the altar at Bethel" (23:17).[26]

The anonymity of these characters and the merging of identities and convictions to which it contributes become a conduit for the narrator's negative views on King Jeroboam and his cultic activities. That Jeroboam's own prophet at Bethel took on not only the prophecy but also the persona of the Judahite indicates the narrator's pro-Judahite stance. The fact that the Judahite had to die because of his unwitting transgression of a command not to partake of food in the vicinity of the outlawed sanctuary underscores the serious nature of his word to Jeroboam.

Anonymity blurs the boundaries between characters and allows their convergence. The instability of the borders between the named and unnamed shows that anonymity itself is not a straightforward category. The converging of character, enhanced by the use of pronouns and the presence of two or more unnamed figures in a single story, does not merely throw obstacles in the way of the reader's attempts to differentiate among characters. It also implies that character traits are not unique to one individual but shared among several. Although these characters are presented as distinct, the converging of character breaks down the borders upon which their individuality depends.

---

[25]According to Simon ("I Kings 13," 116), the fulfillment of the prophecy some three centuries later is presented as added proof of the potency of God's word.

[26]Thomas Dozeman ("The Way of the Man of God from Judah: True and False Prophecy in the Pre-Deuteronomic Legend of 1 Kings 13," *CBQ* 44 [1982]: 382) argues that this latter section was not included in the pre-Deuteronomic legend. Jerome Walsh ("Contexts," 368) brings it into the discussion without, however, considering whether it was originally connected to the story. Simon ("I Kings 13," 109), however, does consider it to be the ending of the story.

7

⊞ ⊞ ⊞

Character Confusion in
the Heavenly Realm

THE BOUNDARIES OF PERSONAL IDENTITY among the human inhabitants of the biblical story world are occasionally unclear; the residents of the heavenly realm can be similarly elusive. That the heavenly realm is populated by a variety of beings in addition to God is intimated from the very beginning of Genesis. Among the heavenly beings are those to whom God suggested, "Let us make humankind in our image" (Gen 1:27) or to whom he expressed his dismay that "the man has become like one of us, knowing good and evil" (Gen 3:22). Some heavenly beings, such as the cherubim, seem akin to animals. God places cherubim and a turning and flaming sword in the garden to guard the way to the tree of life after the expulsion of the first humans from the garden. David describes God as riding a cherub through the heavens (2 Sam 22:11; cf. Ps. 18:10–11); images of cherubim adorn the tabernacle and the temple (Exod 25:18–20; 37:7–9; 1 Kgs 6:23–28). Other beings have some of the characteristics, such as speech, associated with human beings and relate to God as to an earthly monarch. The book of Job depicts "sons of God" (בני האלוהים or בני אלוהים; "heavenly beings" in the NRSV) who present themselves to God periodically (Job 38:7) and among whose number Satan is to be found (Job 1:6; 2:1).[1] Genesis 6:1–4 portrays "sons of God" more provocatively, as the primordial sexual partners of the בנות האדם, "daughters of humans," whose offspring were the heroes

[1]Psalms 29:1; 89:6/7 refer to בני אלים.

of old, "warriors of renown" (Gen 6:4).[2] This later reference ascribes to this group a number of human traits: gender, sexual desire and intercourse, and paternity.

The most prevalent designation for heavenly beings is *messenger* (מלאך), or, more specifically, *a* [or *the*] *messenger of the God/the Lord* (מלאך יהוה or מלאך האלהים). Even this brief survey demonstrates the potential areas of uncertainty regarding the identity of angels. What are the boundaries among divine beings themselves, between divine and human beings, and between divine beings and God himself?

A major contributor to such confusion is the pervasive anonymity of angels. In contrast to the biblical deity, who is identified by numerous names and titles, angels and other members of the divine entourage remain unnamed within the biblical corpus.[3] Anonymity doubtless contributes to scholars' comments concerning angels' vague and elusive characterization[4] and the judgment that "the way in which the beings are thought of never rises above a certain colorlessness and indistinctness."[5] Although the specific functions of biblical angels are only vaguely articulated,[6] their general activities can be extracted from brief remarks by God, the narrator, and other biblical characters. These, in turn, can be used as a basis for examining the presence and impact of character confusion in the divine arena and between the heavenly and human realms.

[2]On the relationship of this passage to ancient Near Eastern mythology, see Robert Graves and Raphael Patai, *Hebrew Myths: The Book of Genesis* (London: Cassell, 1964), 100–107.

[3]Alexander Rofé (*The Belief in Angels in the Bible and in Early Israel* [Jerusalem: Makor, 1979], xxiv [in Hebrew]) argues that angels originally had names, which were later suppressed for theological reasons. Named angels appear frequently in postbiblical literature. Cf. Gerhard von Rad, "מלאך in the OT," *TDNT*, 1: 79; Carol Newsom, "Angels," *ABD* 1: 249. For full-length studies, see Michael Mach, *Entwicklungsstadien des jüdischen Engelglaubens in vorrabbinischer Zeit* (Texte und Studien zum antiken Judentum 34; Tübingen: J. C. B. Mohr [Paul Siebeck], 1992); Saul M. Olyan, *A Thousand Angels Served Him: Exegesis and the Naming of Angels in Ancient Judaism* (Tübingen: J. C. B. Mohr, 1993). Carol Newsom ("Angels," 249) notes that while angels in preexilic texts are not clearly differentiated and exhibit an unclear relationship to God, the exilic and postexilic periods saw an increase in speculation about angels, particularly in prophetic literature.

[4]J. Licht, "מלאך; מלאכים" (Angel, Angels), in אנציקלופדיה מקראית 4:981; Newsom, "Angels," 249; William George Heidt, *Angelology of the Old Testament* (Studies in Sacred Theology 24; Washington, D.C.: Catholic University of America Press, 1949), 8; Mach, *Entwicklungsstadien*, 3, 40.

[5]Gerhard von Rad, *Old Testament Theology*, vol. 1, *The Theology of Israel's Historical Traditions*, trans. D. M. G. Stalker (New York: Harper, 1972), 285.

[6]Olyan, *A Thousand Angels*, 15.

ANGELS IN ACTION

Personal Guides

Some characters attribute the success of their own ventures to the guidance of a divine messenger. In Gen 24:7, Abraham promises his servant that the Lord "will send his angel before you, and you shall take a wife for my son from there." The servant later recasts Abraham's promise for the benefit of Rebecca's family: "The LORD, before whom I walk, will send his angel with you and make your way successful" (Gen 24:40). Jacob attributes his lucrative goat-breeding tactic as well as his decision to leave Laban's household to an angel of God who had given him the strategy in a dream and had ordered him—on God's behalf— to return to the land of his birth (Gen 31:11–13). In his deathbed blessing of his grandsons Ephraim and Manasseh, Jacob evokes "the angel who has redeemed me from all harm" to bless the boys, increase their numbers, and let his own name and that of his ancestors Abraham and Isaac be perpetuated (Gen 48:16).

Among those guided by angels are one or another of the prophets. In 1 Kgs 13:18, one prophet convinces another to go against God's express instructions by saying: "an angel spoke to me by the word of the LORD: Bring him back with you into your house so that he may eat food and drink water." Though these words deceive and ultimately kill the second prophet, they imply that the word of the Lord could be conveyed to the prophet by an angel rather than by the Lord directly. Even the prophet Elijah occasionally receives God's will through an angel rather than directly from God. In 1 Kgs 19:5, Elijah, tired from his attempt to escape from Queen Jezebel's messengers, lies down under the broom bush and falls asleep. An angel comes once, touches him and says, "Get up and eat" (19:5), and a second time, saying, "Get up and eat, otherwise the journey will be too much for you" (19:7). Through their respective messengers, Jezebel and God struggle over the life of Elijah.

A similar interplay between human and superhuman messengers is apparent in 2 Kgs 1:2–4. King Ahaziah, who has injured himself in a fall through the lattice in his upper chamber, sends messengers to inquire of the god Baal-zebub concerning his recovery. An angel of the Lord instructs Elijah to intercept these messengers and provides him with the text of his prophecy: "Say to them, 'Is it because there is no God in Israel that you are going to inquire of Baal-zebub, the god of Ekron?' Now therefore thus says the LORD, 'You [King Ahaziah] shall not leave the bed to which you have gone, but you shall surely die' " (1:3–4). The angel returns in 1:15 to encourage Elijah to confront the king directly, though the prophet had already transmitted God's message to Ahaziah via the king's messengers.

God's Agents in the Exodus

Angels also contribute to the corporate success of Israel in their exodus from Egypt and entry into the land.[7] In Exod 14:19, the narrator describes the formation of the people as they approach the sea with the Egyptians at their heels. The angel of God (מלאך האלהים) and the pillar, which have been leading the Israelites, move to their rear to form a buffer between the Israelites and the Egyptians (14:20). Later, God assures Moses that his angel will go before him (הנה מלאכי ילך לפניך) to the place about which God told him (Exod 32:34) and implies their role in conquest of the land: "I will send an angel before you, and I will drive out the Canaanites, the Amorites, the Hittites, the Perizzites, the Hivites, and the Jebusites" (Exod 33:2).

The angel is not only a medium of divine assistance in the exodus process but also reflects the state of Israel's relationship with God. The divine speech continues: "Go up to a land flowing with milk and honey; but I will not go up among you, or I would consume you on the way, for you are a stiff-necked people" (Exod 33:3). The angel's presence signifies God's absence; it is both the reminder of God's wrath in the aftermath of Israel's construction of the golden calf and the means through which God protects Israel from the consequences of divine anger.

The role of the angel and the basis of his authority are also clarified by God. In Exod 23:20–22, God promises to send:

> an angel in front of you, to guard you on the way and to bring you to the place that I have prepared. Be attentive to him and listen to his voice; do not rebel against him, for he will not pardon your transgression; *for my name is in him*. But if you listen attentively to *his voice* and do *all that I say*, then I will be an enemy to your enemies and a foe to your foes (emphasis added).[8]

The angel's role therefore is not limited to protection and geographical direction but includes authority of the sort which requires Israel's obedience. Listening to the angel's voice is the equivalent of doing God's will. The basis of the angel's authority is God's claim that "my name is in him" (כי שמי בקרבו; Exod 23:21). It is the angel's possession *of* the divine name that allows him to act *in* God's name, as God's representative and ambassador.

Instruments of Destruction

As God's agents, angels are also called on to enact his decrees of destruction on behalf of Israel and against them. In 2 Kgs 19:35, the narrator describes how

---

[7]On the role of angels in the plagues, see Rofé, *Belief*, 155; and Mach, *Entwicklungsstadien*, 44.

[8]Brevard Childs (*The Book of Exodus* [OTL; Philadelphia: Westminster, 1974], 487) argues that the מלאך here is an angel, as is clear from the parallel passages, 32:34; 33:2; and Num 20:16–17.

"the angel of the LORD set out and struck down one hundred eighty-five thousand in the camp of the Assyrians; when morning dawned, they were all dead bodies." In 2 Sam 24:15–17, the Lord sends a pestilence but relents (24:16) when the angel stretched out his hand toward Jerusalem to destroy it. "When David saw the angel who was striking down the people, he said to the LORD, 'I alone have sinned, and I alone have done wickedly; but these sheep, what have they done? Let your hand, I pray, be against me and against my father's house' " (24:17).[9]

Warriors

The angel's role in leading Israel through the desert, battling Israel's enemies, and occasionally punishing God's people themselves implies a military capability. God's warring hosts are mentioned, though not as angels, in the blessing Moses imparts to the Israelites on the eve of his death (Deut 33:2–3):

> The LORD came from Sinai;
>> and dawned from Seir upon us;
>> he shone forth from Mount Paran.
> With him were myriads of holy ones;
>> at his right, a host of his own.
> Indeed, O favorite among peoples,
>> all his holy ones (כל־קדשיו) were in your charge;
> they marched at your heels,
>> accepted direction from you.

Hints of a heavenly host also appear in 2 Kgs 6:17, in which the Lord opens the eyes of Elisha's servant so that he can see a mountain full of horses and chariots of fire all around Elisha.

Harbingers of the Divine Presence

Some angels herald the presence of God or identify the divine domain. The angels in Jacob's dream enact the ongoing traffic between the divine and the human by ascending and descending a ladder connecting earth and sky (Gen 28:12). Their action presages the appearance of the Lord, who speaks to Jacob, identifies himself as the God of his father and grandfather, and reiterates the covenant promises to give Jacob the land and to make his descendants numerous and a source of blessing for others (Gen 28:12–15). Upon awakening, Jacob recognizes his dream as a revelatory experience, in commemoration of which he builds an altar and calls the place Bethel (28:18–19). In Gen 32:2, angels appear

---

[9]P. Kyle McCarter (*II Samuel*, 515–16) suggests that in the original version of the story David saw Yahweh himself; the envoy may have been added to the story later to protect divine transcendence.

again to Jacob, who names the place of the encounter Mahanaim, saying, "This is God's camp!"[10] Similarly, an angel of God (מלאך יהוה) appears to Moses in the flames of the burning bush (Exod 3:2). Thereafter the Lord interacts directly with Moses, and the angel is mentioned no more.

Angels speak in the name of God. Just as Abraham is about to sacrifice Isaac at the Lord's behest (Gen 22:2), the angel of the Lord calls out to him: "Do not lay your hand on the boy or do anything to him; for now I know that you fear God, since you have not withheld your son, your only son, from me" (22:12). In Gen 22:15–16, the angel of the Lord calls a second time from heaven and, as the angel does in 21:17, speaks in the first person in God's name, commending Abraham for his willingness to obey and restating the covenantal promises.[11] In this passage, as in Gen 21:17–19, the life of a child and the existence of a covenant are at stake; the human perceptions of the angel are not visual but auditory. The content of the angel's message (22:12,16) is delivered in the first person singular, implying God as speaker or, at the very least, as composer of the message. Although no explicit indication is given of Abraham's discernment of the angel, his obedience to the angel's words implies his perception that they are the authoritative words of God.

Angels also have some of the traits associated with God. These traits are indirectly imputed to angels by characters who compare David to an angel in one respect or another. In 1 Sam 29:9, Achish tells David: "you are as blameless in my sight as an angel of God (כמלאך אלהים)."[12] In 2 Sam 14:17, the wise woman of Tekoa tells David that "my lord the king is like the angel of God, discerning good and evil," and in 14:20 she says, "My lord has wisdom like the wisdom of the angel of God [כמלאך האלהים] to know all things that are on the earth." Finally, in 2 Sam 19:28, Mephibosheth argues that David should not be slandered because he is like the angel of God (כמלאך האלהים).[13] Although the main concern of these characters is to describe David, their analogies suggest that angels, like God, are blameless (Job 36:23), discerning of good and evil (Psalm 37), wise and all-knowing (Psalm 139), and to be protected from slander (Job 15).

Biblical angels, as we have forged them from the comments of God, the narrator, and other characters, are primarily the mediators of the encounter

---

[10]Rofé (*Belief*, 84–85) points out that the angels whom Jacob encounters at Bethel and Mahanaim do not bring him a message, do not appear to be fulfilling a commission and do not seem to have a real connection to God. Behind these stories, Rofé suggests, lie legends about gods that have been revised to remove hints of polytheism.

[11]In both cases the formulation is very similar to that of Gen 21:17: ויקרא אליו מלאך (22:15). ויקרא מלאך יהוה אל אברהם שנית מן־השמים (22:11); יהוה מן־השמים.

[12]Hertzberg (*I & II Samuel*, 223) describes Achish's comment as "words of exaggerated kindness."

[13]Polzin (*David*, 140) notes that in all three assertions the reader has a much wider perspective on David than do those who praise him.

between the human and divine realms. Appearing at life-changing moments in the lives of individuals and corporate Israel, they convey the words of God and expedite God's will. Their power is not innate but derives from God. The heavenly entourage thus serves God much as royal courtiers, soldiers, and messengers serve their king.

Consistent and harmonious as this construction is, areas of indeterminacy exist. What is the mode of their appearance to others? Are they visible and tangible or perceived through their voices and effects only? Given that the masculine pronoun is used consistently in referring to angels, what role does gender have in their portrayal? Finally, what are the boundaries that separate human beings, angels, and God?

Some of the ambiguity in the angelic portrait is related to their anonymity. Properly named angels could have been counted and distinguished from one another, as, indeed, they were in late- and postbiblical literature. Their role as divine agents may require anonymity, however; their narrative portrayal as the bearers of God's name and the executors of his will points consistently away from any personal and unique identity, as would have been implied by a proper name.

THE BLURRED BOUNDARIES OF ANGELIC IDENTITY

Overlap with a range of human characters is intimated by the Hebrew term for *angel* (מלאך), which is also used to denote messengers. Differentiation between angelic and human messengers is frequently determined by the context and specific mode of reference. In particular, human messengers deliver the messages of other human beings, whereas angels deliver the messages of God. In keeping with this distinction, an angel is referred to as *messenger of the Lord* or *of God* (מלאך יהוה or מלאך האלהים). But problems arise in distinguishing angels from a particular group of human beings—namely, prophets, who are also charged with delivering divine messages.

The equation of the angel's voice and God's speech in Exod 23:22 points to the role of angel as prophet, conveying the words and the will of God to human beings. As prophet, the angel speaks in God's name, frequently using the first person. In many cases, the context allows the reader to determine whether a human or superhuman prophet is at work. But occasionally ambiguity arises. Judges 2:1–5 speaks of an "angel of the LORD" who comes up from Gilgal to Bochim to speak the words of God in the first person. He reminds his Israelite audience (2:4) of God's role in the exodus from Egypt and entry into the land and warns them against making a covenant with the indigenous people, whose altars must be torn down. But, he continues, because the people have already disobeyed this command, "I will not drive them out before you; but they shall become adversaries to you" and their gods a snare (2:1–3). The people meet this announcement with weeping (the literal meaning of Bochim [בכים], 2:5) and sacrifices to the Lord, thereby expressing their belief in the divine source of the distressing message. Similar is the reference in the Song of Deborah to an angel of God who curses the inhabitants of Meroz for not coming to the help of the Lord (Judg 5:23). The messengers in these passages may be either human or divine. In favor of the view that they are divine is their explicit designation as angels of God or the Lord. But the fact that these messengers speak to the people as a whole and not to select individuals, as angels usually do, supports the possibility that they may be human.

Similar difficulties arise in attempting to distinguish clearly between one angel and another. In the first place, it is most unclear as to whether the designation *angel of the Lord/God* presumes the definite article and therefore refers to a distinct individual, as in "the angel of the Lord/God," or whether, in the absence of the definite article, it refers indiscriminately to any member of a class of angels. The Hebrew formulations support either reading. Most scholars choose not to supply the definite article.[14] However, the *NJPSV* and the NRSV translations often differ in their decisions regarding the definite article. For example, the NRSV at 2 Kgs 19:35 has "*the* angel of the Lord," where the *NJPSV* has "*an* angel of the Lord" (emphasis added). These differences in interpretation leave open the question of whether the term *angel of the Lord* (or *the angel of God*) always refers to the same specific being or simply to one of an indefinite number of the Lord's messengers. In favor of the latter view is Gen 28:12, in which Jacob dreams that he sees "angels of God" ascending and descending on a heavenly ladder (Gen 28:12).

Also difficult is the question of whether beings who are not explicitly designated as God's messengers should nevertheless be considered angels. It is often noted that the book of Daniel presents the only named angels in the Hebrew Bible and presages the surge of interest in the personal identity of angels in the second temple period.[15] But are the Gabriel of Daniel 8:16 and the Michael of Daniel 10:21 angels? A negative answer is implied by the absence of the term *angel* (מלאך) from their descriptions. Gabriel is called "a holy one" (אחד קדוש; 8: 13); Michael is "your prince" (שרכם). But the portrayal of Gabriel as the one who speaks to Daniel recalls Zech 2:2–3, which features an angel who talks to the prophet. This parallel and the functions Gabriel and Michael perform suggest but do not confirm their angelic identities.

Finally, the boundaries between angels and God are sometimes indistinct. While it is often clear that an angel acts in God's name, two factors cause

---

[14]Newsom, "Angels," 249. For summaries of scholarship, see Heidt, *Angelology*, 69; Licht, "Angel, angels [מלאך, מלאכים]"; Volkmar Hirth, *Gottes Boten im Alten Testament* (Theologische Arbeiten 32; Berlin: Evangelische Verlaganstalt, 1975), 25–31.

[15]Cf. von Rad, "Angel [מלאך]," 79; Newsom, "Angels," 249.

confusion. One is the apparent interchangeability of the first and third person forms of address. Occasionally, both forms occur within a single speech, as in Gen 21:17–18, in which God hears Ishmael's voice and an angel calls to Hagar from heaven to tell her that "God has heard the voice of the boy where he is" and "I [presumably God] will make a great nation of him." A second is the fact that God frequently appears interchangeably with or alongside his angel. In many cases, there are no narrative indications that the speaker has changed from one to the other. In Exod 3:2, it is an angel who appears to Moses in the burning bush, but in Exod 3:4 it is God who calls to him out of the bush.

These areas of indeterminacy might be attributed to the whim—or perhaps the carelessness—of the narrator or to the vagaries of the redactional process.[16] But a significant number of angel stories play on these confusions. Such stories frequently portray the difficulties faced by a human character in identifying correctly his or her angelic adversary or conversation partner. We now look in more detail at the different ways in which angels are perceived by the characters they encounter.

Angel Not Perceived by a Human (Num 22:22–35)

At one end of the spectrum is the angel who is not perceptible to human beings. Numbers 22:1–21 describes the efforts of Balak, the king of Moab, to hire Balaam, a non-Israelite prophet-diviner, to curse the Israelites, in an attempt to drive them from the land (22:6). On God's command, Balaam initially refuses (22:12). After being further implored, he reconsiders (22:19). God consents, on the condition that Balaam does only as God commands (22:20), and Balaam sets off with the Moabite officials (22:21).

But after Balaam's departure, God becomes angry and places an angel in Balaam's way. This angel is invisible to Balaam but not to the ass upon which Balaam is seated. Three times the angel "with a drawn sword in his hand," blocks the donkey's path, causing it to swerve or otherwise avoid the angel. Three times Balaam responds by beating the donkey. Finally, "the LORD opened the mouth of the donkey" (22:28)[17]; the donkey demands an explanation for his violent behavior, unaware that Balaam has been unable to see the angel. Balaam, incensed but apparently not surprised by the donkey's newfound speaking abilities, declares that if he had a sword he would kill her. This declaration conjures up the image of the angel with drawn sword who had frightened the donkey

---

[16]Eugene Maly ("Genesis," in *The Jerome Bible Commentary*, ed. Raymond E. Brown, et al. [Englewood Cliffs, N.J.: Prentice-Hall, 1968], 21), for example, comments that the uncertainty surrounding the number of guests and their identity in Genesis 18 is clear evidence that a number of independent traditions have been reworked.

[17]Apparently the narrator of this story, unlike that of Genesis 3, had to explain to his reader how it could be that an animal could speak.

in the first place. Calling upon their shared history, the ass forces him to acknowledge that his rash response was not warranted by past experience (22: 30).

The reason for the donkey's words is revealed not by the ass but by the Lord, who "opened the eyes of Balaam" so that he could see the angel for himself (22:31). The angel provides a fulsome explanation for the donkey's behavior and chastisement for Balaam's violent response. Far from punishing her, the angel declares, Balaam should thank his donkey for saving his life. "If it had not turned away from me, surely just now I would have killed you and let it live" (22:33). Most important, the angel conveys God's displeasure at Balaam's mission. When Balaam offers to turn back, the angel permits him to continue, "but speak only what I tell you to speak" (22:35).

This story presents some of the familiar aspects of the angel's typified role. The angel is a warrior, with his sword drawn, who acts on God's behalf as Balaam's adversary to convey his will to Balaam (22:22, 32). As an advocate for Israel, the angel will stand in the way of a non-Israelite about to take an action that might be detrimental to Israel's fortunes. Initially, the very presence of Balaam's adversary is not apparent to him at all. Once seen, however, the adversary's identity as an angel of the Lord is clear. The reader is not told in what form the donkey and later Balaam sees the angel, but it is significant that neither mistakes the angel for a man or other being. The angel bears some resemblance, however, to a human being: He holds a sword in his hand, stands upon the road and speaks intelligibly. More important than the form of the angel is the issue of perception—who can see the angel and who cannot—and the relationship between this perceptive power and other hierarchies of power within the story.

The angel concretizes a power struggle on two levels: between Balaam and his donkey and between God and Balaam. Balaam and his donkey are different species that exist in an interdependent relationship. He provides her with food and shelter; she provides him with transportation and cartage. God and Balaam are also of different species, so to speak. Nevertheless, they, too, are interdependent, though Balaam is not even an Israelite. God oversees Balaam's mission and gives him advice; Balaam provides God with service by prophesying God's words. The story revolves around the power that Balaam wields in each particular relationship. Balaam's power over the donkey is expressed in his expectation of her obedience. Her disobedience to Balaam is caused by her bending to God's will in the form of the angel. Meanwhile, God is standing ready to beat Balaam for future disobedience, by the sword of the angel standing at the wayside.

The two narrative threads are not completely parallel, however. Through divine intervention, the donkey becomes the role model for her human master. Though he ostensibly has power over her, she is superior to him in her ability to see the angel. It requires God to provide Balaam, that seer of repute, with the same ability to see as his donkey has in this story. Moreover, the donkey submits to divine authority after merely seeing the angel, whereas Balaam must be browbeaten with threats before he fully accepts the dictates of God.

The resolution of the story is contained in the angel's words on God's behalf: "Go with the men; but speak only what I tell you to speak" (Num 22: 35). Yet this conclusion does not advance the plot, for it had been stated and accepted in Balaam's second night vision on the eve of his departure (20:20–21). Rather, it demonstrates through humor the divine stake in and control over the lives and abilities of God's creatures, through the play of perceptions and relationships.[18] Here as in the other stories, the angel's anonymity draws attention to his angelic role as God's agent. It also marks his alliance with the donkey, who is similarly anonymous and nonhuman but possesses the human traits of speech, reason, and discernment, more so than the sole human character in the episode.

Angel Perceived as Man

By Manoah (Judges 13)

Judges 13 allows the reader to observe the process by which the human characters, Manoah and his wife, come to recognize the angelic identity of their visitor. The narrator consistently refers to the being whom Manoah and his wife encounter as an angel of God (13:3, 9, 13, 15–18, 20, 21). The sole exception is 13:11a, in which the narrator, speaking from Manoah's perspective, calls the angel "the man." In contrast, Manoah and his wife speak of him as a "man of God," איש אלהים (13:6, 8), or simply "the man," האיש (13:10, 11b). Thus the reader, privy to the "inside information" conveyed by the narrator, watches the characters struggle to recognize the "man's" true identity.[19]

Neither Manoah nor his wife fully realizes the identity of the angel at the

---

[18]On this story see George W. Coats, "The Way of Obedience: Traditio-Historical and Hermeneutical Reflections on the Balaam Story," *Semeia* 24 (1982): 53–79; Peggy L. Day, *An Adversary in Heaven: Satan in the Hebrew Bible* (HSM 43; Atlanta: Scholars Press, 1988); Dennis T. Olson, *The Death of the Old and the Birth of the New: The Framework of the Book of Numbers and the Pentateuch* (BJS 71; Chico, Calif.: Scholars Press, 1985).

[19]See Boling, *Judges*, 219, 222. A similar situation is found in many other biblical stories. See, for example, Judg 6:11, in which Gideon's visitor is identified by the narrator as an angel and, later, as the Lord (6:14, 16). Gideon appears to have an inkling of his visitor's identity (6:15) but does not know for certain until 6:22, after witnessing the theophany in 6:20–21. Similarly, in Genesis 18, the narrator refers to at least one of Abraham's visitors as the Lord (18:1), though when the event is reported from Abraham's point of view, the reference is to three men (18:2). In Abraham's dispute with the Lord over the destruction of Sodom and Gomorrah, it is clear that Abraham is aware of the identity of his partner in dialogue (18:22–33).

outset. The angel appears in human form to the woman, announces the future conception and birth of Samson and prophesies his role as the one who will begin the liberation of the Israelites from the Philistines (13:1–5). After Manoah beseeches God for another visit, the angel reappears to the woman, who leads her husband to him. The angel reiterates his message and ascends to heaven in the flame of the sacrifice he has asked Manoah to provide. This ascent convinces Manoah that he has seen God. Rather than celebrating and commemorating this knowledge, Manoah now fears death. He is reassured by his wife who patiently explains, "If the LORD had meant to kill us, he would not have accepted a burnt offering and a grain offering at our hands, or shown us all these things, or now announced to us such things as these" (13:23).

To readers impatient for certainty, the experience of Manoah might serve only to emphasize the need for the proper name in constructing the identity of the other. But even this tentative assertion is overturned by the biblical text itself. Judges 13 hints that, although anonymity obscures the angel's identity in the eyes of Manoah, it reveals his nature to another more perceptive than this man. The wife of Manoah has questioned her visitor's apparently human identity from the outset. For "his appearance was like that of an angel of God, most awe-inspiring; *I did not ask him where he came from,* and *he did not tell me his name*" (13:6; emphasis added). Her intuition of his angelic nature apparently keeps her from inquiring as to his provenance (intimating a belief that the origins of angels are not to be known) and makes his failure to identify himself by name comprehensible to her. To this woman, in contrast to her husband, the man's anonymity is a marker of identity.

The anonymity of angels simultaneously obscures the individual identity of the angel and reveals it. Manoah's eager request, "What is your name, so that we may honor you when your words come true?" (13:17) is rebuffed by the angel, who says to him, "Why do you ask my name? It is too wonderful" (13:18). In the first instance, this emphatic response indicates that the names of angels are not to be known, a point that emphasizes the woman's foresight in not requesting the "man's" name at their initial encounter (13:6). But at the same time, the absence of the name itself signifies a being whose name is not to be divulged because of his connection to the divine.

The characterization of the angel therefore draws a direct connection between his anonymity and his identity. It is because he is an angel of God that humans are not to know his name. The angel stands in a fairly clear and unambiguous relationship with Manoah and Samson. His primary connection, however elusive, is with the woman. On the one hand, he acts the straightforward part of the annunciating angel. On the other hand, as we noted earlier, the story hints at the possibility of a more intimate encounter. In this respect, the description of this angel differs from that of his biblical counterparts but calls to mind the sons of God who coupled with the daughters of men (Gen 6: 1–4).

By Jacob (Gen 32:25–33)

Like Manoah, Jacob attempts to identify an anonymous individual. The story of Jacob's encounter with a mysterious assailant at the Jabbok River does not contain the word *angel*. Jacob initially perceives his wrestling partner to be a man. He comes to understand his experience as an encounter with God and expresses surprise at his own survival (32:31). The identity of the assailant is hidden not only from the main characters but also from the reader; the narrator refers to the being as "the man" throughout.

The man's initial behavior is combative, perhaps even hostile. He attacks Jacob at night (32:23) and then puts Jacob's hip out of joint before acknowledging defeat (32:26). In 32:27, the man asks to be released, for day is breaking. Jacob, having won the wrestling match, exacts a blessing from the man in exchange for release. The man does not comply immediately. Rather, he requests Jacob's name and then changes it: "You shall no longer be called Jacob, but Israel, for you have striven with God and with humans, and have prevailed" (32:28; 32:29 in Hebrew).[20]

There are two aspects to this nonblessing. First, it raises questions about the assailant's identity. The speech-act which Jacob's name change entails is elsewhere associated with God, suggesting that the assailant may, in fact, have been God. Second, the rationale for the name change seems unrelated to the name itself but reflects on the wrestling match Jacob has just won. It remains unclear as to whether Jacob's success represents his prevailing over humans— since the man is in human form—or with God, either directly or through an angel. The general impression, however, is that the man either is or represents the divinity. The issue is resolved in inner-biblical exegesis: Hos 12:4 states that "[Jacob] strove with the angel and prevailed."[21]

Having given the assailant his name, Jacob asks for the same in return: "Please tell me your name" (הגידה־נא שמך; 32:30; 32:29 in NRSV). Perhaps this request is an attempt at mutuality; after all, Jacob has won the match on equal terms and is now asking for reciprocity of knowledge. But the man demurs: "Why is it that you ask my name?" (למה זה תשאל לשמי; 32:30; 32:29 in NRSV). He then—finally—blesses Jacob and departs. This rebuff is not an obstacle to Jacob's construction of the man's identity but convinces him that he has seen God face to face and survived (32:30).[22] He names the location Peniel in honor of this event, just as he has named other locations—Bethel (28:19), Mahanaim (32:2)—at which he had seen manifestations of the divine presence.

---

[20]An alternate translation refers to "divine and human beings." The Hebrew אלהים can be read either as an epithet for God or more generally as "divine beings."

[21]*NJPS*: "an angel."

[22]This formulation, however, does not necessarily denote an encounter with an angel. Cf. Gen 33:10, in which Jacob says that seeing Esau's face is like seeing the face of God.

The precise meaning of the passage is contested. Speiser suggests that this encounter was a test of Jacob's fitness for the larger tasks that lay ahead.[23] Von Rad points out the story's similarities to the non-Israelite sagas in which the gods, spirits, or demons attack a man, who then extorts something of their identity, their strength, and their secret; in these stories, as in Genesis 32, the superhuman figures must disappear by morning.[24] Other scholars interpret the story as a rite of passage for Jacob, signifying his ascent as respected leader of the tribe,[25] or as a statement of covenantal relationship, according to which Yahweh has the exclusive right to attack Israel or to bless it.[26] Any or all of these suggestions may be defended within the larger context of the Genesis narrative.

Two points are relevant regarding anonymity. First, Jacob interprets his encounter as a face-to-face vision of the divine. Yet the nocturnal setting and the physicality of their contact suggest that touch and not sight is the medium of Jacob's encounter. Second, anonymity is a token in the power struggle between Jacob and the combatant. The story implies a parallel between the physical struggle and the attempt to wrest and manipulate the name of the other. Each party to the physical combat is initially (apparently) anonymous to the other.[27] The parity is broken by Jacob's victory over the assailant. The latter's discovery of and revision to Jacob's name restores the upper hand to him: He has knowledge of Jacob's identity and has taken a fundamental role in its redefinition. Jacob's request for the man's name is similarly an attempt to ascertain his identity, which, if successful, would have returned the balance of power to him. The man's rebuff and his blessing solidify the latter's superior position. Yet Jacob is satisfied, having constructed an identity for the man as God.

By Joshua (Josh 5:13–15)

This story, too, creates ambiguity regarding the identity of an unnamed superhuman figure. While near Jericho, at some unspecified time, Joshua looks up to see a man standing before him, drawn sword in hand (5:13). The man does not reveal his name, nor does Joshua ask directly. Joshua's main concern is not the man's individual identity, but simply his loyalty: "Are you for us or against us?" (5:13; translation mine). In response, the man identifies himself as the captain of the Lord's army, that is, the divine counterpart of Joshua, who

---

[23]*Genesis*, 257.

[24]*Genesis*, 321. This passage has some similarities to Exod 4:24–26, in which "the Lord met [Moses] and tried to kill him" but is protected by Zipporah, who circumcised her son and touched Moses' feet with the foreskin.

[25]Speiser, *Genesis*, 256–57.

[26]Heather A. McKay, "Jacob Makes It across the Jabbok," *JSOT* 38 (1987): 7, 9.

[27]It is conceivable that the assailant already knew Jacob's name and identity; the question in this case would not be a simple request for information but a prelude to the change in Jacob's name and status.

is the captain of Israel's army. This declaration convinces Joshua of the man's superhuman identity; he throws himself to the ground face down and asks, "What do you command your servant, my lord?" (5:14).[28] The captain bids Joshua to remove his sandals because he is standing on holy land, an injunction Joshua immediately obeys.

In this passage, as in Genesis 32, the designation *angel* (מלאך) does not appear. But the man Joshua encounters bears a striking similarity to some of the angels already encountered.[29] Like the angel who interferes with Balaam's journey, the Lord's captain stands with drawn sword. Like the angels seen by Jacob at Bethel and Mahanaim and by Moses at the burning bush, the man identifies sacred space and thereby the presence of God. And like the angel who assisted the Israelites throughout the exodus event and thereafter, he is a warrior who leads battle on behalf of Israel and safeguards God's interests within Israel. Yet despite all this, the absence of the role designation leaves open the possibility that this is some other sort of being altogether. The dramatic act with which Joshua responds to the man's self-identification as the captain of God's army does not confirm his identity. It does reveal, however, Joshua's perception of his visitor as a divine agent through whom the Lord himself may be perceived.

Angel Perceived as God

By the Pregnant Hagar (Gen 16:7–14)

Genesis 16 depicts the banishment of the pregnant Hagar from the household of Abram and Sarai. An angel of the Lord finds her by a spring in the wilderness, calls her by name and role ("Hagar, slave-girl of Sarai"), and inquires about her actions (16:7–8). The angel then directs her to return and submit to Sarai (16:9), prophesies a multitude of descendants (16:10), announces the imminent birth of her first descendant, and describes his life journey. According to the angel, Hagar's son, Ishmael:

> shall be a wild ass of a man,
> with his hand against everyone,
>   and everyone's hand against him;
> and he shall live at odds with all his kin.(16:12)

Hagar responds by naming "the LORD who spoke to her, 'You are El-roi'; for she said, 'Have I really seen God and remained alive after seeing him?' "

---

[28]According to Boling (*Joshua* [AB 6; New York, Doubleday, 1975], 196), Joshua's bravery in approaching the warrior is paired with a slowness of discernment.

[29]Boling (*Joshua*, 198) refers to this figure as an angel, despite the absence of the term מלאך.

(16:13). This divine appellation is incorporated into the name of the well where these events occurred, Beer-lahai-roi ("well of the Living One who sees me"; 16:14).

The angel plays the role of prophet, conveying God's intentions and his words to Hagar. Although the prophecy pertains to her specific situation, it has broader implications in light of the covenant motif that has dominated Genesis to this point. The circumstances and literary context of Hagar's pregnancy, arranged by Sarai in an attempt to acquire offspring (16:2), might suggest that Hagar is the one through whom God's covenantal promises to Abram will be fulfilled. The angel's communique in 16:10, "I will so greatly multiply your offspring that they cannot be counted for multitude," echoes God's covenantal promises to Abram in Gen 12:2 and 15:5. The prophecy that Ishmael will be at odds with his kin, however, does not fit with the positive tone of the covenantal promises to Abram, that in him all families will be blessed (12:3) and that his offspring shall inherit the land (15:18). This contrast suggests that the covenant hinted at in the angel's words to Hagar is not the one that God had established with Abram.

The reliability of the angel's prophecy is called into question, however, by later events as narrated in Genesis. For a man at odds with all his kin, Ishmael shows a remarkable degree of compliance with family obligations. He returns to bury Abraham, an act in which he cooperates with his brother Isaac (25:9), and he gives his daughter (named Mahalath in 28:9 and Basemath in 36:3) in marriage to Esau. Though he lives in the wilderness (21:20–21), he is not "a wild ass of a man," at least with respect to the social conventions related to mortality and marriage.

The discrepancies between the prophecy and future events, however, are not evident to Hagar or acknowledged by the narrator. According to 16:13, both take the prophecy as God's words. Hagar herself is moved to name the Lord "El-roi" (16:13), meaning "God who sees" or the "God of seeing." Her explanation of this name is difficult, however. The Hebrew הגם הלם ראיתי אחרי ראי is translated variously as "Have I really seen God and remained alive after seeing him?" (NRSV) or "Have I not gone on seeing after He saw me!" (NJPSV). In either case, the varied repetition of the verb *see* draws attention to the absence of any indication within the story itself that she had, in fact, seen either the angel or God. The angel finds her (ימצאה) and speaks with her, but her perceptions of him are not recounted. Her act of naming the Lord, however, testifies to her interpretation of this encounter and its significance.[30]

---

[30]Von Rad (*Genesis*, 193–94) considers the angel of the Lord here to be God in human form. In his words, "this strange shift between a divine and a human subject . . . is the intended result of an apparently intensive inner revision of very old traditions . . . [which] told quite directly of extremely spectacular divine appearances at definite places. Those

By Hagar with Ishmael (Gen 21:17–19)

Similar motifs appear in Hagar's second encounter with an angel. Hagar has been banished again from the household of Abram and Sarai, now called Abraham and Sarah (17:5, 15). This time she must leave, along with her son Ishmael. Hagar weeps over the impending death of the boy. God hears the boy's cry, and an angel of the Lord (מלאך אלהים) calls from heaven with reassurances that "God heard the voice of the boy" and with instructions to lift the boy up and hold him tight, "for I will make a great nation of him" (21:17–18). God then opens Hagar's eyes to see a well, and she saves her son with its water.

Here, too, the angel acts as God's prophet, communicating God's words in both the third and first persons. But the angel does not act alone as God's representative, for, as the narrator states, God himself opens Hagar's eyes to see the well. This divine activity modifies the absoluteness and even the necessity of the angel's role as God's agent. Hagar's encounter with the divine is therefore twofold: She hears God's words through the voice of the angel and experiences God's action in her newfound ability to see the well.

The two passages featuring Hagar maintain a measure of differentiation between the Lord and his angel. God is the authority and power whose instructions and prophecies are conveyed to human beings by his messenger. But this clarity is blurred at two points. The first is Hagar's assertion that her auditory encounter with the angel amounts to seeing and being seen by the Lord. The second concerns the activity of both God and the angel in ensuring Ishmael's survival. The latter point raises the question of why divine communication to people is mediated by an angel if God himself can enter the scene directly.

Angel as Man and God

By Abraham and Lot (Genesis 18–19)

The issue of differentiation between God and angels emerges forcefully in Genesis 18–19. The difficulty is introduced in the very first words of the episode. In Gen 18:1, the narrator declares, "The LORD appeared to Abraham [literally: him] by the oaks of Mamre, as he sat at the entrance of his tent in the heat of the day." What *Abraham* saw, however, was a group of "three men standing near him" (שלשה אנשים; 18:2). The uncertainty created by the apparent contradiction between what really happened (according to the narrator) and what Abraham perceived continues in Abraham's gracious invitation: "My lord, if I find favor with you, do not pass by your servant" (18:2).

---

who came later . . . understood it in such a way that not Yahweh but Yahweh's angel appeared."

This invitation poses two problems. The first concerns the number of visitors entertained by Abraham. Depending upon its vocalization, אדני can denote "my lords" (*NJPSV*), "my lord" (NRSV), or "my (divine) Lord."[31] This range of possibilities allows for narrative irony: the "lord(s)" whom Abraham addresses so politely is (are), in fact, the Lord, as the reader already knows and as Abraham will soon discover. The Masoretic choice of the first option creates a second problem: In the remainder of the verse, Abraham addresses his visitor(s) in the second person singular (e.g., תעבר, עבדך, עיניך). This contradiction can be harmonized, as Speiser has done, by suggesting that Abraham turns to one of the three as leader in 18:2 while including all three out of courtesy in 18: 4–5.[32] But even such harmonization does not mask the dissonance among the narrator's simple assertion of a visit by the Lord, the narrator's assertion that Abraham saw three men, and Abraham's own confusing comments regarding their number. The visitors' acceptance of Abraham's hospitality does nothing to challenge his perception that they are human beings.

Throughout the detailed description of the offer and preparation of the meal (Gen 18:3–8), the visitors speak in concert and are spoken of in the plural. A shift occurs between 18:9 and 18:10. In 18:9 "they" inquire as to Sarah's presence. After being told that she is in the tent, "one" prophesies: "I will surely return to you in due season, and your wife Sarah shall have a son" (Gen 18:10). In announcing the impending birth, this speech signals a change in theme, from hospitality to annunciation. The promise of a son to Sarah fills the void left by the unexpected pronouncement to Hagar in Genesis 16 concerning the fate of Abraham's erstwhile heir. It also begins to close the gap between the narrator's identification of the Lord as the one appearing to Abraham and Abraham's initial ignorance of the provenance and identity of his visitors.

The visitor's prophecy of the impending conception and birth is repeated in 18:13–14 by the Lord, who also queries Abraham as to Sarah's incredulous response to the prophecy in 18:10–12. The near-verbatim repetition of the prophecy by a speech identified as God's (שוב אשוב אליך) creates confusion as to the identity of the one who had proclaimed it the first time. Is the speaker of 18:10 also the Lord? Or is the Lord repeating the words of one of the angels? These questions relate to a more fundamental confusion: Is the Lord one of the visitors, an additional visitor, or is he somehow made manifest in the three acting as one?[33]

---

[31]Speiser (*Genesis*, 129) suggests that present pointing of אדני is probably influenced by the explicit mention of Yahweh in v. 1.

[32]*Genesis*, 129.

[33]In his fourth homily on Genesis, Origen equates all three men with the Lord, though he does not explicitly develop a trinitarian interpretation in this context. Origen, *Homilies*

Support for the view that the Lord is one of the three visitors is found in the continuation of the story. In 18:16, the narrator indicates that the men (האנשים), in unspecified number, set out from Abraham's abode, while the Lord stayed behind to inform Abraham of his plans to destroy Sodom and Gomorrah. After heated negotiation with Abraham over the necessary number of righteous people required to save the cities, "the LORD went his way . . . and Abraham returned to his place" (18:33). Immediately thereafter, "two angels" (שני מלאכים) appear to Lot in Sodom (19:1). It would seem that the third of Abraham's visitors was the Lord, who stayed behind. This conclusion also suggests that it is this particular visitor who is the Lord of 18:1.

The setting of Genesis 19 parallels that of the previous chapter. Lot is sitting at the gateway of his dwelling in Sodom, just as Abraham was sitting at the entrance to his abode. Like Abraham, Lot offers hospitality, in similar language, referring to his visitors as אדני; unlike 18:3, the vocalization in 19:2 simply implies a masculine plural addressee. And, like Abraham, Lot apparently simply perceives the strangers as men. The readers know differently, however, thanks to the narrator, who has already designated them as angels (19:1). In contrast to their behavior with Abraham, however, the visitors initially refuse Lot's hospitality, finally relenting only after he has implored them strongly (19:3).

The Sodomites, too, perceive the visitors as men. Whereas Lot presses his hospitality on them, the Sodomites demand access to Lot's guests "that we may know them" (19:5). Lot's concern for his visitors impels him to offer his two daughters instead. The angels forestall violence by bringing Lot inside the house and striking the men outside with blindness (19:10–11). Although the narrator at this point refers to them as men, their knowledge of the events outside the door and their ability to perform miracles are consistent with the angelic role with which they have been identified in 19:1.

At this point, the two reveal their commission to Lot: They are to destroy Sodom but save Lot and his family (19:12–13). Lot believes his visitors' words and urges his family to leave, but his sons-in-law are skeptical. In the morning, the angels—now referred to as such—urge Lot on (19:15). In the face of his procrastination, they finally seize Lot and his wife and daughters, bring them out of the city and leave them there, instructing them to flee without looking back (19:16–17). Lot's response, using the polite language with which he has addressed them throughout, is to plead that he and his family not be forced to remain there but that they be allowed to go to a city in the vicinity (19:20). This conclusion to the episode maintains inconsistency in the ways in which both Lot and the narrator refer to the visitors. In 19:18, Lot refers to them as

---

on Genesis and Exodus, trans. Ronald E. Heine (Fathers of the Church, 71; Washington: Catholic University of America, 1981), 108.

אֲדֹנָי, now pointed to mean "my Lord," and, like Abraham in Gen. 18:3, uses the second person singular.[34] In 19:21, the narrator also switches to the singular, in referring to only one who responds favorably to Lot's request: "he said to him" (וַיֹּאמֶר אֵלָיו). Finally, in 19:24, it is the Lord who is said to have "rained on Sodom and Gomorrah sulfur and fire . . . out of heaven."[35]

In this lengthy episode, the visitors perform aspects of the typical angelic role: They prophesy the destruction of the cities and the impending conception and birth of a son to Abraham and Sarah. The stories also reveal that angels can take human form and perform minor miracles, such as striking the Sodomites blind. But uncertainties remain. Do angels eat and drink or not? Does their ready acceptance of Abraham's hospitality and reluctant acquiescence to that offered by Lot reflect a judgment of the relative status of Abraham and Lot vis-à-vis God or some aspect of their angelic identity? Most important, the varying designations in Genesis 18–19 confound attempts to identify the three visitors. Indistinctness pertains not only to the relationship between the Lord and the visitors but also to the two angels, who almost always act in concert and are thus only minimally differentiated from one another. The beginning of Genesis 19 momentarily resolves the difficulties of Genesis 18 by specifying two angels, thereby implying that the third visitor to Abraham's tent was the Lord. But the final reference to the Lord as the one who destroys the two cities implies that he is performing the duties that he had earlier relegated to the angels. The contradictions can be harmonized by arguing that the narrator does not mean that the Lord himself rained destruction upon the cities but only that he authorized this destruction. Nevertheless, this harmonizing move may be resisted and the ambiguities permitted to stand.

The anonymity of the angels contributes greatly to the confusion surrounding the nature of the visitors, their number, their identities, and their relationship to one another. Proper names for all visitors would have gone some distance in resolving these problems, as later re-tellers of the story, including Jewish and Christian commentators, recognized.[36] The contrast between the definite naming of the Lord and the indefiniteness of the angels is illusory in light of angels' ability to speak and act in God's name. And the question remains: If God can enter the human realm to do these things himself, why are angels needed? Does it make a difference whether God is perceived directly or through

---

[34]The NRSV translates אֲדֹנָי here as "my lords," implying the use of the second person plural throughout this speech, though the *BHS*/MT vocalize the word as singular. In the use of the expression "your servant has found favor with you" (מָצָא עַבְדְּךָ חֵן בְּעֵינֶיךָ), 19:19 echoes 18:3 very strongly.

[35]For a comparison to the flood story, see Claus Westermann, *Genesis: An Introduction* (Minneapolis: Fortress, 1992), 52.

[36]The angels are named Michael, Gabriel, and Raphael in b. Baba Mezia 86b; Gen. Rab. 50:2.

his angels? Their anonymity in any case is consistent with their lack of unique individuation; they speak in concert or in God's name and have no personalities to speak of.

By Gideon (Judg 6:11–40)

Similar confusion appears in Gideon's encounter with an angel. At the outset of Judges 6, the Israelites are suffering under Midianite rule, a situation the narrator attributes to the Lord's punishment for Israelite evildoing (6:1). When the people cry out to the Lord after seven years of oppression, the Lord responds both directly and through two agents. The first is a prophet, who, speaking in the Lord's name, reiterates the exodus history, the monotheistic imperative, and the Israelites' violation thereof (6:8–10). The second is the angel of the Lord, who does not appear to the Israelites as a whole but to Gideon, who was engaged in hiding wheat from the Midianites (6:11).

Gideon's story has affinities with both Genesis 18 and Exodus 3. Like Abraham's visitors in Genesis 18, the angel appears unexpectedly under an oak tree. As in Exodus 3, the angel is involved in the recruitment of an unsuspecting Israelite for a major leadership role in liberating the Israelites from oppression. In all three stories, the angel not only speaks the Lord's words but also heralds the Lord's presence.

Gideon's angel is nowhere called a man. Rather, he is consistently designated "angel" by the narrator. It takes some time, however, for Gideon to recognize him as such. The angel greets Gideon by proclaiming, "The LORD is with you, you mighty warrior" (6:12). This greeting conveys the Lord's approval of Gideon, foreshadows Gideon's future role in the liberation of his people, and implies its success.[37] Gideon's response, however, relates to none of these aspects. Rather, he takes the angel's singular word עמך ("with you") as a collective reference to Israel and sets the conversation in the context of Israel's plight. From Gideon's perspective, the Lord is not with Israel but has cast them off (6:13).

Gideon's initial perception of the angel is difficult to gauge; his use of the polite form of address אדני carries the same ambiguity here as it does in Genesis 18 and 19. But in 6:14 the Lord enters the picture. The abruptness of this entry raises the same question as in Genesis 18: What is the relationship between the Lord and the angel? The story provides no clues for addressing this question. The Lord formally commissions Gideon to deliver Israel from the Midianites; Gideon appears oblivious to this change, although the continued use of the address אדני carries the possibility that he does recognize the Lord.

Like Moses before him, Gideon attempts to avoid the commission by denying his ability to fulfill it (6:15). The Lord identifies himself to Gideon by

---

[37]Cf. Judg 6:16, in which the Lord promises Gideon: "But I will be with you, and you shall strike down the Midianites, every one of them."

using a variant of the divine name that is reminiscent of God's self-identification in Exod 3:14 (אהיה; 6:16). The Lord promises that he will aid Gideon and bring him victory against the Midianites. Gideon then devises a test to authenticate the identity of his dialogue partner and hence assess the validity of the commission (6:17). The Lord agrees to wait until Gideon's return (6:18). The narrator then details Gideon's preparation and presentation of meat, broth, and unleavened cakes.

The angel now reappears as Gideon's dialogue partner. The angel instructs Gideon to put the cakes on a rock and pour out the broth. After this, "the angel of the LORD reached out the tip of the staff that was in his hand, and touched the meat and the unleavened cakes; and fire sprang up from the rock and consumed the meat and the unleavened cakes; and the angel of the LORD vanished from his sight" (6:21). The angel's pyrotechnic display of miraculous sacrifice satisfies Gideon that he has, indeed, seen the angel of the Lord.

He begs the Lord for help, apparently overcome with awe at this realization (6:22). The Lord reassures him that he shall not die (6:23). Gideon, like others who have encountered angels, builds an altar to the Lord and names it. The name, "The LORD is peace" (יהוה שלום; 6:24), reflects the terms of their initial encounter and also anticipates a satisfactory conclusion to Gideon's military career. From that point on, communication between Gideon and the Lord remains close, direct, and unmediated. Nevertheless, the story conditions, if only slightly, the reliability of God's words and promises of military success. Gideon does, indeed, succeed in liberating the Israelites from Midianite rule (8:28), but along the way he strays into idolatrous practices (8:27). Nevertheless, the narrator's final assessment of Gideon focuses on "all the good that he had done to Israel" (8:35).

This story completely blurs the boundaries between the angel and the Lord, a blurring aided by the angel's anonymity. They each speak and act in the Lord's name, suggesting either that they are one and the same or that they are both present on the scene. Perhaps Gideon is unknowingly caught up in a three-way conversation, while the hearers of the story relate the visible messenger to his invisible commander. Gideon's request for a sign follows upon his first awareness that he has encountered the Lord, but the successful execution of the sign convinces him that he has seen the angel of the Lord. This contrasts with Hagar, who interpreted her encounter with an angel as a vision of the Lord. This recognition, however, attends the disappearance of the angel (6:21), at which point Gideon is left only with the Lord.

Insofar as the distinctions between angels and men are not immediately visible to other biblical characters or to their readers, they permit narrative play on the fine line between appearance and reality. Angels may be present even when we cannot see them; angels may appear in the form of a man and take on the attributes of physical strength, attractiveness, and sexuality, all of which are then recast once the angel's identity is revealed.

More difficult to account for is the blurring of the angelic and divine identities. Like other anonymous figures, angels move events along—for example, by showing Israel the way through the desert, assuring the survival of Ishmael and Isaac, and announcing the birth of Samson. Angels also help to highlight the personal traits of the characters alongside whom they act. Moses is responsive to angelic appearances in unusual vegetation; Balaam the seer is less perceptive than his beast of burden; Gideon is a hesitant leader. And certainly some stories imply a worldview in which human behavior and experiences are shaped by the divine will. Crucial events in the life of the individual and of the covenant community are seen as determined by God and enacted through a mediator. Human beings are dependent on God, who communicates with humankind in a variety of ways, both directly and through agents. These agents are not important for who they are in and of themselves, and the question of whether they have either name or identity is left open. Hence, just as human messengers convey information between two parties separated by physical distance, divine messengers allow communication between two parties—God and human beings—separated by metaphysical distance.

This hypothesis is undone, however, by the ongoing willingness of God to speak directly to the people and by the people's persistence in seeing the divine in the appearance of his angel. Although the angel is a mouthpiece of God, God does not hesitate to speak directly. The angel substitutes for God and also acts alongside God. The presence of the angel does not denote the absence of God or his distance from his people. The angel heralds and introduces God, thereby preparing the individual for a divine encounter; he also stands in for God, imparts his words, and guides his subjects.

It may be more appropriate to think about angels not as filling the theological need for a mediator but as a set of beings who, like servants, messengers, wise women, and prophets, were simply an accepted part of Israelite personal and historical experience, on the one hand, and an integral part of the divine realm on the other hand. As such, they needed narrative acknowledgment just as much as did the human dramatis personae. What results from their narrative portrayal is a sketch of the varied population of the heavenly arena and an outline of the integral and complex relationship between the divine and human realms as well as the angelic traffic between them. The inability of the reader to pin down the parameters of the divine-human relationship and the roles of angels within it maintains the sense of God's ultimate unpredictability and unknowability.

The anonymity of angels is absolute and impenetrable. It draws attention to their angelic role and its various aspects; angels are portrayed as prophets and warriors, agents of salvation and destruction, and instruments of personal and collective revelation, though never as women or as having attributes that are elsewhere strongly associated with women. Though the angels who visit Lot in Sodom exercise judgment on how to avert the gang rape of his daughters and convince the family as a whole to depart the doomed city, angels usually act only as God wishes them to and display no personal ambition or will.

These observations raise the possibility that, unlike all other unnamed characters, the angels of God do not have names or individual identities within the world implied by the narrative. Their names, identities, and superhuman abilities are derived from God, whose name lives within them.

8

⬖ ⬖ ⬖

Crossing the Threshold between Reader and Text

A NONYMITY can call into question the boundaries between characters, between the human and divine realms, and between the inhabitants of the heavens themselves. But there remains one last border, that between the reader outside the text and the characters firmly ensconced within. This chapter considers the impact of anonymity on this final frontier.

The distinction between reader and character would seem to be inherent in the reading situation itself. After all, the text as such is housed in a book, scroll, tape, or other medium; the reader may pick up or put down the text at will. But the physical distinctness of reader and text quickly loses clarity when we consider the complex imaginative exercise that reading entails. Indeed, the perennial power of narrative lies precisely in its ability to endow characters with a life that spills out from the narrative at the same time as it carries the reader imaginatively into the story itself.[1]

The open door between reader and text is like Jacob's ladder, which allows traffic between heaven and earth. Neither door nor ladder, however, dissolves the boundary between the two realms they connect. Despite their readiness to be transported by the magic of biblical narrative, readers frequently remain conscious of their linguistic, geographical, and chronological distance from the ancient Near Eastern context of the biblical texts and their original audiences.

[1]The power of fiction in the experience of the reader is emphasized by Joseph Gold, *Read for Your Life: Literature as a Life Support System* (Markham, Ont.: Fitzhenry and Whiteside, 1990).

Academic readers, and no doubt many others, attempt to silence their inner voices in order to listen to the text itself.[2] These readers maintain their separation from the text and its characters better to understand the place of these figures within the story world conjured up from the text.

The distinction between the reader and the characters within the text can be maintained, even if one does not silence one's inner voices and explicitly allows one's own concerns to enter into efforts to construct character. Readings of Lot's daughters and the Levite's concubine are sharpened by contemporary discussions of rape and abuse and the growing awareness that wives and children are not always safe within the domestic sphere.[3] Less tragic but nevertheless problematic for many women and men are issues of role conflict, in the competing demands of work and family and among the roles of child, parent, and spouse.

For me as an academic reader of the Bible, maintaining the borders between reader and text is not only comfortable but also necesary. These borders allow me to approach the text and its characters with sympathy, as I might a friend. In doing so, I accept and even welcome the fact that my own personal identity will influence the interaction and may, in turn, be altered by the characters I meet.

The Reader in the Text

Postmodern literature and theory, however, challenge us to go beyond such a stance to become a part of the text itself. We turn to Thomas Docherty for guidance as to what this process might entail. Docherty notes that identification with a particular character permits the reader's sympathy "but locks the reader within his or her discrete self."[4] Instead, Docherty suggests, the reader should read with empathy, which "allows the reader to read ecstatically, finding subjectivity always beyond his or her self."[5] Empathy understood in this way is made possible by postmodern fiction, which deliberately omits or rejects those aspects of mimetic characterization that lead the reader to posit a distinct and separate identity for the characters and to endow them with a past, present, and future in a story world analogous to some "real world" outside the text. The anonymity of character is one important aspect of this impersonal mode of

---

[2]So Yair Zakovitch, "Bible, Bible on the Wall," *Jerusalem Report*, January 26, 1995, p. 48, in a review of Judith A. Kates and Gail Twersky Reimer, eds., *Reading Ruth: Contemporary Women Reclaim a Sacred Story* (New York: Ballantine, 1994); and Christina Büchman and Celina Spiegel, eds., *Out of the Garden: Women Writers on the Bible* (New York: Ballantine, 1993).

[3]Trible, *Texts of Terror*, 1–2, 86.

[4]*Reading (Absent) Character*, 86.

[5]*Reading (Absent) Character*, 86.

characterization.[6] The empathy demanded by impersonality of character allows the reader to impersonate many subject positions. In doing so, the reader loses identity as a nameable self. The freedom of the reader is the release from his or her own subjectivity that is experienced in the endeavor to occupy the subject positions left vacant by anonymous characters. This attempt, in turn, permits the modification of the reader's sense of self.[7]

Biblical narrative, too, presents the reader with a series of subject positions, if only because its epic and episodic nature entails a long sequence of narratives and a seemingly endless set of narrative protagonists. Despite the patent presence of unnamed characters in both postmodern literature and biblical narrative, the two differ in the roles accorded to these figures. Even in the case of the bit players, anonymous characters in biblical narrative are not absent in the same way as are the characters in the novels of Robbe-Grillet and Saurraute. Unlike the unnamed figures in the *nouveau roman*, anonymous biblical characters, except for the occupants of the heavenly realm perhaps, *have* names and personal identity and history within the story world, even if we readers are not privy to them.

THE READER AS CHARACTER

Although the text does not require the dissolution of the boundary between reader and narrative, it does permit it. Or, to be more precise, there are readers who have given themselves permission to encounter unnamed characters in personal ways. Patricia J. Williams's "In Search of Pharaoh's Daughter"[8] provides an example. Williams tells of her adoption of a son one week after then–Vice President of the United States Dan Quayle denounced the fictional television character Murphy Brown for bearing a child as a single parent. Recounting the social resistance that she has experienced, even as a woman privileged with financial security, career, and time, Williams sews "a patchwork of tales" that echo in her mind after rereading the account of Moses' many mothers in Exod 2:1–10.[9] Above all, she resonates with the figure of Pharaoh's daughter, who likewise challenged, or perhaps merely ignored, social expectation by adopting a child without the participation of a husband but in community with others, across the boundaries of religion, class, and neighborhood.[10] The anecdote that concludes the patchwork is set at a glitzy New York Christmas party, where Williams mingles with a high-powered crowd. When a beautiful ex-model

---

[6]*Docherty, Reading (Absent) Character*, passim.
[7]*Docherty, Reading (Absent) Character*, 84–85.
[8]In Büchman and Spiegel, eds., *Out of the Garden*, 54–71.
[9]Williams, "Search," 56.
[10]Williams, "Search," 71.

expounds on the need for Third World countries to limit reproduction, Williams turns away, "too pained to respond, and push[es] through the Tom Wolfe-ish crowd, in search of Pharaoh's daughter."[11] Throughout the article, quotations from Exodus 1–2 alternate with stories of and reflections on contemporary urban life. By its conclusion, Williams has brought the unnamed daughter of Pharaoh into her own life not only as a paradigm but also as a sister whose companionship she actively seeks.

Williams has not so much freed herself from her subjectivity by her empathy with the Pharaoh's daughter as she has invited this unnamed adoptive mother into her own subjectivity. In doing so, Williams has declined the text's open offer to enter its narrative world and, instead, has brought one of its characters into her own. In this way, Williams illustrates that a personal encounter with an unnamed biblical character allows one not only to construct the character's identity but also to call upon the character in constructing one's own. No merging of character occurs, however. Williams still speaks of Pharaoh's daughter in the third person, as someone with an existence separate from herself.

It is a rare reader who truly overcomes the boundaries between reader and character.[12] Docherty acknowledges the difficulty of such a merging even in the reading of those postmodern novels that actively encourage it.[13] Perhaps the only biblical text in which such a merging is close to possible is the Song of Songs. Several factors contribute. One is the abundant use of first-person pronouns. In reading the text, the readers can take on the voices of the narrators and thereby become the lovers themselves: "As a lily among brambles, so is my love among maidens. As an apple tree among the trees of the wood, so is my beloved among young men" (Song 2:2–3). Also significant are the absence of a strong narrative component and the universality of the erotic theme. Because the text is only tenuously tied to a narrative context, the reader is not required to situate the text outside the universal realm of erotic love. The first-person narration, vivid language, and erotic theme dissolve the distance between reader and text. As Athalya Brenner describes:

> When I read the Song of Songs I do it, first and foremost and mainly, for the delight of translating the text into personal images. My senses are quickly involved, I can smell and see and taste and hear and yes, almost touch the

[11]Williams, "Search," 71.

[12]This state may be partially achieved by those who accept the text's value system as binding not only within the story world constructed from the text but also in the lives of the readers themselves. See, for example, Naomi H. Rosenblatt and Joshua Horwitz, *Wrestling with Angels: What the First Family of Genesis Teaches Us about Our Spiritual Identity, Sexuality, and Personal Relationships* (New York: Delacorte, 1995).

[13]*Reading (Absent) Character*, 71–72.

sometimes elusive referents of the written word. I am deeply affected by it, as I expect to be, in spite of the textual and linguistic difficulties, regardless of the basic problematics of this collection of love lyrics.[14]

READER AS NARRATOR

Song of Songs aside, it would seem that the boundaries between character and reader cannot easily be dissolved. The gate remains open for the reader to enter the text to meet the characters in their own environment and for the characters to emerge into the readers' own story. Strong as the links between reader and character might be, reading the Bible presupposes a second, more fundamental confrontation: that between the reader and the narrator. Although in some fictions the narrator is separate from the authorial voice, such is not the case in much of biblical narrative.[15] Indeed, the biblical narrator is not only the authorial voice but also the voice of divine authority. Whereas "the recent experimental novelist, in an age of scepticism and relativism, seems to feel that a writer must circumvent any suggestion that the fiction is being manipulated as it might be by a godlike author,"[16] our biblical narrator had no such compunctions. Though the Bible credits Moses with transmitting God's laws to Israel, it is the narrator who conveys them to the reader.

The narrator's authority is also experienced as his power over the reader. The narrator guides the reader to the correct—that is, the narrator's own— interpretation of events. The statement that Solomon's foreign wives led him to idolatry and hence to his downfall as king (1 Kgs 11:4), for example, is not a factual assertion but rather an expression of the narrator's disapproval of exogamy and his hypothesis concerning the reason for Solomon's royal failure.

In presenting the authoritative story, the narrator frequently suppresses alternative versions. The narrator exonerates Joseph and upholds his virtue while discrediting the version told by Potiphar's wife. This story, along with the paradigmatic vignettes such as the account of the man who violates the sabbath by gathering wood (Num 15:32–36), express the narrator's worldview and value system.

Finally, the narrator expresses his authority and power through his portrayal of character, including the quantity and type of information conveyed and the narrative context into which characters are placed. The narrator has the power over the name, number, and nature of narrative details. He can consign a character to the role of bit player or give the character a starring role in her or his

---

[14]"An Afterword," in *A Feminist Companion to the Song of Songs*, ed. Athalya Brenner (Sheffield: Sheffield Academic Press, 1993), 279.

[15]For an analysis of relationships among narrator, narratee, author, and reader, see Seymour Chatman, *Story and Discourse: Narrative Structure in Fiction and Film* (Ithaca, N.Y.: Cornell University Press, 1978), 147 and passim.

[16]Docherty, *Reading (Absent) Character*, 60.

very own pericope. Of course, we do not know whether the narrator tells us all he knows or whether he edits or fabricates and, if so, to what extent and in what ways. But certain texts suggest that the narrator knows more than he tells. In 1 Kgs 16:14, for example, the narrator refers the reader to "the Book of the Annals of the Kings of Israel" for the "rest of the acts of Elah, and all that he did." Although this does not demonstrate that the narrator knows the contents of those annals, at the very least he knows that his own account is incomplete.

In the face of the narrator's authority and power, the reader has two choices. Though they can be described separately, the reader is not bound to choose one over the other or to be consistent in her or his choice. The first is to accept the narrator's authority by remaining within the bounds of the narrator's story and accepting the value system as authoritative. The alternative is to resist the narrator's authority. This resistance might entail accepting the story of Potiphar's wife rather than Joseph's version as communicated and endorsed by the narrator, though it is only because the narrator has included her story that such resistance is possible at all. Resistance might also entail rejecting aspects of the narrator's value system, such as the proscription of homosexuality (Lev 18:22). In doing so, the reader overrides the authority of the narrator in favor of an alternate authority, such as the authority of Potiphar's wife to tell her own story, or validates a contemporary acceptance of homosexuality over against the limited forms of sexual expression espoused by the narrator.

Perhaps the most widespread form of resistance, however, concerns the narrator's portrayal of the characters. Readers from the immediate postbiblical period and onward have transgressed the narrator's silence concerning the names of anonymous characters by providing them with proper names of their own choosing. Ancient readers named Manoah's wife Eluma (*BibAnt*, 42), Zlelponith (b. Baba Batra 91a) and Hazlelponi (Numbers Rabbah 10:5). They identified the unnamed servant of Abraham charged with finding a wife for Isaac with, and as, the Damascan Eliezer, whom Abraham regretfully considers to be his probable heir in the absence of natural offspring (Gen 15:2–3).[17] More recently, similar moves have been made by a number of feminist critics. Alice Bach calls Potiphar's wife Met-em-enet[18]; Mieke Bal names Jephthah's daughter Bath (בת; daughter), Samson's Timnite wife Kallah (כלה; bride), and the Levite's concubine Beth (בית; house).[19] Bal explains why she has named the unnamed:

---

[17]This identification is also made by von Rad and other modern commentators, based on the description of the servant as being in charge of all that is Abraham's, a situation that would befit the heir-designate of Genesis 15. See von Rad, *Genesis*, 254. Certainly the name Eliezer is used in popular articles or articles by nonspecialists, e.g., Dahlia Haitovsky, "Rosso's 'Rebecca and Eliezer at the Well,' " *Gazette des beaux arts* 123 (1994): 111–22. For detailed discussion of postbiblical namings of biblical women, see Tal Ilan, "Biblical Women's Names in the Apocryphal Traditions," *JSP* 11 (1993): 3–67.

[18]"Breaking Free," passim.

[19]*Death*, 43, 78, 90.

To name this nameless character [Bath] is to violate the biblical text. Not to name her is to violate her with the text, endorsing the text's ideological position. I feel it is not only acceptable, but necessary, to take some critical distance from the alienating anonymity of the character without, however, losing sight of the structure of subjectivity that it signifies. Therefore, I will give this woman a name, but a name which stresses her dependence and her state. In order to make her speakable, I will call her what she most basically is: Jephthah's daughter, Bath-J, or briefer, Bath. Bath-J versus J: the inequality, the dependence, and yet the acknowledgment of this woman as a full character resounds in this name.[20]

Bal's speech-acts can also be seen as spurning the narrator who has failed to provide the name himself.

Arguing that the anonymity of Jephthah's daughter encourages readers not to view her as a person in her own right,[21] J. Cheryl Exum proposes to over-interpret the text by naming her Bath-Shever, "daughter of the break," a name intended to evoke the sound of the name "Bath Sheba" and to signify:

the role feminist criticism plays in breaking open the text's phallocentric ideology and exposing the buried and encoded messages it gives to women. Both naming the woman and making her the focus of our inquiry are interpretive moves that restore her to the subject position the androcentric narrative destroys.[22]

Not only can the text be violated by transforming anonymous characters into named ones but also the characters themselves can be abducted from their narrative contexts and placed in entirely new surroundings and genres. Lot's unnamed wife becomes the central image of author Rebecca Goldstein's musings on midrash, her father's righteousness, and the different senses in which one does or does not "look back."[23] Raphael pictured her transformation into a pillar of salt in his 1508 painting *Abraham and Lot Fleeing from Sodom*.[24] Noah's wife emerges from the pages of Genesis to take part in a variety of other creations. In a cartoon by Mort Gerberg, she watches as the venerable Noah stands on a ladder and paints the name "Noah's Ark" on the ark's hull, and she asks indignantly, "What about MY Name?" The caption is ambiguous. The caption's use of upper case for "Name" implies that God is the complainer, while the picture clearly indicates Noah's wife, hands on hips, mouth wide open,

---

[20]*Death*, 43.

[21]Exum, *Fragmented*, 176.

[22]*Fragmented*, 177.

[23]"Looking Back."

[24]Logge, Vatican; reproduced in Susan Wright, *The Bible in Art* (New York: Todri, 1996), 24–25.

as speaker.[25] "Mrs. Noah" is on center stage in Robert Duncan's poem, "The Ballad of Mrs Noah" (1960). The poem depicts her as having a comfortable domain within the Holy Boat, with her own hearth, two cats, two books, two cooking pots, two pints of porter, two pecks of peas, and "a stir in her stew of memories." She converses with the lowly worm, the sleeping cat, and the searching crow and receives the olive shoot brought by the dove, a "Branch of All-Cheer," which she may wear on her nightgown as a boa.[26] She is also prominent in Timothy Findley's imaginative story of the Flood, *Not Wanted on the Voyage*.[27] The midrashic name for Noah's wife, Naamah, is adopted in the children's story *A Prayer for the Earth: The Story of Naamah, Noah's Wife*, by Sandy Eisenberg Sasso, which describes her as the one who ensured the survival of vegetation.[28]

As figures in novels, poems, cartoons, and artwork, biblical characters serve different narrators than the one whose mark is evident in the biblical corpus. Narrative authority is also exercised by academics even when they attempt a meticulous separation between themselves and the text. After all, biblical exegesis and its accounts in articles and books are themselves "stories of reading," though often couched in the idiom of objective, scientific research.[29] In our stories, the scholar is the narrator, though the stuff of her narration includes the characters and other materials provided by the biblical narrator. Or, to put it another way, scholars usurp the godlike control that the biblical narrator exerts over his characters.

Indeed, scholars treat characters like dolls. Though endowed by their manufacturers with certain features and personalities, dolls can be arranged and rearranged, dressed and undressed, and provided with dialogue and narrative context at the whim of the one who plays with them. Scholars, too, play with characters and other narrative elements, rearrange them, categorize them, expound upon them, and bring them into play with elements from which their biblical context had kept them separate. Even when scholars do not name the unnamed or write new stories for them, we re-create them in our own image or, at least, according to our own specifications, as surely as God fashioned

[25]Mort Gerberg, *More All-Jewish Cartoons, Yet* (New York: Putnam, 1987), reprinted in *Moment*, October 1994/Heshvan 5755, 6.

[26]Richard Ellman and Robert O'Clair, eds., *Modern Poems: An Introduction to Poetry* (New York: Norton, 1976, 358–60; reprinted from Robert Duncan, *The Opening of the Field* (New York: Grove, 1960).

[27]Toronto: Pebble Productions, 1984.

[28]Woodstock, Vt.: Jewish Lights Publishing, 1996.

[29]The term "stories of reading" is used by Janice Capel Anderson. See "Feminist Criticism: The Dancing Daughter," in *Mark and Method: New Approaches in Biblical Studies*, ed. Janice Capel Anderson and Stephen D. Moore (Minneapolis: Fortress, 1992), 110.

human beings to his liking and the narrator created character from the raw materials, whether traditional or imaginative, at his disposal. In this way, scholars, too, blur the lines between reader and text.

But perhaps we have insisted on too great a differentiation between narrator and character. After all, the narrator, like his characters, exists solely within the text. The narrator, too, is unnamed yet has taken on personality and identity by means of his narration. Notice, for example, that I speak of him in the singular and in the masculine, despite the absence of explicit narrative indicators of either of these traits. That I speak of him in the singular does not deny the multiple authorship of the text but rather indicates my sense that, beyond its variations and ambiguities, biblical narrative conveys an overall unity of worldview. That I speak of him in the masculine is not a statement of my views about the "historical" identity of the narrator or the author who created him but rather a comment on my own inability to hear the narrator speak in anything but male tones. The narrator has come to life for me as a male, though he is not oblivious to women. He is androcentric in his concerns, though not incapable of focusing on female characters. He espouses a patriarchal set of values, which he frequently subverts himself. His political views, sexual mores, and personal favorites among his cast of characters are also clear. He sees the reign of King David as the pinnacle of Israel's history and is firmly convinced that homosexuality is an abomination. He prefers Abraham to Lot and Deborah to Samson. Though we meet only through his creation, our relationship blows hot and cold. I delight in his artistry, in his characters, and in the stories he tells. I resent the power that I perceive him to be exerting over my own readings of the text. Although he is unaware of my existence, I suspect he would be both delighted and grieved at the readiness of his readers to ride roughshod over his creation.

Biblical narrative does not easily permit erasure of the boundaries between reader and character, and readers of biblical narrative are not particularly ready to dissolve their own subjectivities into that of the characters within the text. But the metaphor of the open door allows us to see the interchange between reader and character and, more important perhaps, between reader and narrator. The reader may be a tourist, ready for a time to set aside his or her own concerns to experience a new terrain and meet the locals. Some readers prefer more intense relationships and invite their new friends home with them. Other readers take up residence within the text as a rival to the narrator, raiding his stock of characters and stories in order to build a new edifice by telling a new story in words or images. Anonymity not only allows readers to construct the character's personal identity on a basis other than the proper name but also invites us to examine our own.

Conclusion

THE ANONYMOUS CHARACTERS of narrative are as real to me as any literary figures can be. The sense of reality that they convey to me does not mask the fictional nature of my interpretive framework itself. Indeed, the category I have called "anonymous characters of biblical narrative" exists entirely in my imagination. There is no indication within the text that these characters have more in common with one another than they do with other figures within the narrative. And why, indeed, should the unnamed daughters of Lot share a narrative category with, say, the Cushite messenger, when they could be communing with named daughters like Dinah and Rebecca? And who is to say that the Queen of Sheba should sojourn with the young Saul's servant boy and not with the named foreign monarchs in her immediate narrative context?

It is, of course, the reader—in this case, myself—who has placed these characters together. The groupings are not mutually exclusive; the categories of *daughters* or of *monarchs* are no less meaningful than the category of anonymous characters, and most unnamed characters could be grouped successfully with a range of other biblical figures, named and not named. It is the very diversity in role designations, the quality and degree of narrative attention they are given, the specific situations in which they find themselves, and the evaluative judgments that they call forth either implicitly or explicitly that makes them so interesting and yet so difficult to subsume under a single heading.

Any reader is free to arrange these figures at her or his whim. In this study, however, I have argued that anonymity, the single feature by which I have connected these diverse figures, contributes in a significant and unique way to our efforts to construct our readings of the characters and the stories in which they appear.

Anonymity is a negative feature; it focuses not on what is present within the text but on what is absent from it. Whereas the proper name ascribes stability, unity, and individuality to the named figure, its absence calls these aspects into question. Yet anonymity in and of itself is not meaningful beyond the fact that it designates the absence of the proper name; that is, we cannot know what the person is, whether he or she is important, and how we might relate to the person, based on anonymity alone.

The absence of the proper name may cohere so well with other gaps, such as the absence of the character's words or deeds from the narrative, that the construction of character is possible only if the reader applies a serious imaginative effort to the task. In the story of the medium of Endor, anonymity is a veil over personal identity that enhances the theme of secrecy developed by other details, such as the nocturnal setting, the illicit nature of the medium's activity, and King Saul's attempts to mask his own identity. In the tragedies of the doomed daughters, anonymity can signify the death of identity, a demise that foreshadows their own.

For many characters, however, the absence of the proper name does not consign them to narrative oblivion but simply requires that the readers interact with, analyze, or construct the unnamed character on a basis other than the proper name. Indeed, the principal effect of the absence of a proper name is to focus the reader's attention on the role designations that flood into the gap that anonymity denotes. Focus on role designations, in turn, allows us to construct identity in the locus between the role designation and the character's narrative portrayal. In doing so, we compare the stereotypical behaviors associated with the role in biblical narrative and the particular ways in which the unnamed character fulfills or does not fulfill the role, or we look at the degree to which he or she stretches its limits or calls its very contours into question. The character's individuality, character traits, and modes of interaction—that is, her or his personal identity—emerge from this comparison.

Another effect of anonymity is to challenge the notion that personal identity is a stable, fixed, and unified entity. Anonymous characters highlight the permeability of personal identity, which allows them to stand in for one another, as do Micah's son and the Levite he hires to care for his shrine, or to recall a range of named characters in the way that the Timnite woman contrasts with other biblical brides such as Rebecca, Rachel, and Zipporah.

The generic nature of role designations lends a paradigmatic quality to the unnamed characters, even when personal identity is very much apparent. Most meaningful to me, for example, are the women who are caught in the web of the competing demands that their various social roles require. Their extreme fates do not promise death or incest for all women and men who must similarly negotiate the pressure of multiple roles, but they do suggest the universality of this experience, which sometimes seems so symptomatic of the late twentieth century. The wayward wives, in turn, illustrate the potential for relationships outside the marital relationship. Except for Potiphar's wife, other women in this category, such as the primordial woman, Manoah's wife and the Shunammite woman, illustrate the potential (and sometimes literal) fruitfulness of such encounters. It is true that named characters may also be paradigmatic for the reader. But the presence of the proper name ascribes definitive character so that paradigmatic quality and permeability are secondary to the uniqueness of the individual instead of in tension with them as with anonymous characters.

With the exception of angels, who may have no name and no personal identity, and presumably the two talking animals, the snake in Eden and Balaam's donkey, anonymity is a relative rather than an absolute characteristic of these characters. Anonymity, like identity, exists in the relationship between ourselves and others. Anonymous characters are defined in relation to ourselves. In this sense, we encounter unnamed biblical characters in the same way as we meet the unnamed in our world.

In considering biblical characters, the reader is in much the same position as Jacob and Manoah, who confronted the anonymous beings they encountered with the urgent question: "What is your name?" Whereas named characters provide a simple answer through their proper names, unnamed characters rebuff the question as directly as did the heavenly beings with whom Jacob and Manoah conversed. Nevertheless, unnamed angels and human beings alike permit themselves to be known at least partially through their role designations, words and actions.

But the parallel between the reader and the two biblical men may be pushed further. Jacob, Manoah, and other figures are changed by their encounter despite—or perhaps because of—the anonymity of the angels. Jacob becomes Israel; Manoah becomes the father of Samson. Gideon becomes a warrior, and Balaam a true prophet of God. Knowledge and awareness are expanded by the encounter; they now know more of their world for having encountered figures whom they clearly never expected to confront in their lifetimes. Similarly, readers gain a measure of self-knowledge; insofar as they take on the roles that are depicted in the stories, they can consider how they apply in a more personal fashion. Furthermore, both Jacob and Manoah exert some sort of power over the unnamed figures. Jacob bests his assailant in a wrestling match, whereas Manoah induces God to have the unnamed angel return to his household and show himself directly to Manoah. Similarly, the reader decides how to construct characters, whether and how to compare them with others, or whether to ignore them altogether.

One of the judgments that readers are called upon to make concerns the relationship between the social world as implied in the text or read out of it and the "real world" in which the narrative was created and read. Does anonymity reflect the social world, or it is a literary construct only?

One way to address this question is to look at gender distribution. The biblical tendency to indeterminacy frustrates even the most concerted efforts to determine the number and proportion of male and female unnamed characters. In the first place, the large number of group characters make a headcount virtually impossible. Second, the categories of named and unnamed are themselves not always clear-cut, as we have seen. A tally of individual actors in the narrative (excluding those who are merely mentioned, as in genealogical lists) indicates a total of approximately 390 named males and 100 unnamed males, compared to a total of approximately 50 named females and 46 unnamed females. Uncertain as these figures are, they do indicate that while there are more anonymous male than female characters, a much higher proportion of female characters than male characters are unnamed. These observations help to explain why I, and—I would venture—many other readers of biblical narrative, initially associated anonymity with female biblical figures.

The associations among anonymity, gender, and literary and societal suppression or oppression are similarly unclear. Anonymous men outnumber anonymous women. Further, all of the men who victimize the Levite's concubine are unnamed (Judges 19). Many biblical victims are named women, such as Dinah (Genesis 34) and David's daughter Tamar (2 Samuel 13), who are raped; others are named men, such as Uriah the Hittite, whose death in war was mandated by David (2 Sam 11:15), or unnamed men, such as the Amalekite messenger whom David ordered killed over his role in the death of Saul (2 Sam 1:15). Conversely, unnamed women such as the medium of Endor (1 Samuel 28), the wise woman of Tekoa (2 Sam 14), and the Queen of Sheba (1 Kings 10), are hardly victimized and, indeed, exert some power over the named male characters—kings all—with whom they interact. The presence of unnamed kings, prophets, and priests also argues against the view that anonymity within the narrative reflects the hierarchies of Israelite society.

Nevertheless, one clear pattern does emerge. Except for the bit players, who are themselves a miscellaneous grouping, no role designations are shared among both unnamed men and unnamed women. This pattern is obvious in the case of priests, all of whom are male, and wise women, who are by definition female. It is also true of those categories that would not seem to require segregation on the basis of gender. Yet unnamed servants, messengers, and prophets are almost invariably male, whereas unnamed kinfolk are primarily female. Surely this distribution does not reflect Israelite society, which knew female servants and no doubt female message-bearers, and certainly had roughly the same number of men defined by familial designations as women at any given time.

This pattern may, however, reflect the worldview of the narrator. For the narrator, for example, angels are real, though not always visible. Though they are not human, they take male form on occasion, generally but not always refraining from liaisons with the daughters of men. The narrator seems to relish tales of war and political intrigue, which occupy the books of Samuel and Kings and provide occupation for a multitude of messengers and armor-bearers. In the domestic realm, stories of unnamed women uphold and perpetuate the values of sexual fidelity and procreation, while providing just enough basis for a resistant reader to question them:

The absence of the proper name destabilizes the link between name and identity and even the notion of fixed identity itself; anonymity launches us into an uncertain realm in which the stability of personal identity cannot be taken for granted. But anonymity does not suppress the personal identities of the anonymous; it does not prevent us from seeking them out and fashioning their individuality. Further, entering their company does not require, or even allow, us readers to leave ourselves behind.

The ways in which we construct anonymous character, delight in, or deplore the contrast or coherence between role designations, and engage with the permeability of personal identity involve us in the text as more than innocent bystanders. In allowing ourselves the freedom to engage the characters and bring them into proximity with others and with ourselves, we not only construct their identities but also our own.

SELECTED BIBLIOGRAPHY

Abrams, M. H. "The Deconstructive Angel." In *Modern Criticism and Theory: A Reader*, ed. D. Lodge, 265–76. London: Longman, 1988.

Aitken, Kenneth T. "The Wooing of Rebekah: A Study in the Development of the Tradition." *JSOT* 30 (1984): 3–23.

Albright, William Foxwell. *Archaeology and the Religion of Israel*. Baltimore: Johns Hopkins University Press, 1956.

Alter, Robert. *The Art of Biblical Narrative*. New York: Basic, 1981.

———. "How Convention Helps Us Read: The Case of the Bible's Annunciation Type-Scene." Prooftexts 3 (1983): 115–30.

Amit, Yairah. " 'There was a man whose name was . . .': Redactional Variation and Its Tendencies" (in Hebrew). *Beth Mikra* 30 (1985): 388–99.

———. "Three Variations on the Death of Saul" (in Hebrew). *Beth Mikra* 30 (1985): 92–102.

Arnold, Bill T. "The Amalekite's Report of Saul's Death: Political Intrigue or Incompatible Sources?" *Journal of the Evangelical Theological Society* 32 (1989): 289–98.

Auld, A. Graeme. *Joshua, Judges, and Ruth*. Philadelphia: Westminster Press, 1984.

Aycock, D. Alan. "The Fate of Lot's Wife: Structural Mediation in Biblical Mythology." In *Structuralist Interpretations of Biblical Myth*, ed. Edmund Leach and D. Alan Aycock, 113–19. Cambridge: Cambridge University Press, 1983.

———. "Potiphar's Wife: Prelude to a Structural Exegesis." *Man*, n.s. 27 (1992): 479–94.

Bach, Alice. "Breaking Free of the Biblical Frame-up: Uncovering the Woman in Genesis 39." In *A Feminist Companion to Genesis*, 318–42. Sheffield: JSOT Press, 1993.

Bal, Mieke. *Death and Dissymmetry: The Politics of Coherence in the Book of Judges.* Chicago: University of Chicago Press, 1988.

———. *Femmes imaginaires: l'Ancien Testament au risque d'une narratologie critique.* Utrecht: HES Publishers; Paris: A. G. Nizet, 1986.

———. *Lethal Love: Feminist Literary Readings of Biblical Love Stories.* Bloomington: Indiana University Press, 1987.

Bar-Efrat, Shimon. "Literary Modes and Methods in Biblical Narrative in View of 2 Samuel 10–20 and 1 Kings 1–2." *Immanuel* 8 (1978): 20–22.

———. *Narrative Art in the Bible.* JSOTSup 70. Sheffield: Almond Press, 1989.

Barton, John. "Classifying Biblical Criticism." *JSOT* 29 (1984): 19–35.

Bassler, Jouette. "Adam, Eve, and the Pastor: The Use of Genesis 2–3 in the Pastoral Epistles." In *Genesis 1–3 in the History of Exegesis: Intrigue in the Garden,* ed. Gregory Allen Robbins. Lewiston, N.Y.: Edwin Mellen Press, 1988.

Bellefontaine, Elizabeth. "Customary Law and Chieftainship: Judicial Aspects of 2 Samuel 14.4–21." *JSOT* 38 (1987): 47–72.

Bellis, Alice Ogden. *Helpmates, Harlots, Heroes: Women's Stories in the Hebrew Bible.* Louisville, Ky.: Westminster/John Knox, 1994.

Bellis, Peter J. *No Mysteries out of Ourselves: Identity and Textual Formation in the Novels of Herman Melville.* Philadelphia: University of Philadelphia Press, 1990.

Berlin, Adele. *Poetics and Interpretation of Biblical Narrative.* Sheffield: Almond Press, 1983.

———. "Point of View in Biblical Narrative." In *A Sense of Text: The Art of Language in the Study of Biblical Literature,* ed. Stephen A. Geller et al., 71–113. JQR Supplement. Winona Lake, Ind.: Eisenbrauns, 1982.

Beuken, W. A. M. "I Samuel 28: The Prophet as 'Hammer of Witches.'" *JSOT* 6 (1978): 3–17.

———. "No Wise King without a Wise Woman." In *New Avenues in the Study of the Old Testament: A Collection of Old Testament Studies Published on the Occasion of the Fiftieth Anniversary of the Oudtestamentisch Werkgezelschap and the Retirement of Prof. Dr. M. J. Mulder,* ed. A. S. van der Woude, 1–21. Oudtestamentische Studien 25. Leiden: Brill, 1989.

Bird, Phyllis. "The Harlot as Heroine: Narrative Art and Social Presupposition in Three Old Testament Texts." *Semeia* 46 (1989): 119–39.

Bird, Phyllis A. "Images of Women in the Old Testament." In *Religion and Sexism: Images of Woman in the Jewish and Christian Traditions,* ed. Rosemary Radford Ruether, 41–88. New York: Simon and Schuster, 1974.

———. "Male and Female He Created Them: Gen 1:27b in the Context of the Priestly Account of Creation." *HTR* 74 (1981): 129–60.

Bledstein, Adrien Janis, "Is Judges a Woman's Satire of Men Who Played God?" In *A Feminist Companion to Judges,* ed. Athalya Brenner, 34–54. Sheffield: Sheffield University Press, 1993.

Blenkinsopp, J. *A History of Prophecy in Israel.* Philadelphia: Westminster, 1983.

———. "Structure and Style in Judges 13–16." *JBL* 82 (1963): 65–76.

Boling, Robert G. *Joshua.* AB 6. New York: Doubleday, 1975.

———. *Judges.* AB 6A. New York: Doubleday, 1975.

Boose, Lynda E., "The Father's House and the Daughter in It: The Structures of Western Culture's Daughter-Father Relationship." In *Daughters and Fathers*, ed. Lynda E. Boose and Betty S. Flowers, 19–74. Baltimore: Johns Hopkins University Press, 1989.

Booth, Wayne C. "Distance and Point of View: An Essay in Classification." In *The Theory of the Novel*, ed. P. Stevick, 87–107. New York: Free Press, 1967.

Brenner, Athalya. "An Afterword." In *A Feminist Companion to the Song of Songs*, ed. Athalya Brenner. Sheffield: Sheffield Academic Press, 1993.

———, ed. *A Feminist Companion to Judges*. Sheffield: Sheffield University Press, 1993.

———. *The Israelite Woman: Social Role and Literary Type in Biblical Narrative*. Biblical Seminars 2. Sheffield: JSOT Press, 1985.

Brenner, Athalya, and Fokelien van Dijk-Hemmes. *On Gendering Texts: Female and Male Voices in the Hebrew Bible*. Leiden: Brill, 1993.

Brinker, Menachem. "Versimilitude, Conventions, and Belief." *NLH* 14 (1983): 253–76.

Browne, Elizabeth. "Samson: Riddle and Paradox." *Bible Today* 22 (1984): 160–67.

Brueggemann, Walter. *First and Second Samuel*. Louisville, Ky.: Westminster/John Knox Press, 1990.

Büchman, Christina, and Celina Spiegel, eds. *Out of the Garden: Women Writers on the Bible*. New York: Ballantine, 1993.

Burney, C. F. *The Book of Judges*. London: Rivingtons, 1918.

Camp, Claudia. *Wisdom and the Feminine in the Book of Proverbs*. Decatur, Ga.: Almond Press, 1985.

———. "The Wise Women of 2 Samuel: A Role Model for Women in Early Israel?" *CBQ* 43 (1981): 14–29.

Camp, Claudia V., and Carole R. Fontaine, "The Words of the Wise and Their Riddles." In *Text and Tradition: The Hebrew Bible and Folklore*, ed. Susan Niditch, 127–51. Atlanta: Scholars Press, 1990.

Campbell, Antony F. *Of Prophets and Kings: A Late Ninth-Century Document (1 Samuel 1–2 Kings 10)*. CBQ Monograph Series 17. Washington, D.C.: Catholic Biblical Association, 1986.

Carter, Ronald. "The Placing of Names: Sequencing in Narrative Openings." *Leeds Studies in English* 18 (1987): 89–100.

Chatman, Seymour. *Coming to Terms: The Rhetoric of Narrative in Fiction and Film*. Ithaca, N.Y.: Cornell University Press, 1990.

———. *Story and Discourse: Narrative Structure in Fiction and Film*. Ithaca, N.Y.: Cornell University Press, 1978.

Childs, Brevard S. *The Book of Exodus*. OTL. Philadelphia: Westminster, 1974.

———. "The Exegetical Significance of Canon for the Study of the Old Testament." *VTSup* (1977):66–80.

Cixous, Helene. "The Character of 'Character' " *NLH* 5 (1974): 383–402.

———. "Sorties." In *Modern Criticism and Theory: A Reader*, ed. D. Lodge, 286–93. London: Longman, 1988.

Clines, David J. A. "The Significance of the 'Sons of God' Episode (Genesis 6:1–4) in the Context of the 'Primeval History' (Genesis 1–11)." *JSOT* 13 (1979): 34–46.

———. "X, X Ben Y, Ben Y: Personal Names in Hebrew Narrative Style." *VT* 22 (1972): 266–87.

Clines, David J. A., and Tamara C. Eskenazi, eds. *Telling Queen Michal's Story: An Experiment in Comparative Interpretation.* JSOTSup 119; Sheffield: JSOT Press, 1991.

Coats, George W. "Parable, Fable, and Anecdote: Storytelling in the Succession Narrative." *Int* 35 (1981): 368–82.

———. "The Way of Obedience: Traditio-Historical and Hermeneutical Reflections on the Balaam Story." *Semeia* 24 (1982): 53–79.

Cogan, Mordechai, and Hayim Tadmor. *II Kings.* AB 11. Garden City, N.Y.: Doubleday, 1988.

Coggins, Richard. "On Kings and Disguises." *JSOT* 50 (1991): 55–62.

Cohen, Jeremy. *"Be Fertile and Increase, Fill the Earth and Master It": The Ancient and Medieval Career of a Biblical Text.* Ithaca, N.Y.: Cornell University Press, 1989.

Cohen, Martin A. "The Role of the Shilonite Priesthood in the United Monarchy of Ancient Israel." *HUCA* 36 (1965): 59–98.

Cohen, Shaye J. D. "Solomon and the Daughter of Pharaoh: Intermarriage, Conversion, and the Impurity of Women." *JANESCU* 16–17 (1984–85): 23–37.

Cohn, Robert L. "Convention and Creativity in the Book of Kings: The Case of the Dying Monarch." *CBQ* 47 (1985): 606–8.

———. "Literary Technique in the Jeroboam Narrative." *ZAW* 97 (1985): 23–35.

Crenshaw, James L. *Prophetic Conflict: Its Effect upon Israelite Religion.* Berlin: Walter de Gruyter, 1971.

———. *Samson: A Secret Betrayed, a Vow Ignored.* Atlanta: John Knox Press, 1978.

———. "The Samson Saga: Filial Devotion or Erotic Attachment?" *ZAW* 86 (1974): 470–504.

Culler, Jonathan. *Structuralist Poetics.* London: Routledge and Kegan Paul, 1975.

Daube, David. *The Exodus Pattern in the Bible.* London: Faber and Faber, 1963.

Davies, Gordon Fay. *Israel in Egypt: Reading Exodus 1–2.* JSOTSup 135. Sheffield: JSOT Press, 1992.

Day, Peggy L. *An Adversary in Heaven: Satan in the Hebrew Bible.* HSM 43. Atlanta: Scholars Press, 1988.

———. "From the Child Is Born the Woman: The Story of Jephthah's Daughter." In *Gender and Difference in Ancient Israel,* ed. Peggy L. Day, 58–74. Minneapolis: Fortress, 1989.

De Man, Paul. "The Resistance to Theory." In *Modern Criticism and Theory: A Reader,* ed. D. Lodge, 355–71. London: Longman, 1988.

Dell, Katharine J. "Review of J. Cheryl Exum, *Fragmented Women: Feminist (Sub)versions of Biblical Narratives.*" *VT* 44 (1994): 407–10.

Derrida, Jacques. "Structure, Sign and Play in the Discourse of the Human Sciences." In *Modern Criticism and Theory: A Reader,* ed. D. Lodge, 108–23. London: Longman, 1988.

Detweiler, Robert. "What Is a Sacred Text?" *Semeia* 31 (1985): 213–30.

Deurloo, K. A. "The King's Wisdom in Judgement: Narration as Example (I Kings iii)." In *New Avenues in the Study of the Old Testament,* ed. A. S. van der Woude, 11–21. Leiden: Brill, 1989.

Docherty, Thomas. *Reading (Absent) Character: Towards a Theory of Characterization in Fiction.* Oxford: Clarendon, 1983.

Donaldson, Laura. "Cyborgs, Ciphers, and Sexuality: Re-theorizing Literary and Biblical Character." *Semeia* 63 (1993): 90–92.

Dozeman, Thomas B. "The Way of the Man of God from Judah: True and False Prophecy in the Pre-Deuteronomic Legend of 1 Kings 13." *CBQ* 44 (1982): 379–93.

Dragga, Sam. "In the Shadow of the Judges: The Failure of Saul." *JSOT* 38 (1987): 39–46.

Driver, S. R. *The Book of Exodus*. Rev. ed. Cambridge: Cambridge University Press, 1953.

Eichrodt, Walther. *Ezekiel: A Commentary*. Trans. Cosslett Quin. OTL. Philadelphia: Westminster, 1970.

Eissfeldt, Otto. *The Old Testament: An Introduction*. New York: Harper and Row, 1965.

Ellington, John. "Man and Adam in Genesis 1–5." *BT* 30 (1979): 201–5.

Eslinger, Lyle. "Inner-Biblical Exegesis and Inner-Biblical Allusion: The Question of Category." *VT* 42 (1992): 47–58.

Exum, J. Cheryl. "Aspects of Symmetry and Balance in the Samson Saga." *JSOT* 19 (1981): 3–29.

———. *Fragmented Women: Feminist (Sub)versions of Biblical Narratives*. Valley Forge, Pa.: Trinity Press International, 1993.

———. "On Judges 11." In *A Feminist Companion to Judges*, ed. Athalya Brenner, 131–44. Sheffield: JSOT Press, 1993.

———. "Promise and Fulfillment: Narrative Art in Judges 13." *JBL* 99 (1980): 43–59.

———. "The Theological Dimension of the Samson Saga." *VT* 33 (1983): 30–45.

———. " 'You Shall Let Every Daughter Live': A Study of Exodus 1:8–2:10." *Semeia* 28 (1983): 63–82. Reprinted in *A Feminist Companion to Exodus to Deuteronomy*, ed. Athalya Brenner, 37–61. Sheffield: Sheffield University Press, 1994.

Exum, J. Cheryl, and J. William Whedbee. "Isaac, Samson, and Saul: On the Comic and Tragic Visions." *Semeia* 32 (1984): 5–40.

Fewell, Danna Nolan. "Feminist Reading of the Hebrew Bible: Affirmation, Resistance and Transformation." *JSOT* 39 (1987): 77–87.

Fields, Weston W. "The Motif 'Night as Danger' Associated with Three Biblical Destruction Narratives." In *"Sha 'arei Talmon": Studies in the Bible, Qumran, and the Ancient Near East Presented to Shemaryahu Talmon*, ed. M. Fishbane and E. Tov, 17–32. Winona Lake, Ind.: Eisenbrauns, 1992.

Fish, Stanley. "Why No One's Afraid of Wolfgang Iser: Review of *The Act of Reading: A Theory of Aesthetic Response*. Baltimore: Johns Hopkins University Press, 1978." *Diacritics* 11 (1981): 2–13.

Fishbane, Michael. "Recent Work on Biblical Narrative: Review of Bar-Efrat, *Literary Modes and Methods in the Biblical Narrative*; Fokkelman, *Narrative Art in Genesis*; and Licht, *Storytelling in the Bible*." *Prooftexts* 1 (1981): 99–104.

———. *Text and Texture: Close Readings of Selected Biblical Texts*. New York: Schocken, 1979.

Flesch, William. "Anonymity and Unhappiness in Proust and Wittgenstein." *Criticism* 29 (1987): 459–76.

Fokkelman, J. P. *Narrative Art and Poetry in the Books of Samuel*. Vol. 1, *King David*. Assen, The Netherlands: Van Gorcum, 1981.

————. *Narrative Art and Poetry in the Books of Samuel.* Vol. II, *The Crossing Fates.* Assen, The Netherlands: Van Gorcum, 1986.

————. *Narrative Art in Genesis.* 2d ed. Sheffield: JSOT Press, 1991.

————. "Structural Remarks on Judges 9 and 19." In *"Sha 'arei Talmon": Studies in the Bible, Qumran, and the Ancient Near East Presented to Shemaryahu Talmon,* ed. M. Fishbane and E. Tov, 33–45. Winona Lake, Ind.: Eisenbrauns, 1992.

Fontaine, Carole. "The Bearing of Wisdom on the Shape of 2 Samuel 11–12 and 1 Kings 3." *JSOT* 34 (1986): 61–77.

Forster, E. M. *Aspects of the Novel.* London: Edward Arnold, 1927.

Foucault, Michel. "What Is an Author?" In *Modern Criticism and Theory: A Reader,* ed. D. Lodge, 197–210. London: Longman, 1988.

Fowler, Robert M. "Who Is 'The Reader' in Reader Response Criticism?" *Semeia* 31 (1985): 5–23.

Friedman, Norman. "The Point of View in Fiction: The Development of a Critical Concept." In *The Theory of the Novel,* ed. P. Stevick, 108–37. New York: Free Press, 1967.

Fuchs, Esther. "The Literary Characterization of Mothers and Sexual Politics in the Hebrew Bible." *Semeia* 46 (1989): 151–66.

————. "Marginalization, Ambiguity, Silencing: The Story of Jephthah's Daughter." In *A Feminist Companion to Judges,* ed. Athalya Brenner, 116–30. Sheffield: JSOT Press, 1993.

Furman, Nelly. "His Story versus Her Story: Male Genealogy and Female Strategy in the Jacob Cycle." *Semeia* 46 (1989): 141–49.

Garsiel, Moshe. "Homiletic Name-Derivations as a Literary Device in the Gideon Narrative: Judges VI–VIII." *VT* 43 (1993): 302–17.

Gass, William H. "The Concept of Character in Fiction." In *Essentials of the Theory of Fiction,* ed. P. D. Murphy and M. J. Hoffman, 267–76. Durham, N.C.: Duke University Press, 1988.

Geller, Stephen A. "Through Windows and Mirrors into the Bible: History, Literature, and Language in the Study of the Text." In *A Sense of Text: The Art of Language in the Study of Biblical Literature; Papers from a Symposium at the Dropsie College for Hebrew and Cognate Learning, May 11, 1982,* 3–40. *Jewish Quarterly Review* Supplement 1982. Winona Lake, Ind.: Eisenbrauns, 1982.

Genette, Gérard. *Fiction and Diction.* Trans. Catherine Porter. Ithaca, N.Y.: Cornell University Press, 1993.

Gevaryahu, Chaim. "The Return of the Exile to God's Estate in the Parable of the Wise Woman of Tekoa" (in Hebrew). *Beth Mikra* 36 (1969): 10–33.

Ginzberg, Louis. *Legends of the Jews.* Vol. 2. Philadelphia: Jewish Publication Society, 1910.

Goitein, S. D. "Women as Creators of Biblical Genres." *Prooftexts* 8 (1988): 1–34.

Gold, Joseph. *Read for Your Life: Literature as a Life Support System.* Markham, Ont.: Fitzhenry and Whiteside, 1990.

Goldstein, Rebecca. "Looking Back at Lot's Wife." In *Out of the Garden: Women Writers on the Bible,* ed. Christina Büchman and Celina Spiegel, 3–12. New York: Ballantine, 1993.

Graetz, Naomi. "Dinah the Daughter." In *A Feminist Companion to Genesis*, ed. Athalya Brenner, 306–17. Sheffield: JSOT Press, 1993.

Graffy, Adrian. "The Literary Genre of Isaiah 5,1–7." *Biblica* 60 (1979): 400–9.

Graves, Robert, and Raphael Patai. *Hebrew Myths: The Book of Genesis*. London: Cassell, 1964.

Gray, G. Buchanan. "Angel." In *Encyclopaedia Biblica*, Vol. 1. London: Adam and Charles Black, 1899.

Gray, John. *I and II Kings: A Commentary*. 2d rev. ed. OTL. London: SCM Press, 1970.

Greene, John T. *Balaam and His Interpreters: A Hermeneutical History of the Balaam Traditions*. BJS 244. Atlanta: Scholars Press, 1992.

———. *The Role of the Messenger and Message in the Ancient Near East*. BJS 169. Atlanta: Scholars Press, 1989.

Greenstein, Edward L. "Biblical Narratology: Review of Crenshaw, *Samson: A Secret Betrayed*; Fishbane, *Text and Texture*; Gunn, *The Story of King David*; Gunn, *The Fate of King Saul*; and Sasson, *Ruth*." *Prooftexts* 1 (1981): 201–6.

———. "Deconstruction and Biblical Narrative." *Prooftexts* 9 (1989): 43–71.

———. "The Riddle of Samson." *Prooftexts* 1 (1981): 237–60.

Grimm, Dieter. "Der Name des Gottesboten in Richter 13." *Biblica* 62 (1981): 92–99.

Gros Louis, Kenneth R. R. "The Book of Judges." In *Literary Interpretations of Biblical Narratives*, ed. J. S. Ackerman, T. S. Warshaw, and K. R. R. Gros Louis, 141–62. Nashville: Abingdon, 1974.

Gross, Walter. "Lying Prophet and Disobedient Man of God in 1 Kings 13." *Semeia* 15 (1979): 97–135.

Gunn, David M. *The Fate of King Saul: An Interpretation of a Biblical Story*. JSOTSup 14. Sheffield: JSOT, 1980.

———. *The Story of King David: Genre and Interpretations*. JSOTSup 6. Sheffield: JSOT Press, 1978.

Hagan, Harry. "Deception as Motif and Theme in 2 Sm 9–20; 1 Kgs 1–2." *Biblica* 60 (1979): 301–26.

Haitovsky, Dahlia. "Rosso's 'Rebecca and Eliezer at the Well,' " *Gazette des beaux arts* 123 (1994): 111–22.

Haran, Menahem. *Temples and Temple Service in Ancient Israel: An Inquiry into the Character of Cult Phenomena and the Historical Setting of the Priestly School*. Oxford: Clarendon, 1978.

Harvey, W. J. *Character and the Novel*. London: Chatto and Windus, 1965.

Hauser, Alan J. "Judges 5: Parataxis in Hebrew Poetry," *JBL* 99 (1980): 23–41.

Heidt, William George. *Angelology of the Old Testament*. Studies in Sacred Theology 24. Washington, D.C.: Catholic University of America Press, 1949.

Hertzberg, Hans Wilhelm. *I & II Samuel: A Commentary*. Philadelphia: Westminster, 1964.

Hirsch, E. D., Jr. "Beyond Convention?" *NLH* 14 (1983): 388–97.

Hirth, Volkmar. *Gottes Boten im Alten Testament*. Theologische Arbeiten 32. Berlin: Evangelische Verlaganstalt, 1975.

Hochman, Baruch. *Character in Literature*. Ithaca, N.Y.: Cornell University Press, 1985.

Hoftijzer, J. "David and the Tekoite Woman." *VT* 20 (1970): 19–44.

Hollis, Susan Tower. "The Woman in Ancient Examples of the Potiphar's Wife Motif, K2111." In *Gender and Difference in Ancient Israel*, ed. Peggy L. Day, 28–42. Minneapolis: Fortress, 1989.

Hurowitz, Victor Avigdor. "Joseph's Enslavement of the Egyptians (Genesis 47:13–26) in Light of Famine Texts from Mesopotamia." *RB* 101 (1994): 355–62.

Ilan, Tal. "Biblical Women's Names in the Apocryphal Traditions." *JSP* 11 (1993): 3–67.

———. "Notes on the Distribution of Jewish Women's Names in Palestine in the Second Temple and Mishnaic Periods." *JJS* 40 (1989): 186–200.

Iser, Wolfgang. *The Implied Reader: Patterns of Communication in Prose Fiction from Bunyan to Beckett*. Baltimore: Johns Hopkins University Press, 1974.

James, Henry. "The Art of Fiction." In *Henry James on the Theory and Practice of Fiction*, ed. William R. Veeder and Susan M. Griffin, 165–83. Chicago: University of Chicago Press, 1986.

Janzen, J. Gerald. "A Certain Woman in the Rhetoric of Judges 9." *JSOT* 38 (1987): 33–37.

Jauss, Hans Robert. "Levels of Identification of Hero and Audience." *NLH* 5 (1974): 283–317.

Jeansonne, Sharon Pace. "The Characterization of Lot in Genesis." *BTB* 18/4 (1988): 123–29.

———. *The Women of Genesis: From Sarah to Potiphar's Wife*. Minneapolis: Fortress, 1990.

Jefferson, Ann. *The Nouveau Roman and the Poetics of Fiction*. Cambridge: Cambridge University Press, 1980.

———. "Structuralism and Post-Structuralism." In *Modern Literary Theory: A Comparative Introduction*. 2d ed. Ed. A. Jefferson and D. Robey, 92–121. London: B. T. Batsford, 1986.

Jenkins, Allan K. "A Great Name: Genesis 12:2 and the Editing of the Pentateuch." *JSOT* 10 (1978): 41–57.

Jones, Gwilyn. *1 and 2 Kings*. New Century Commentary. Grand Rapids: Eerdmans, 1984.

Kates, Judith A., and Gail Twersky Reimer, eds. *Reading Ruth: Contemporary Women Reclaim a Sacred Story*. New York: Ballantine, 1994.

Klein, Lillian R. "A Spectrum of Female Characters." In *A Feminist Companion to Judges*, ed. Athalya Brenner. Sheffield: JSOT Press, 1993.

———. *The Triumph of Irony in the Book of Judges*. Sheffield: Almond Press, 1988.

Koch, Klaus. *The Growth of the Biblical Tradition: The Form-Critical Method*. Scribner Studies in Biblical Interpretation. New York: Scribner's, 1969.

Kselman, John S. "The Book of Genesis: A Decade of Scholarly Research." *Int* 45 (1991): 380–92.

Kugel, James L. *In Potiphar's House: The Interpretive Life of Biblical Texts*. San Francisco: Harper, 1990.

———. "On the Bible and Literary Criticism." *Prooftexts* 2 (1982): 217–36.

———. "On the Bible as Literature." *Prooftexts* 2 (1982): 323–32.

Landes, Daniel. "A Vow of Death." In *Confronting Omnicide: Jewish Reflections on Weapons of Mass Destruction*, ed. Daniel Landes, 5–11. Northvale, N.J.: Jason Aronson, 1991.

Lanser, Susan S. "(Feminist) Criticism in the Garden: Inferring Genesis 2–3." *Semeia* 41 (1988): 67–84.

Lasine, Stuart. "Guest and Host in Judges 19: Lot's Hospitality in an Inverted World." *JSOT* 29 (1984): 37–59.

———. "Jehoram and the Cannibal Mothers (2 Kings 6.24–33): Solomon's Judgment in an Inverted World." *JSOT* 50 (1991): 27–53.

———. "The Riddle of Solomon's Judgment and the Riddle of Human Nature in the Hebrew Bible." *JSOT* 45 (1989): 61–86.

———. "The Ups and Downs of Monarchical Justice: Solomon and Jehoram in an Intertextual World." *JSOT* 59 (1993): 37–53.

Lassner, Jacob. *Demonizing the Queen of Sheba: Boundaries of Gender and Culture in Postbiblical Judaism and Medieval Islam.* Chicago: University of Chicago Press, 1993.

Lemke, Werner E. "The Way of Obedience: 1 Kings 13 and the Structure of the Deuteronomistic History." In *Magnalia Dei, the Mighty Acts of God*, ed. Frank Moore Cross, et al. 301–26. Garden City, N.Y.: Doubleday, 1976.

Licht, Jacob. "מלאכים ;מלאך" (Angel, Angels). In אנציקלופדיה מקראית, *Entsiklopedyah mikra'it* = *Encyclopaedia Biblica* 4:975–90. 9 vols. Jerusalem: Mosad Bialik 1965–88.

———. *Storytelling in the Bible.* Jerusalem: Magnes Press, 1978.

Lindblom, J. *Prophecy in Ancient Israel.* Philadelphia: Fortress, 1973.

Long, Burke O. "A Figure at the Gate: Readers, Reading, and Biblical Theologians." In *Canon, Theology, and Old Testament Interpretation: Essays in Honor of Brevard S. Childs*, ed. D. L. Peterson, R. R. Wilson, and G. M. Tucker, 166–86. Philadelphia: Fortress, 1988.

———. *1 Kings.* The Forms of the Old Testament Literature 9. Grand Rapids: Eerdmans, 1984.

———. "The 'New' Biblical Poetics of Alter and Sternberg." *JSOT* 51 (1991): 71–84.

———. *2 Kings.* The Forms of the Old Testament Literature 10. Grand Rapids: Eerdmans, 1991.

———. "The Shunammite Woman." *BibRev* 7 (1991): 13–19, 42.

McCarter, P. Kyle, Jr. *I Samuel.* AB 8. Garden City, N.Y.: Doubleday, 1980.

———. *II Samuel.* AB 9. Garden City, N.Y.: Doubleday, 1984.

Mach, Michael. *Entwicklungsstadien des jüdischen Engelglaubens in vorrabbinischer Zeit.* Texte und Studien zum antiken Judentum 34. Tübingen: J. C. B. Mohr (Paul Siebeck), 1992.

McKay, Heather A. "Jacob Makes It across the Jabbok." *JSOT* 38 (1987): 3–13.

McKenzie, John L. *The World of the Judges.* Englewood Cliffs, N.J.: Prentice-Hall, 1966.

Maclean, Ian. "Reading and Interpretation." In *Modern Literary Theory: A Comparative Introduction.* 2d ed. Ed. A. Jefferson and D. Robey, 122–44. London: B. T. Batsford, 1986.

Magonet, Jonathan. "The Names of God in Biblical Narratives." In *Words Remembered, Texts Renewed: Essays in Honor of John F.A. Sawyer*, ed. J. Davre, et. al., 80–96. JSOTSup 195. Sheffield: JSOT Press, 1995.

———. "The Themes of Genesis 2–3." In *Walk in the Garden: Biblical, Iconographical and Literary Images of Eden*, ed. P. Morris and D. Sawyer, 39–46. JSOTSup 136. Sheffield: JSOT Press, 1992.

Mailloux, Steven. "Convention and Context." *NLH* 14 (1983): 399–407.

Maly, Eugene. "Genesis." In *The Jerome Biblical Commentary*, ed. Raymond E. Brown, et al. Englewood Cliffs, N.J.: Prentice-Hall, 1968.

Margalith, Othniel. "The Legends of Samson/Heracles." *VT* 37 (1987): 63–70.

———. "More Samson Legends." *VT* 36 (1986): 397–405.

Martin, James D. *The Book of Judges.* Cambridge: Cambridge University Press, 1975.

Martin, Wallace. *Recent Theories of Narrative.* Ithaca, N.Y.: Cornell University Press, 1986.

Meier, Samuel A. *The Messenger in the Ancient Semitic World.* HSM 45. Atlanta: Scholars Press, 1988.

Mettinger, Tryggve N. D. *King and Messiah: The Civil and Sacral Legitimation of the Israelite Kings.* Lund: LiberLöromedel/Gleerup, 1976.

Meyers, Carol. *Discovering Eve: Ancient Israelite Women in Context.* New York: Oxford University Press, 1988.

Milgrom, Jacob. *The JPS Torah Commentary: Numbers.* Philadelphia: JPS, 1990.

Miscall, Peter D. "Biblical Narrative and Categories of the Fantastic." *Semeia* 60 (1992): 39–51.

———. "Jacques Derrida in the Garden of Eden." *USQR* 44 (1990): 1–9.

———. *The Workings of Old Testament Narrative.* Philadelphia: Fortress; Chico, Calif.: Scholars Press, 1983.

Mitchell, Juliet. "Femininity, Narrative and Psychoanalysis." In *Modern Criticism and Theory: A Reader*, ed. D. Lodge, 425–30. London: Longman, 1988.

Moi, Toril. "Feminist Literary Criticism." In *Modern Literary Theory: A Comparative Introduction*, ed. A. Jefferson and D. Robey, 204–21. London: B.T. Batsford, 1986.

Montgomery, James A. *The Books of Kings.* ICC. New York: Scribner's, 1951.

Moore, George Foot. *A Critical and Exegetical Commentary on the Book of Judges.* New York: Scribner's, 1895.

Moore, Michael S. *The Balaam Traditions: Their Character and Development.* SBLDS 113. Atlanta: Scholars Press, 1990.

Mullen, E. Theodore, Jr. *The Assembly of Gods: The Divine Council in Canaanite and Early Hebrew Literature.* HSM 24. Chico, Calif.: Scholars Press, 1980.

Natanson, Maurice. *Anonymity: A Study in the Philosophy of Alfred Schutz.* Bloomington: Indiana University Press, 1986.

———. *Phenomenology, Role, and Reason: Essays on the Coherence and Deformation of Social Reality.* Springfield, Ill.: Charles C. Thomas, 1974.

———. "Solipsism and Sociality." *NLH* 5 (1974): 237–44.

Naveh, Joseph. "Nameless People." *Israel Exploration Journal* 40 (1990): 109–23.

Newsom, Carol A. "Angels." In *ABD* 1: 248–53.

Niditch, Susan. "Samson as Culture Hero, Trickster, and Bandit: The Empowerment of the Weak." *CBQ* 52 (1990): 608–24.

———. "The 'Sodomite' Theme in Judges 19–20: Family, Community, and Social Disintegration." *CBQ* 44 (1982): 365–78.

Noth, Martin. *Exodus: A Commentary.* OTL. Philadelphia: Westminster, 1962.

———. *A History of Israel.* New York: Harper and Row, 1960.

———. *Könige.* BKAT 9/1. Neukirchen: Neukirchener Verlag, 1968.

Olson, Dennis T. *The Death of the Old and the Birth of the New: The Framework of the Book of Numbers and the Pentateuch.* BJS 71. Chico, Calif.: Scholars Press, 1985.

Olyan, Saul M. *A Thousand Angels Served Him: Exegesis and the Naming of Angels in Ancient Judaism.* Tübingen: J. C. B. Mohr, 1993.

Origen, *Homilies on Genesis and Exodus.* Trans. Ronald E. Heine. Fathers of the Church 71. Washington: Catholic University of America, 1981.

Pardes, Ilana. *Countertraditions in the Bible: A Feminist Approach.* Cambridge: Harvard University Press, 1992.

Phelan, James. *Reading People, Reading Plots.* Chicago: University of Chicago Press, 1989.

Polzin, Robert. *David and the Deuteronomist: A Literary Study of the Deuteronomic History, Part III.* Bloomington: Indiana University Press, 1993.

———. *Moses and the Deuteronomist: A Literary Study of the Deuteronomic History, Part I.* Bloomington: Indiana University Press, 1993.

———. *Samuel and the Deuteronomist: A Literary Study of the Deuteronomic History, Part II.* Bloomington: Indiana University Press, 1993.

Pope, Marvin. *Job,* AB 15. Garden City, N.Y.: Doubleday, 1964.

Price, Martin. *Forms of Life: Character and Moral Imagination in the Novel.* New Haven: Yale University Press, 1983.

———. "People of the Book: Character in Forster's *A Passage to India.*" *Critical Inquiry* 1 (1974–75): 602–22.

Pritchard, James B. *Ancient Near Eastern Texts.* 2d. ed. Princeton, N.J.: Princeton University Press, 1955.

———, ed. *Solomon and Sheba.* London: Phaidon, 1974.

Propp, William H. "That Bloody Bridegroom (Exodus IV 24–6)." *VT* 43 (1993): 495–518.

Pyper, Hugh S. "Judging the Wisdom of Solomon: The Two-Way Effect of Intertextuality." *JSOT* 59 (1993): 23–36.

Ramsay, George W. "Is Name-Giving an Act of Dominion in Genesis 2.23 and Elsewhere?" *CBQ* 50 (1988): 24–35.

Rappaport, Nessa. "The Woman Who Lost Her Names." In *The Woman Who Lost Her Names: Selected Writings by American Jewish Women,* ed. J. W. Mazow, 135–42. San Francisco: Harper and Row, 1980.

Redford, Donald B. *Egypt, Canaan, and Israel in Ancient Times.* Princeton, N.J.: Princeton University Press, 1992.

———. *A Study of the Biblical Story of Joseph.* VTSup 20. Leiden: Brill, 1970.

Rehm, Merlin D. "Levites and Priests." In *ABD* 4: 297–310.

Reinhartz, Adele. "Anonymous Female Characters in the Books of Kings." In *A Feminist Companion to Samuel and Kings,* ed. Athalya Brenner, 43–65. Sheffield: JSOT Press, 1994.

———. "Samson's Mother: An Unnamed Protagonist." *JSOT* 55 (1992): 25–37. Reprinted in *A Feminist Companion to Judges,* ed. Athalya Brenner, 157–170. Sheffield: Sheffield Academic Press, 1993.

———. "Anonymity and Characterization in the Books of Samuel." *Semeia* 63 (1993): 117–41.

Reis, Pamela Tamarkind, "Eating the Blood: Saul and the Witch of Endor." *JSOT* 73 (1997): 3–23.

———. "Vindicating God: Another Look at 1 Kings XIII." *VT* 44 (1994): 376–86.

Revell, E. J. *The Designation of the Individual: Expressive Usage in Biblical Narrative.* Kampen, The Netherlands: Kok Pharos, 1996.

Rimmon-Kenan, Shlomith. *Narrative Fiction: Contemporary Poetics.* London: Methuen, 1983.

Robbe-Grillet, Alain. *For a New Novel: Essays on Fiction.* Trans. R. Howard. New York: Grove Press, 1965.

———. *La Jalousie.* Paris: Les Éditions de Minuit, 1959.

Robertson, David. *The Old Testament and the Literary Critic.* Philadelphia: Fortress, 1977.

Rofé, Alexander. *The Belief in Angels in the Bible and in Early Israel* (in Hebrew). Jerusalem: Makor, 1979.

———. "The Classification of the Prophetical Stories." *JBL* 89 (1970): 427–40.

Rosenberg, Joel W. "The Garden Story Forward and Backward: The Non-Narrative Dimension of Gen. 2–3." *Prooftexts* 1 (1981): 1–27.

Rosenblatt, Naomi H., and Joshua Horwitz. *Wrestling with Angels: What the First Family of Genesis Teaches Us about Our Spiritual Identity, Sexuality, and Personal Relationships.* New York: Delacorte, 1995.

Roth, Wolfgang. "The Wooing of Rebekah: A Tradition-Critical Study of Genesis 24." *CBQ* 34 (1972): 177–87.

Rouillard, H. "L'ânesse de Balaam: analyse littéraire de Nomb., XXII, 24–35." *RB* 87 (1980): 211–41.

Safren, Jonathan D. "Balaam and Abraham." *VT* 38 (1988): 105–13.

Sakenfeld, Katharine Doob. "In the Wilderness, Awaiting the Land: The Daughters of Zelophehad and Feminist Interpretation." *Princeton Seminary Bulletin* 9 (1988): 179–96.

Samuel, Maurice. *Certain People of the Book.* New York: Union of American Hebrew Congregations, 1955.

Sarna, Nahum. *The JPS Torah Commentary: Exodus.* Philadelphia: JPS, 1991.

———. *The JPS Torah Commentary: Genesis.* Philadelphia: JPS, 1989.

———. *Understanding Genesis.* New York: Schocken, 1966.

Sarraute, Nathalie. *Portrait d'un inconnu.* Paris: Gallimard, 1956.

Satterthwaite, Philip. " 'No King in Israel': Narrative Criticism and Judges 17–21." *Tyndale Bulletin* 44 (1993): 75–88.

Savran, George W. "Beastly Speech: Intertextuality, Balaam's Ass and the Garden of Eden." *JSOT* 64 (1994): 33–55.

———. *Telling and Retelling: Quotation in Biblical Narrative.* Bloomington: Indiana University Press, 1988.

Sawyer, Deborah. "Resurrecting Eve? Feminist Critique of the Garden of Eden." In *Walk in the Garden: Biblical, Iconographical and Literary Images of Eden*, ed. P. Morris and D. Sawyer, 273–89. JSOTSup 136. Sheffield: JSOT Press, 1992.

Schottroff, Willy. "Der Zugriff des Königs auf die Töchter: zur Fronarbeit von Frauen im Alten Israel." *ET* 49 (1989): 268–85.

Schuller, Eileen. "Feminist Biblical Hermeneutics: Genesis 1–3 as a Test Case." In *Gender, Genre and Religion: Feminist Reflections*, ed. Morny Joy and Eva K. Neumaier-Dargyay, 31–46. Waterloo, Ont.: Wilfrid Laurier Press, 1995.

———. "Women of the Exodus in Biblical Retellings of the Second Temple Period." In *Gender and Difference in Ancient Israel*, ed. Peggy L. Day, 178–94. Minneapolis: Fortress, 1989.

Searle, John R. "Proper Names." *Mind* 67 (1958): 166–73.

Segert, Stanislav. "Paranomasia in the Samson Narrative in Judges XIII–XVI." *VT* 34 (1984): 454–61.

Seybold, Donald A. "Paradox and Symmetry in the Joseph Narrative." In *Literary Interpretations of Biblical Narratives*, ed. Kenneth R. R. Gros Louis, et al., 59–73. Nashville: Abingdon, 1974.

Shields, Mary E. "Subverting a Man of God, Elevating a Woman: Role and Power Reversals in 2 Kings 4." *JSOT* 58 (1993): 59–69.

Showalter, Elaine. "Feminist Criticism in the Wilderness." In *Modern Criticism and Theory: A Reader*, ed. D. Lodge, 330–53. London: Longman, 1988.

Siebert-Hommes, Jopie. "Die Geburtsgeschichte des Mose innerhalb des Erzählzusammenhangs von Exodus I und II." *VT* 42 (1992): 398–404.

———. "Twelve Women in Exodus 1 and 2: The Role of Daughters and Sons in the Stories concerning Moses." *Amsterdamse Cahiers voor Exegeses en Bijbelse Theologie* 9 (1988):47–58.

Simon, Uriel. "A Balanced Story: The Stern Prophet and the Kind Witch." *Prooftexts* 8 (1988): 164–65.

———. "I Kings 13: A Prophetic Sign—Denial and Persistence." *HUCA* 47 (1976): 81–117.

———. "Minor Characters in Biblical Narrative." *JSOT* 46 (1990): 11–19.

Skinner, John. *A Critical and Exegetical Commentary on Genesis*. ICC. Edinburgh: T. and T. Clark, 1930.

Smith, Henry Preserved. *A Critical and Exegetical Commentary on the Books of Samuel*. ICC 8. New York: Scribner's, 1904.

Snaith, Norman H. *1 and 2 Kings*. Nashville: Abingdon, 1954.

Soggin, J. Alberto. *Judges: A Commentary*. OTL. Philadelphia: Westminster, 1981.

Speiser, E. A. *Genesis*. AB 1. New York: Doubleday, 1964.

Steinberg, Naomi. "Alliance or Descent? The Functions of Marriage in Genesis." *JSOT* 51 (1991): 45–55.

———. "Gender Roles in the Rebekah Cycle." *USQR* 39 (1984): 175–88.

Sternberg, Meir. *The Poetics of Biblical Narrative: Ideological Literature and the Drama of Reading*. Bloomington: Indiana University Press, 1985.

Teugels, Lise. "The Anonymous Matchmaker: An Enquiry into the Characterization of the Servant of Abraham in Genesis 24." *JSOT* 65 (1995): 13–23.

Thompson, Yakov. "Samson in Timnah: Judges 14–15: Form and Function." *Dor le Dor* 15 (1986–87): 249–55.

Trible, Phyllis. "Bringing Miriam out of the Shadows," *BibRev* 5 (1989): 14–25, 34.

———. *God and the Rhetoric of Sexuality*. Philadelphia: Fortress, 1978.

———. "Subversive Justice: Tracing the Miriam Traditions." In *Justice and the Holy:*

Essays in Honor of Walter Harrelson, ed. Douglas A. Knight and Peter J. Paris, 99–109. Atlanta: Scholars Press, 1989.

————. *Texts of Terror: Literary-Feminist Readings of Biblical Narratives.* Philadelphia: Fortress, 1984.

Turner, Laurence A. "Lot as Jekyll and Hyde: A Reading of Genesis 18–19." In *The Bible in Three Dimensions: Essays in Celebration of Forty Years of Biblical Studies in the University of Sheffield,* ed. David J. A. Clines, et al., 85–101. JSOTSup 87. Sheffield: JSOT Press, 1990.

Unterman, Jeremiah. "The Literary Influence of 'The Binding of Isaac' (Genesis 22) on 'The Outrage at Gibeah' (Judges 19)." *HAR* 4 (1980): 161–67.

Urbrock, William J. "Sisera's Mother in Judges 5 and Haim Gouri's *Immo.*" *HAR* 11 (1987): 423–34.

Van Dijk-Hemmes, Fokkelien. "The Metaphorization of Woman in Prophetic Speech: An Analysis of Ezekiel XXIII." *VT* 43 (1993): 162–70.

Van Seters, John. *Abraham in History and Tradition.* New Haven: Yale University Press, 1975.

————. *The Life of Moses: The Yahwist as Historian in Exodus-Numbers.* Louisville, Ky.: Westminster/John Knox Press, 1994.

Van Winkle, D. W. "1 Kings XIII: True and False Prophecy." *VT* 39 (1989): 31–43.

Vergote, J. *Joseph en Égypte: Genèse chap. 37–50 à la lumière des études égyptologiques récentes.* Orientalia et Biblica Lovaniensia 3. Louvain: Publications Universitaires, 1959.

Von Rad, Gerhard. "מלאך; in the OT." In *TDNT* 1:76–78.

————. *Genesis: A Commentary.* Rev. ed. OTL. Philadelphia: Westminster, 1972.

————. *Old Testament Theology.* Vol. 1, *The Theology of Israel's Historical Traditions.* Trans. D. M. G. Stalker. New York: Harper, 1972.

Vorster, Willem. "Readings, Readers and the Succession Narrative: An Essay on Reception." *ZAW* 98 (1986): 351–62.

Walsh, Jerome. "The Contexts of 1 Kings XIII." *VT* 39 (1989): 355–70.

————. *1 Kings.* Berit Olam: Studies in Hebrew Narrative and Poetry. Collegeville, Minn.: Liturgical Press, 1996.

Webb, Barry G. *The Book of the Judges: An Integrated Reading.* JSOTSup 46. Sheffield: JSOT Press, 1987.

Weems, Renita J. "The Hebrew Women Are Not Like the Egyptian Women: The Ideology of Race, Gender and Sexual Reproduction in Exodus 1." *Semeia* 59 (1992): 25–34.

Weinsheimer, Joel. "Theory of Character: Emma." *Poetics Today* 1 (1979): 185–211.

Westbrook, Raymond. *Property and the Family in Biblical Law.* JSOTSup 113. Sheffield: JSOT Press, 1991.

Westermann, Claus. *Genesis: An Introduction.* Minneapolis: Fortress, 1992.

————. *Genesis 12–36: A Commentary.* Trans. John J. Scullion, S.J. Minneapolis: Augsburg, 1985.

Wharton, James A. "The Secret of Yahweh: Story and Affirmation in Judges 13–16." *Int* 27 (1973): 48–66.

Whitelam, Keith. *The Just King: Monarchical Judicial Authority in Ancient Israel.* JSOTSup 12. Sheffield: JSOT Press, 1979.

Williams, James G. *Women Recounted: Narrative Thinking and the God of Israel.* Sheffield: Almond Press, 1982.

Williams, Patricia J. "In Search of Pharaoh's Daughter." In *Out of the Garden: Women Writers on the Bible,* ed. Christina Büchmann and Celina Spiegel, 54–71. New York: Ballantine, 1993.

Wilson, Rawdon. "The Bright Chimera: Character as a Literary Theme." *Critical Inquiry* 5 (1978–79): 725–49.

———. "On Character: A Reply to Martin Price." *Critical Inquiry* 2 (1975–76): 191–98.

Wilson, Robert R. "The Hardening of Pharaoh's Heart." *CBQ* 41 (1979): 18–36.

Woolf, Virginia. "Mr. Bennett and Mrs. Brown." In *Approaches to the Novel: Material for a Poetics.* Rev. ed., ed. R. Scholes. Scranton: Chandler, 1966.

Wright, Austin M. *The Formal Principle in the Novel.* Ithaca, N.Y.: Cornell University Press, 1982.

Wright, Susan. *The Bible in Art.* New York: Todri, 1996.

Yates, Roy. "Angels in the Old Testament." *Irish Theological Quarterly* 38 (1971): 164–67.

Yee, Gale A. " 'Fraught with Background': Literary Ambiguity in II Samuel 11." *Int* 42 (1988): 240–53.

Zakovitch, Yair. *On Three . . . and on Four* (in Hebrew). Jerusalem: Makor, 1979.

———. "The Woman's Rights in the Biblical Law of Divorce." *The Jewish Law Annual* 4 (1981): 28–46.

Zakovitch, Yair, and Avigdor Shinan, "Rebecca's Fall from the Camel: On the Metamorphosis of a Strange Traditional Tale" (in Hebrew). *Ha-Sifrut* 29 (1979): 104–9.

INDEX OF SCRIPTURAL CITATIONS

HEBREW BIBLE (in NRSV order)

EARLY CHRISTIAN LITERATURE

INDEX OF MODERN AUTHORS

SUBJECT INDEX

218